Behavioral Patterns

Chain of Responsibility (223) Avoid coupling the sender of a request to its receiver by giving more than one object a chance to handle the request. Chain the receiving objects and pass the request along the chain until an object handles it.

Command (233) Encapsulate a request as an object, thereby letting you parameterize clients with different requests, queue or log requests, and support undoable operations.

Interpreter (243) Given a language, define a represention for its grammar along with an interpreter that uses the representation to interpret sentences in the language.

Iterator (257) Provide a way to access the elements of an aggregate object sequentially without exposing its underlying representation.

Mediator (273) Define an object that encapsulates how a set of objects interact. Mediator promotes loose coupling by keeping objects from referring to each other explicitly, and it lets you vary their interaction independently.

Memento (283) Without violating encapsulation, capture and externalize an object's internal state so that the object can be restored to this state later.

✓ **Observer (293)** Define a one-to-many dependency between objects so that when one
Dependents object changes state, all its dependents are notified and updated automatically.

State (305) Allow an object to alter its behavior when its internal state changes. The object will appear to change its class.

Strategy (315) Define a family of algorithms, encapsulate each one, and make them interchangeable. Strategy lets the algorithm vary independently from clients that use it.

Template Method (325) Define the skeleton of an algorithm in an operation, deferring some steps to subclasses. Template Method lets subclasses redefine certain steps of an algorithm without changing the algorithm's structure.

Visitor (331) Represent an operation to be performed on the elements of an object structure. Visitor lets you define a new operation without changing the classes of the elements on which it operates.

Addison-Wesley Professional Computing Series

Brian W. Kernighan, Consulting Editor

Please see our web site (http://www.awl.com/cseng/series/professionalcomputing) for more information on these titles.

Design Patterns

Design Patterns
Elements of Reusable Object-Oriented Software

Erich Gamma

Richard Helm

Ralph Johnson

John Vlissides

ADDISON-WESLEY
An imprint of Addison Wesley Longman, Inc.

Reading, Massachusetts   Harlow, England   Menlo Park, California
Berkeley, California   Don Mills, Ontario   Sydney
Bonn   Amsterdam   Tokyo   Mexico City

The publisher offers discounts on this book when ordered in quantity for special sales. For more information please contact:

    Corporate & Professional Publishing Group
    Addison-Wesley Publishing Company
    One Jacob Way
    Reading, Massachusetts 01867

Library of Congress Cataloging-in-Publication Data
Design Patterns : elements of reusable object-oriented software /
    Erich Gamma . . . [et al.].
        p.   cm. -- (Addison-Wesley professional computing series)
    Includes bibliographical references and index.
    ISBN 0-201-63361-2
    1. Object-oriented programming (Computer science)   2. Computer
software--Reusability.   I. Gamma, Erich.   II. Series.
    QA76.64.D47   1994
    005.1'2--dc20   94-34264
                                              CIP

Text printed on recycled and acid-free paper.

ISBN 0-201-63361-2
17 1819202122 CRW 02 01 00 99

17th Printing   June 1999

To Karin
—E.G.

To Sylvie
—R.H.

To Faith
—R.J.

To Dru Ann and Matthew
Joshua 24:15b
—J.V.

Praise for *Design Patterns: Elements of Reusable Object-Oriented Software*

"This is one of the best written and wonderfully insightful books that I have read in a great long while...this book establishes the legitimacy of patterns in the best way: not by argument but by example."
   — **Stan Lippman,** *C++ Report*

"...this new book by Gamma, Helm, Johnson, and Vlissides promises to have an important and lasting impact on the discipline of software design. Because *Design Patterns* bills itself as being concerned with object-oriented software alone, I fear that software developers outside the object community may ignore it. This would be a shame. This book has something for everyone who designs software. All software designers use patterns; understanding better the reusable abstractions of our work can only make us better at it."
   — **Tom DeMarco,** *IEEE Software*

"Overall, I think this book represents an extremely valuable and unique contribution to the field because it captures a wealth of object-oriented design experience in a compact and reusable form. This book is certainly one that I shall turn to often in search of powerful object-oriented design ideas; after all, that's what reuse is all about, isn't it?"
   — **Sanjiv Gossain,** *Journal of Object-Oriented Programming*

"This much-anticipated book lives up to its full year of advance buzz. The metaphor is of an architect's pattern book filled with time-tested, usable designs. The authors have chosen 23 patterns from decades of object-oriented experience. The brilliance of the book lies in the discipline represented by that number. Give a copy of *Design Patterns* to every good programmer you know who wants to be better."
   — **Larry O'Brien,** *Software Development*

"The simple fact of the matter is that patterns have the potential to permanently alter the software engineering field, catapulting it into the realm of true elegant design. Of the books to date on this subject, *Design Patterns* is far and away the best. It is a book to be read, studied, internalized, and loved. The book will forever change the way you view software."
   — **Steve Bilow,** *Journal of Object-Oriented Programming*

"*Design Patterns* is a powerful book. After a modest investment of time with it, most C++ programmers will be able to start applying its "patterns" to produce better software. This book delivers intellectual leverage: concrete tools that help us think and express ourselves more effectively. It may fundamentally change the way you think about programming.
   — **Tom Cargill,** *C++ Report*

Contents

Preface

This book isn't an introduction to object-oriented technology or design. Many books already do a good job of that. This book assumes you are reasonably proficient in at least one object-oriented programming language, and you should have some experience in object-oriented design as well. You definitely shouldn't have to rush to the nearest dictionary the moment we mention "types" and "polymorphism," or "interface" as opposed to "implementation" inheritance.

On the other hand, this isn't an advanced technical treatise either. It's a book of **design patterns** that describes simple and elegant solutions to specific problems in object-oriented software design. Design patterns capture solutions that have developed and evolved over time. Hence they aren't the designs people tend to generate initially. They reflect untold redesign and recoding as developers have struggled for greater reuse and flexibility in their software. Design patterns capture these solutions in a succinct and easily applied form.

The design patterns require neither unusual language features nor amazing programming tricks with which to astound your friends and managers. All can be implemented in standard object-oriented languages, though they might take a little more work than *ad hoc* solutions. But the extra effort invariably pays dividends in increased flexibility and reusability.

Once you understand the design patterns and have had an "Aha!" (and not just a "Huh?") experience with them, you won't ever think about object-oriented design in the same way. You'll have insights that can make your own designs more flexible, modular, reusable, and understandable—which is why you're interested in object-oriented technology in the first place, right?

A word of warning and encouragement: Don't worry if you don't understand this book completely on the first reading. We didn't understand it all on the first writing! Remember that this isn't a book to read once and put on a shelf. We hope you'll find yourself referring to it again and again for design insights and for inspiration.

This book has had a long gestation. It has seen four countries, three of its authors' marriages, and the birth of two (unrelated) offspring. Many people have had a part in its development. Special thanks are due Bruce Anderson, Kent Beck, and André Weinand for their inspiration and advice. We also thank those who reviewed drafts of the manuscript: Roger Bielefeld, Grady Booch, Tom Cargill, Marshall Cline, Ralph Hyre, Brian Kernighan, Thomas Laliberty, Mark Lorenz, Arthur Riel, Doug Schmidt, Clovis Tondo, Steve Vinoski, and Rebecca Wirfs-Brock. We are also grateful to the team at Addison-Wesley for their help and patience: Kate Habib, Tiffany Moore, Lisa Raffaele, Pradeepa Siva, and John Wait. Special thanks to Carl Kessler, Danny Sabbah, and Mark Wegman at IBM Research for their unflagging support of this work.

Last but certainly not least, we thank everyone on the Internet and points beyond who commented on versions of the patterns, offered encouraging words, and told us that what we were doing was worthwhile. These people include but are not limited to Jon Avotins, Steve Berczuk, Julian Berdych, Matthias Bohlen, John Brant, Allan Clarke, Paul Chisholm, Jens Coldewey, Dave Collins, Jim Coplien, Don Dwiggins, Gabriele Elia, Doug Felt, Brian Foote, Denis Fortin, Ward Harold, Hermann Hueni, Nayeem Islam, Bikramjit Kalra, Paul Keefer, Thomas Kofler, Doug Lea, Dan LaLiberte, James Long, Ann Louise Luu, Pundi Madhavan, Brian Marick, Robert Martin, Dave McComb, Carl McConnell, Christine Mingins, Hanspeter Mössenböck, Eric Newton, Marianne Ozkan, Roxsan Payette, Larry Podmolik, George Radin, Sita Ramakrishnan, Russ Ramirez, Alexander Ran, Dirk Riehle, Bryan Rosenburg, Aamod Sane, Duri Schmidt, Robert Seidl, Xin Shu, and Bill Walker.

We don't consider this collection of design patterns complete and static; it's more a recording of our current thoughts on design. We welcome comments on it, whether criticisms of our examples, references and known uses we've missed, or design patterns we should have included. You can write us care of Addison-Wesley, or send electronic mail to design-patterns@cs.uiuc.edu. You can also obtain softcopy for the code in the Sample Code sections by sending the message "send design pattern source" to design-patterns-source@cs.uiuc.edu. And now there's a Web page at http://st-www.cs.uiuc.edu/users/patterns/DPBook/DPBook.html for late-breaking information and updates.

Mountain View, California	E.G.
Montreal, Quebec	R.H.
Urbana, Illinois	R.J.
Hawthorne, New York	J.V.

August 1994

Foreword

All well-structured object-oriented architectures are full of patterns. Indeed, one of the ways that I measure the quality of an object-oriented system is to judge whether or not its developers have paid careful attention to the common collaborations among its objects. Focusing on such mechanisms during a system's development can yield an architecture that is smaller, simpler, and far more understandable than if these patterns are ignored.

The importance of patterns in crafting complex systems has been long recognized in other disciplines. In particular, Christopher Alexander and his colleagues were perhaps the first to propose the idea of using a pattern language to architect buildings and cities. His ideas and the contributions of others have now taken root in the object-oriented software community. In short, the concept of the design pattern in software provides a key to helping developers leverage the expertise of other skilled architects.

In this book, Erich Gamma, Richard Helm, Ralph Johnson, and John Vlissides introduce the principles of design patterns and then offer a catalog of such patterns. Thus, this book makes two important contributions. First, it shows the role that patterns can play in architecting complex systems. Second, it provides a very pragmatic reference to a set of well-engineered patterns that the practicing developer can apply to crafting his or her own specific applications.

I'm honored to have had the opportunity to work directly with some of the authors of this book in architectural design efforts. I have learned much from them, and I suspect that in reading this book, you will also.

Grady Booch

Chief Scientist, Rational Software Corporation

Guide to Readers

This book has two main parts. The first part (Chapters 1 and 2) describes what design patterns are and how they help you design object-oriented software. It includes a design case study that demonstrates how design patterns apply in practice. The second part of the book (Chapters 3, 4, and 5) is a catalog of the actual design patterns.

The catalog makes up the majority of the book. Its chapters divide the design patterns into three types: creational, structural, and behavioral. You can use the catalog in several ways. You can read the catalog from start to finish, or you can just browse from pattern to pattern. Another approach is to study one of the chapters. That will help you see how closely related patterns distinguish themselves.

You can use the references between the patterns as a logical route through the catalog. This approach will give you insight into how patterns relate to each other, how they can be combined with other patterns, and which patterns work well together. Figure 1.1 (page 12) depicts these references graphically.

Yet another way to read the catalog is to use a more problem-directed approach. Skip to Section 1.6 (page 24) to read about some common problems in designing reusable object-oriented software; then read the patterns that address these problems. Some people read the catalog through first and *then* use a problem-directed approach to apply the patterns to their projects.

If you aren't an experienced object-oriented designer, then start with the simplest and most common patterns:

- Abstract Factory (page 87)
- Adapter (139)
- Composite (163)
- Decorator (175)
- Factory Method (107)
- Observer (293)
- Strategy (315)
- Template Method (325)

It's hard to find an object-oriented system that doesn't use at least a couple of these patterns, and large systems use nearly all of them. This subset will help you understand design patterns in particular and good object-oriented design in general.

Chapter 1

Introduction

Designing object-oriented software is hard, and designing *reusable* object-oriented software is even harder. You must find pertinent objects, factor them into classes at the right granularity, define class interfaces and inheritance hierarchies, and establish key relationships among them. Your design should be specific to the problem at hand but also general enough to address future problems and requirements. You also want to avoid redesign, or at least minimize it. Experienced object-oriented designers will tell you that a reusable and flexible design is difficult if not impossible to get "right" the first time. Before a design is finished, they usually try to reuse it several times, modifying it each time.

Yet experienced object-oriented designers do make good designs. Meanwhile new designers are overwhelmed by the options available and tend to fall back on non-object-oriented techniques they've used before. It takes a long time for novices to learn what good object-oriented design is all about. Experienced designers evidently know something inexperienced ones don't. What is it?

One thing expert designers know *not* to do is solve every problem from first principles. Rather, they reuse solutions that have worked for them in the past. When they find a good solution, they use it again and again. Such experience is part of what makes them experts. Consequently, you'll find recurring patterns of classes and communicating objects in many object-oriented systems. These patterns solve specific design problems and make object-oriented designs more flexible, elegant, and ultimately reusable. They help designers reuse successful designs by basing new designs on prior experience. A designer who is familiar with such patterns can apply them immediately to design problems without having to rediscover them.

An analogy will help illustrate the point. Novelists and playwrights rarely design their plots from scratch. Instead, they follow patterns like "Tragically Flawed Hero" (Macbeth, Hamlet, etc.) or "The Romantic Novel" (countless romance novels). In the same way, object-oriented designers follow patterns like "represent states with objects"

1

and "decorate objects so you can easily add/remove features." Once you know the pattern, a lot of design decisions follow automatically.

We all know the value of design experience. How many times have you had design *déjà-vu*—that feeling that you've solved a problem before but not knowing exactly where or how? If you could remember the details of the previous problem and how you solved it, then you could reuse the experience instead of rediscovering it. However, we don't do a good job of recording experience in software design for others to use.

The purpose of this book is to record experience in designing object-oriented software as **design patterns**. Each design pattern systematically names, explains, and evaluates an important and recurring design in object-oriented systems. Our goal is to capture design experience in a form that people can use effectively. To this end we have documented some of the most important design patterns and present them as a catalog.

Design patterns make it easier to reuse successful designs and architectures. Expressing proven techniques as design patterns makes them more accessible to developers of new systems. Design patterns help you choose design alternatives that make a system reusable and avoid alternatives that compromise reusability. Design patterns can even improve the documentation and maintenance of existing systems by furnishing an explicit specification of class and object interactions and their underlying intent. Put simply, design patterns help a designer get a design "right" faster.

None of the design patterns in this book describes new or unproven designs. We have included only designs that have been applied more than once in different systems. Most of these designs have never been documented before. They are either part of the folklore of the object-oriented community or are elements of some successful object-oriented systems—neither of which is easy for novice designers to learn from. So although these designs aren't new, we capture them in a new and accessible way: as a catalog of design patterns having a consistent format.

Despite the book's size, the design patterns in it capture only a fraction of what an expert might know. It doesn't have any patterns dealing with concurrency or distributed programming or real-time programming. It doesn't have any application domain-specific patterns. It doesn't tell you how to build user interfaces, how to write device drivers, or how to use an object-oriented database. Each of these areas has its own patterns, and it would be worthwhile for someone to catalog those too.

1.1   What Is a Design Pattern?

Christopher Alexander says, "Each pattern describes a problem which occurs over and over again in our environment, and then describes the core of the solution to that problem, in such a way that you can use this solution a million times over, without ever doing it the same way twice" [AIS+77, page x]. Even though Alexander was talking about patterns in buildings and towns, what he says is true about object-oriented design patterns. Our solutions are expressed in terms of objects and interfaces instead of walls and doors, but at the core of both kinds of patterns is a solution to a problem in a context.

In general, a pattern has four essential elements:

1. The **pattern name** is a handle we can use to describe a design problem, its solutions, and consequences in a word or two. Naming a pattern immediately increases our design vocabulary. It lets us design at a higher level of abstraction. Having a vocabulary for patterns lets us talk about them with our colleagues, in our documentation, and even to ourselves. It makes it easier to think about designs and to communicate them and their trade-offs to others. Finding good names has been one of the hardest parts of developing our catalog.

2. The **problem** describes when to apply the pattern. It explains the problem and its context. It might describe specific design problems such as how to represent algorithms as objects. It might describe class or object structures that are symptomatic of an inflexible design. Sometimes the problem will include a list of conditions that must be met before it makes sense to apply the pattern.

3. The **solution** describes the elements that make up the design, their relationships, responsibilities, and collaborations. The solution doesn't describe a particular concrete design or implementation, because a pattern is like a template that can be applied in many different situations. Instead, the pattern provides an abstract description of a design problem and how a general arrangement of elements (classes and objects in our case) solves it.

4. The **consequences** are the results and trade-offs of applying the pattern. Though consequences are often unvoiced when we describe design decisions, they are critical for evaluating design alternatives and for understanding the costs and benefits of applying the pattern.

   The consequences for software often concern space and time trade-offs. They may address language and implementation issues as well. Since reuse is often a factor in object-oriented design, the consequences of a pattern include its impact on a system's flexibility, extensibility, or portability. Listing these consequences explicitly helps you understand and evaluate them.

Point of view affects one's interpretation of what is and isn't a pattern. One person's pattern can be another person's primitive building block. For this book we have concentrated on patterns at a certain level of abstraction. *Design patterns* are not about designs such as linked lists and hash tables that can be encoded in classes and reused as is. Nor are they complex, domain-specific designs for an entire application or subsystem. The design patterns in this book are *descriptions of communicating objects and classes that are customized to solve a general design problem in a particular context.*

A design pattern names, abstracts, and identifies the key aspects of a common design structure that make it useful for creating a reusable object-oriented design. The design pattern identifies the participating classes and instances, their roles and collaborations, and the distribution of responsibilities. Each design pattern focuses on a particular object-oriented design problem or issue. It describes when it applies, whether it can be applied in view of other design constraints, and the consequences and trade-offs of its use. Since we must eventually implement our designs, a design pattern also provides sample C++ and (sometimes) Smalltalk code to illustrate an implementation.

Although design patterns describe object-oriented designs, they are based on practical solutions that have been implemented in mainstream object-oriented programming languages like Smalltalk and C++ rather than procedural languages (Pascal, C, Ada) or more dynamic object-oriented languages (CLOS, Dylan, Self). We chose Smalltalk and C++ for pragmatic reasons: Our day-to-day experience has been in these languages, and they are increasingly popular.

The choice of programming language is important because it influences one's point of view. Our patterns assume Smalltalk/C++-level language features, and that choice determines what can and cannot be implemented easily. If we assumed procedural languages, we might have included design patterns called "Inheritance," "Encapsulation," and "Polymorphism." Similarly, some of our patterns are supported directly by the less common object-oriented languages. CLOS has multi-methods, for example, which lessen the need for a pattern such as Visitor (page 331). In fact, there are enough differences between Smalltalk and C++ to mean that some patterns can be expressed more easily in one language than the other. (See Iterator (257) for an example.)

1.2   Design Patterns in Smalltalk MVC

The Model/View/Controller (MVC) triad of classes [KP88] is used to build user interfaces in Smalltalk-80. Looking at the design patterns inside MVC should help you see what we mean by the term "pattern."

MVC consists of three kinds of objects. The Model is the application object, the View is its screen presentation, and the Controller defines the way the user interface reacts to user input. Before MVC, user interface designs tended to lump these objects together. MVC decouples them to increase flexibility and reuse.

MVC decouples views and models by establishing a subscribe/notify protocol between them. A view must ensure that its appearance reflects the state of the model. Whenever the model's data changes, the model notifies views that depend on it. In response, each view gets an opportunity to update itself. This approach lets you attach multiple views to a model to provide different presentations. You can also create new views for a model without rewriting it.

The following diagram shows a model and three views. (We've left out the controllers for simplicity.) The model contains some data values, and the views defining a spreadsheet, histogram, and pie chart display these data in various ways. The model communicates with its views when its values change, and the views communicate with the model to access these values.

views

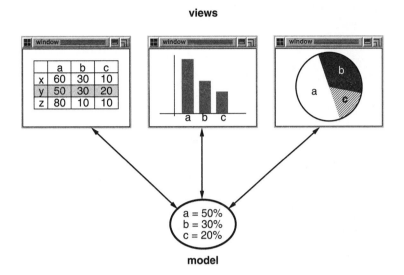

model

Taken at face value, this example reflects a design that decouples views from models. But the design is applicable to a more general problem: decoupling objects so that changes to one can affect any number of others without requiring the changed object to know details of the others. This more general design is described by the Observer (page 293) design pattern.

Another feature of MVC is that views can be nested. For example, a control panel of buttons might be implemented as a complex view containing nested button views. The user interface for an object inspector can consist of nested views that may be reused in a debugger. MVC supports nested views with the CompositeView class, a subclass of View. CompositeView objects act just like View objects; a composite view can be used wherever a view can be used, but it also contains and manages nested views.

Again, we could think of this as a design that lets us treat a composite view just like we treat one of its components. But the design is applicable to a more general problem, which occurs whenever we want to group objects and treat the group like an individual object. This more general design is described by the Composite (163) design pattern. It lets you create a class hierarchy in which some subclasses define primitive objects (e.g., Button) and other classes define composite objects (CompositeView) that assemble the primitives into more complex objects.

MVC also lets you change the way a view responds to user input without changing its visual presentation. You might want to change the way it responds to the keyboard, for example, or have it use a pop-up menu instead of command keys. MVC encapsulates the response mechanism in a Controller object. There is a class hierarchy of controllers, making it easy to create a new controller as a variation on an existing one.

A view uses an instance of a Controller subclass to implement a particular response strategy; to implement a different strategy, simply replace the instance with a different kind of controller. It's even possible to change a view's controller at run-time to let the view change the way it responds to user input. For example, a view can be disabled so that it doesn't accept input simply by giving it a controller that ignores input events.

The View-Controller relationship is an example of the Strategy (315) design pattern. A Strategy is an object that represents an algorithm. It's useful when you want to replace the algorithm either statically or dynamically, when you have a lot of variants of the algorithm, or when the algorithm has complex data structures that you want to encapsulate.

MVC uses other design patterns, such as Factory Method (107) to specify the default controller class for a view and Decorator (175) to add scrolling to a view. But the main relationships in MVC are given by the Observer, Composite, and Strategy design patterns.

1.3   Describing Design Patterns

How do we describe design patterns? Graphical notations, while important and useful, aren't sufficient. They simply capture the end product of the design process as relationships between classes and objects. To reuse the design, we must also record the decisions, alternatives, and trade-offs that led to it. Concrete examples are important too, because they help you see the design in action.

We describe design patterns using a consistent format. Each pattern is divided into sections according to the following template. The template lends a uniform structure to the information, making design patterns easier to learn, compare, and use.

Pattern Name and Classification

The pattern's name conveys the essence of the pattern succinctly. A good name is vital, because it will become part of your design vocabulary. The pattern's classification reflects the scheme we introduce in Section 1.5.

Intent

A short statement that answers the following questions: What does the design pattern do? What is its rationale and intent? What particular design issue or problem does it address?

Also Known As

Other well-known names for the pattern, if any.

Motivation

A scenario that illustrates a design problem and how the class and object structures in the pattern solve the problem. The scenario will help you understand the more abstract description of the pattern that follows.

Applicability

What are the situations in which the design pattern can be applied? What are examples of poor designs that the pattern can address? How can you recognize these situations?

Structure

A graphical representation of the classes in the pattern using a notation based on the Object Modeling Technique (OMT) [RBP+91]. We also use interaction diagrams [JCJO92, Boo94] to illustrate sequences of requests and collaborations between objects. Appendix B describes these notations in detail.

Participants

The classes and/or objects participating in the design pattern and their responsibilities.

Collaborations

How the participants collaborate to carry out their responsibilities.

Consequences

How does the pattern support its objectives? What are the trade-offs and results of using the pattern? What aspect of system structure does it let you vary independently?

Implementation

What pitfalls, hints, or techniques should you be aware of when implementing the pattern? Are there language-specific issues?

Sample Code

Code fragments that illustrate how you might implement the pattern in C++ or Smalltalk.

Known Uses

Examples of the pattern found in real systems. We include at least two examples from different domains.

Related Patterns

What design patterns are closely related to this one? What are the important differences? With which other patterns should this one be used?

The appendices provide background information that will help you understand the patterns and the discussions surrounding them. Appendix A is a glossary of terminology we use. We've already mentioned Appendix B, which presents the various notations. We'll also describe aspects of the notations as we introduce them in the upcoming discussions. Finally, Appendix C contains source code for the foundation classes we use in code samples.

1.4   The Catalog of Design Patterns

The catalog beginning on page 79 contains 23 design patterns. Their names and intents are listed next to give you an overview. The number in parentheses after each pattern name gives the page number for the pattern (a convention we follow throughout the book).

Abstract Factory (87) Provide an interface for creating families of related or dependent objects without specifying their concrete classes.

Adapter (139) Convert the interface of a class into another interface clients expect. Adapter lets classes work together that couldn't otherwise because of incompatible interfaces.

Bridge (151) Decouple an abstraction from its implementation so that the two can vary independently.

Builder (97) Separate the construction of a complex object from its representation so that the same construction process can create different representations.

Chain of Responsibility (223) Avoid coupling the sender of a request to its receiver by giving more than one object a chance to handle the request. Chain the receiving objects and pass the request along the chain until an object handles it.

Command (233) Encapsulate a request as an object, thereby letting you parameterize clients with different requests, queue or log requests, and support undoable operations.

Composite (163) Compose objects into tree structures to represent part-whole hierarchies. Composite lets clients treat individual objects and compositions of objects uniformly.

Decorator (175) Attach additional responsibilities to an object dynamically. Decorators provide a flexible alternative to subclassing for extending functionality.

Facade (185) Provide a unified interface to a set of interfaces in a subsystem. Facade defines a higher-level interface that makes the subsystem easier to use.

Factory Method (107) Define an interface for creating an object, but let subclasses decide which class to instantiate. Factory Method lets a class defer instantiation to subclasses.

Flyweight (195) Use sharing to support large numbers of fine-grained objects efficiently.

Interpreter (243) Given a language, define a represention for its grammar along with an interpreter that uses the representation to interpret sentences in the language.

Iterator (257) Provide a way to access the elements of an aggregate object sequentially without exposing its underlying representation.

Mediator (273) Define an object that encapsulates how a set of objects interact. Mediator promotes loose coupling by keeping objects from referring to each other explicitly, and it lets you vary their interaction independently.

Memento (283) Without violating encapsulation, capture and externalize an object's internal state so that the object can be restored to this state later.

Observer (293) Define a one-to-many dependency between objects so that when one object changes state, all its dependents are notified and updated automatically.

Prototype (117) Specify the kinds of objects to create using a prototypical instance, and create new objects by copying this prototype.

Proxy (207) Provide a surrogate or placeholder for another object to control access to it.

Singleton (127) Ensure a class only has one instance, and provide a global point of access to it.

State (305) Allow an object to alter its behavior when its internal state changes. The object will appear to change its class.

Strategy (315) Define a family of algorithms, encapsulate each one, and make them interchangeable. Strategy lets the algorithm vary independently from clients that use it.

Template Method (325) Define the skeleton of an algorithm in an operation, deferring some steps to subclasses. Template Method lets subclasses redefine certain steps of an algorithm without changing the algorithm's structure.

Visitor (331) Represent an operation to be performed on the elements of an object structure. Visitor lets you define a new operation without changing the classes of the elements on which it operates.

1.5   Organizing the Catalog

Design patterns vary in their granularity and level of abstraction. Because there are many design patterns, we need a way to organize them. This section classifies design patterns so that we can refer to families of related patterns. The classification helps you

		Purpose		
		Creational	**Structural**	**Behavioral**
Scope	**Class**	Factory Method (107)	Adapter (class) (139)	Interpreter (243)
				Template Method (325)
	Object	Abstract Factory (87)	Adapter (object) (139)	Chain of Responsibility (223)
		Builder (97)	Bridge (151)	Command (233)
		Prototype (117)	Composite (163)	Iterator (257)
		Singleton (127)	Decorator (175)	Mediator (273)
			Facade (185)	Memento (283)
			Flyweight (195)	Observer (293)
			Proxy (207)	State (305)
				Strategy (315)
				Visitor (331)

Table 1.1: Design pattern space

learn the patterns in the catalog faster, and it can direct efforts to find new patterns as well.

We classify design patterns by two criteria (Table 1.1). The first criterion, called **purpose**, reflects what a pattern does. Patterns can have either **creational**, **structural**, or **behavioral** purpose. Creational patterns concern the process of object creation. Structural patterns deal with the composition of classes or objects. Behavioral patterns characterize the ways in which classes or objects interact and distribute responsibility.

The second criterion, called **scope**, specifies whether the pattern applies primarily to classes or to objects. Class patterns deal with relationships between classes and their subclasses. These relationships are established through inheritance, so they are static—fixed at compile-time. Object patterns deal with object relationships, which can be changed at run-time and are more dynamic. Almost all patterns use inheritance to some extent. So the only patterns labeled "class patterns" are those that focus on class relationships. Note that most patterns are in the Object scope.

Creational class patterns defer some part of object creation to subclasses, while Creational object patterns defer it to another object. The Structural class patterns use inheritance to compose classes, while the Structural object patterns describe ways to assemble objects. The Behavioral class patterns use inheritance to describe algorithms and flow of control, whereas the Behavioral object patterns describe how a group of objects cooperate to perform a task that no single object can carry out alone.

There are other ways to organize the patterns. Some patterns are often used together. For example, Composite is often used with Iterator or Visitor. Some patterns are alternatives: Prototype is often an alternative to Abstract Factory. Some patterns result in similar designs even though the patterns have different intents. For example, the structure diagrams of Composite and Decorator are similar.

Yet another way to organize design patterns is according to how they reference each other in their "Related Patterns" sections. Figure 1.1 depicts these relationships graphically.

Clearly there are many ways to organize design patterns. Having multiple ways of thinking about patterns will deepen your insight into what they do, how they compare, and when to apply them.

1.6   How Design Patterns Solve Design Problems

Design patterns solve many of the day-to-day problems object-oriented designers face, and in many different ways. Here are several of these problems and how design patterns solve them.

Finding Appropriate Objects

Object-oriented programs are made up of objects. An **object** packages both data and the procedures that operate on that data. The procedures are typically called **methods** or **operations**. An object performs an operation when it receives a **request** (or **message**) from a **client**.

Requests are the *only* way to get an object to execute an operation. Operations are the *only* way to change an object's internal data. Because of these restrictions, the object's internal state is said to be **encapsulated**; it cannot be accessed directly, and its representation is invisible from outside the object.

The hard part about object-oriented design is decomposing a system into objects. The task is difficult because many factors come into play: encapsulation, granularity, dependency, flexibility, performance, evolution, reusability, and on and on. They all influence the decomposition, often in conflicting ways.

Object-oriented design methodologies favor many different approaches. You can write a problem statement, single out the nouns and verbs, and create corresponding classes and operations. Or you can focus on the collaborations and responsibilities in your system. Or you can model the real world and translate the objects found during analysis into design. There will always be disagreement on which approach is best.

Many objects in a design come from the analysis model. But object-oriented designs often end up with classes that have no counterparts in the real world. Some of these are low-level classes like arrays. Others are much higher-level. For example, the Composite (163) pattern introduces an abstraction for treating objects uniformly that doesn't have a physical counterpart. Strict modeling of the real world leads to a system that reflects today's realities but not necessarily tomorrow's. The abstractions that emerge during design are key to making a design flexible.

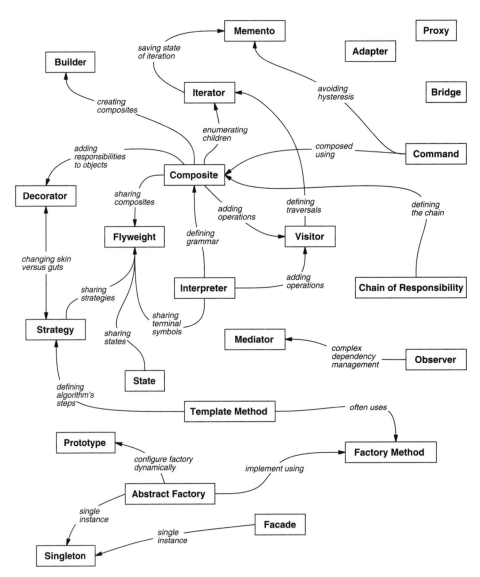

Figure 1.1: Design pattern relationships

Design patterns help you identify less-obvious abstractions and the objects that can capture them. For example, objects that represent a process or algorithm don't occur in nature, yet they are a crucial part of flexible designs. The Strategy (315) pattern describes how to implement interchangeable families of algorithms. The State (305) pattern represents each state of an entity as an object. These objects are seldom found during analysis or even the early stages of design; they're discovered later in the course of making a design more flexible and reusable.

Determining Object Granularity

Objects can vary tremendously in size and number. They can represent everything down to the hardware or all the way up to entire applications. How do we decide what should be an object?

Design patterns address this issue as well. The Facade (185) pattern describes how to represent complete subsystems as objects, and the Flyweight (195) pattern describes how to support huge numbers of objects at the finest granularities. Other design patterns describe specific ways of decomposing an object into smaller objects. Abstract Factory (87) and Builder (97) yield objects whose only responsibilities are creating other objects. Visitor (331) and Command (233) yield objects whose only responsibilities are to implement a request on another object or group of objects.

Specifying Object Interfaces

Every operation declared by an object specifies the operation's name, the objects it takes as parameters, and the operation's return value. This is known as the operation's **signature**. The set of all signatures defined by an object's operations is called the **interface** to the object. An object's interface characterizes the complete set of requests that can be sent to the object. Any request that matches a signature in the object's interface may be sent to the object.

A **type** is a name used to denote a particular interface. We speak of an object as having the type "Window" if it accepts all requests for the operations defined in the interface named "Window." An object may have many types, and widely different objects can share a type. Part of an object's interface may be characterized by one type, and other parts by other types. Two objects of the same type need only share parts of their interfaces. Interfaces can contain other interfaces as subsets. We say that a type is a **subtype** of another if its interface contains the interface of its **supertype**. Often we speak of a subtype *inheriting* the interface of its supertype.

Interfaces are fundamental in object-oriented systems. Objects are known only through their interfaces. There is no way to know anything about an object or to ask it to do anything without going through its interface. An object's interface says nothing about its implementation—different objects are free to implement requests differently. That means two objects having completely different implementations can have identical interfaces.

When a request is sent to an object, the particular operation that's performed depends on *both* the request *and* the receiving object. Different objects that support identical requests may have different implementations of the operations that fulfill these requests. The run-time association of a request to an object and one of its operations is known as **dynamic binding**.

Dynamic binding means that issuing a request doesn't commit you to a particular implementation until run-time. Consequently, you can write programs that expect an object with a particular interface, knowing that any object that has the correct interface will accept the request. Moreover, dynamic binding lets you substitute objects that have identical interfaces for each other at run-time. This substitutability is known as **polymorphism**, and it's a key concept in object-oriented systems. It lets a client object make few assumptions about other objects beyond supporting a particular interface. Polymorphism simplifies the definitions of clients, decouples objects from each other, and lets them vary their relationships to each other at run-time.

Design patterns help you define interfaces by identifying their key elements and the kinds of data that get sent across an interface. A design pattern might also tell you what *not* to put in the interface. The Memento (283) pattern is a good example. It describes how to encapsulate and save the internal state of an object so that the object can be restored to that state later. The pattern stipulates that Memento objects must define two interfaces: a restricted one that lets clients hold and copy mementos, and a privileged one that only the original object can use to store and retrieve state in the memento.

Design patterns also specify relationships between interfaces. In particular, they often require some classes to have similar interfaces, or they place constraints on the interfaces of some classes. For example, both Decorator (175) and Proxy (207) require the interfaces of Decorator and Proxy objects to be identical to the decorated and proxied objects. In Visitor (331), the Visitor interface must reflect all classes of objects that visitors can visit.

Specifying Object Implementations

So far we've said little about how we actually define an object. An object's implementation is defined by its **class**. The class specifies the object's internal data and representation and defines the operations the object can perform.

Our OMT-based notation (summarized in Appendix B) depicts a class as a rectangle with the class name in bold. Operations appear in normal type below the class name. Any data that the class defines comes after the operations. Lines separate the class name from the operations and the operations from the data:

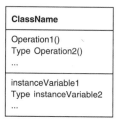

Return types and instance variable types are optional, since we don't assume a statically typed implementation language.

Objects are created by **instantiating** a class. The object is said to be an **instance** of the class. The process of instantiating a class allocates storage for the object's internal data (made up of **instance variables**) and associates the operations with these data. Many similar instances of an object can be created by instantiating a class.

A dashed arrowhead line indicates a class that instantiates objects of another class. The arrow points to the class of the instantiated objects.

New classes can be defined in terms of existing classes using **class inheritance**. When a **subclass** inherits from a **parent class**, it includes the definitions of all the data and operations that the parent class defines. Objects that are instances of the subclass will contain all data defined by the subclass and its parent classes, and they'll be able to perform all operations defined by this subclass and its parents. We indicate the subclass relationship with a vertical line and a triangle:

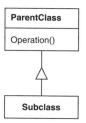

An **abstract class** is one whose main purpose is to define a common interface for its subclasses. An abstract class will defer some or all of its implementation to operations defined in subclasses; hence an abstract class cannot be instantiated. The operations that an abstract class declares but doesn't implement are called **abstract operations**. Classes that aren't abstract are called **concrete classes**.

Subclasses can refine and redefine behaviors of their parent classes. More specifically, a class may **override** an operation defined by its parent class. Overriding gives subclasses a chance to handle requests instead of their parent classes. Class inheritance lets you define classes simply by extending other classes, making it easy to define families of objects having related functionality.

The names of abstract classes appear in slanted type to distinguish them from concrete classes. Slanted type is also used to denote abstract operations. A diagram may include pseudocode for an operation's implementation; if so, the code will appear in a dog-eared box connected by a dashed line to the operation it implements.

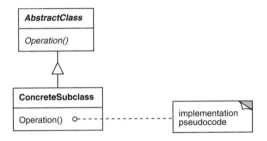

A **mixin class** is a class that's intended to provide an optional interface or functionality to other classes. It's similar to an abstract class in that it's not intended to be instantiated. Mixin classes require multiple inheritance:

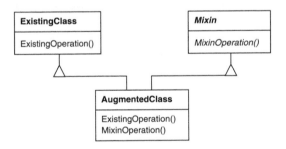

Class versus Interface Inheritance

It's important to understand the difference between an object's *class* and its *type*.

An object's class defines how the object is implemented. The class defines the object's internal state and the implementation of its operations. In contrast, an object's type only refers to its interface—the set of requests to which it can respond. An object can have many types, and objects of different classes can have the same type.

Of course, there's a close relationship between class and type. Because a class defines the operations an object can perform, it also defines the object's type. When we say that an object is an instance of a class, we imply that the object supports the interface defined by the class.

Languages like C++ and Eiffel use classes to specify both an object's type and its implementation. Smalltalk programs do not declare the types of variables; consequently, the compiler does not check that the types of objects assigned to a variable are subtypes of the variable's type. Sending a message requires checking that the class of the receiver implements the message, but it doesn't require checking that the receiver is an instance of a particular class.

It's also important to understand the difference between class inheritance and interface inheritance (or subtyping). Class inheritance defines an object's implementation in terms of another object's implementation. In short, it's a mechanism for code and representation sharing. In contrast, interface inheritance (or subtyping) describes when an object can be used in place of another.

It's easy to confuse these two concepts, because many languages don't make the distinction explicit. In languages like C++ and Eiffel, inheritance means both interface and implementation inheritance. The standard way to inherit an interface in C++ is to inherit publicly from a class that has (pure) virtual member functions. Pure interface inheritance can be approximated in C++ by inheriting publicly from pure abstract classes. Pure implementation or class inheritance can be approximated with private inheritance. In Smalltalk, inheritance means just implementation inheritance. You can assign instances of any class to a variable as long as those instances support the operation performed on the value of the variable.

Although most programming languages don't support the distinction between interface and implementation inheritance, people make the distinction in practice. Smalltalk programmers usually act as if subclasses were subtypes (though there are some well-known exceptions [Coo92]); C++ programmers manipulate objects through types defined by abstract classes.

Many of the design patterns depend on this distinction. For example, objects in a Chain of Responsibility (223) must have a common type, but usually they don't share a common implementation. In the Composite (163) pattern, Component defines a common interface, but Composite often defines a common implementation. Command (233), Observer (293), State (305), and Strategy (315) are often implemented with abstract classes that are pure interfaces.

Programming to an Interface, not an Implementation

Class inheritance is basically just a mechanism for extending an application's functionality by reusing functionality in parent classes. It lets you define a new kind of object rapidly in terms of an old one. It lets you get new implementations almost for free, inheriting most of what you need from existing classes.

However, implementation reuse is only half the story. Inheritance's ability to define families of objects with *identical* interfaces (usually by inheriting from an abstract class) is also important. Why? Because polymorphism depends on it.

When inheritance is used carefully (some will say *properly*), all classes derived from an abstract class will share its interface. This implies that a subclass merely adds or overrides operations and does not hide operations of the parent class. *All* subclasses can then respond to the requests in the interface of this abstract class, making them all subtypes of the abstract class.

There are two benefits to manipulating objects solely in terms of the interface defined by abstract classes:

1. Clients remain unaware of the specific types of objects they use, as long as the objects adhere to the interface that clients expect.

2. Clients remain unaware of the classes that implement these objects. Clients only know about the abstract class(es) defining the interface.

This so greatly reduces implementation dependencies between subsystems that it leads to the following principle of reusable object-oriented design:

> *Program to an interface, not an implementation.*

Don't declare variables to be instances of particular concrete classes. Instead, commit only to an interface defined by an abstract class. You will find this to be a common theme of the design patterns in this book.

You have to instantiate concrete classes (that is, specify a particular implementation) somewhere in your system, of course, and the creational patterns (Abstract Factory (87), Builder (97), Factory Method (107), Prototype (117), and Singleton (127)) let you do just that. By abstracting the process of object creation, these patterns give you different ways to associate an interface with its implementation transparently at instantiation. Creational patterns ensure that your system is written in terms of interfaces, not implementations.

Putting Reuse Mechanisms to Work

Most people can understand concepts like objects, interfaces, classes, and inheritance. The challenge lies in applying them to build flexible, reusable software, and design patterns can show you how.

Inheritance versus Composition

The two most common techniques for reusing functionality in object-oriented systems are class inheritance and **object composition**. As we've explained, class inheritance lets you define the implementation of one class in terms of another's. Reuse by subclassing is often referred to as **white-box reuse**. The term "white-box" refers to visibility: With inheritance, the internals of parent classes are often visible to subclasses.

Object composition is an alternative to class inheritance. Here, new functionality is obtained by assembling or *composing* objects to get more complex functionality. Object composition requires that the objects being composed have well-defined interfaces. This style of reuse is called **black-box reuse**, because no internal details of objects are visible. Objects appear only as "black boxes."

Inheritance and composition each have their advantages and disadvantages. Class inheritance is defined statically at compile-time and is straightforward to use, since it's supported directly by the programming language. Class inheritance also makes it easier to modify the implementation being reused. When a subclass overrides some but not all operations, it can affect the operations it inherits as well, assuming they call the overridden operations.

But class inheritance has some disadvantages, too. First, you can't change the implementations inherited from parent classes at run-time, because inheritance is defined at compile-time. Second, and generally worse, parent classes often define at least part of their subclasses' physical representation. Because inheritance exposes a subclass to details of its parent's implementation, it's often said that "inheritance breaks encapsulation" [Sny86]. The implementation of a subclass becomes so bound up with the implementation of its parent class that any change in the parent's implementation will force the subclass to change.

Implementation dependencies can cause problems when you're trying to reuse a subclass. Should any aspect of the inherited implementation not be appropriate for new problem domains, the parent class must be rewritten or replaced by something more appropriate. This dependency limits flexibility and ultimately reusability. One cure for this is to inherit only from abstract classes, since they usually provide little or no implementation.

Object composition is defined dynamically at run-time through objects acquiring references to other objects. Composition requires objects to respect each others' interfaces, which in turn requires carefully designed interfaces that don't stop you from using one object with many others. But there is a payoff. Because objects are accessed solely through their interfaces, we don't break encapsulation. Any object can be replaced at run-time by another as long as it has the same type. Moreover, because an object's implementation will be written in terms of object interfaces, there are substantially fewer implementation dependencies.

Object composition has another effect on system design. Favoring object composition over class inheritance helps you keep each class encapsulated and focused on one task. Your classes and class hierarchies will remain small and will be less likely to grow into unmanageable monsters. On the other hand, a design based on object composition will have more objects (if fewer classes), and the system's behavior will depend on their interrelationships instead of being defined in one class.

That leads us to our second principle of object-oriented design:

Favor object composition over class inheritance.

Ideally, you shouldn't have to create new components to achieve reuse. You should be able to get all the functionality you need just by assembling existing components through object composition. But this is rarely the case, because the set of available components is never quite rich enough in practice. Reuse by inheritance makes it easier to make new components that can be composed with old ones. Inheritance and object composition thus work together.

Nevertheless, our experience is that designers overuse inheritance as a reuse technique, and designs are often made more reusable (and simpler) by depending more on object composition. You'll see object composition applied again and again in the design patterns.

Delegation

Delegation is a way of making composition as powerful for reuse as inheritance [Lie86, JZ91]. In delegation, *two* objects are involved in handling a request: a receiving object delegates operations to its **delegate**. This is analogous to subclasses deferring requests to parent classes. But with inheritance, an inherited operation can always refer to the receiving object through the `this` member variable in C++ and `self` in Smalltalk. To achieve the same effect with delegation, the receiver passes itself to the delegate to let the delegated operation refer to the receiver.

For example, instead of making class Window a subclass of Rectangle (because windows happen to be rectangular), the Window class might reuse the behavior of Rectangle by keeping a Rectangle instance variable and *delegating* Rectangle-specific behavior to it. In other words, instead of a Window *being* a Rectangle, it would *have* a Rectangle. Window must now forward requests to its Rectangle instance explicitly, whereas before it would have inherited those operations.

The following diagram depicts the Window class delegating its Area operation to a Rectangle instance.

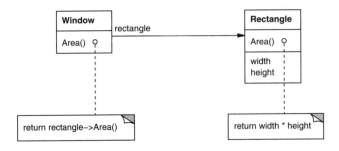

A plain arrowhead line indicates that a class keeps a reference to an instance of another class. The reference has an optional name, "rectangle" in this case.

The main advantage of delegation is that it makes it easy to compose behaviors at run-time and to change the way they're composed. Our window can become circular at run-time simply by replacing its Rectangle instance with a Circle instance, assuming Rectangle and Circle have the same type.

Delegation has a disadvantage it shares with other techniques that make software more flexible through object composition: Dynamic, highly parameterized software is harder to understand than more static software. There are also run-time inefficiencies, but the human inefficiencies are more important in the long run. Delegation is a good design choice only when it simplifies more than it complicates. It isn't easy to give rules that tell you exactly when to use delegation, because how effective it will be depends on the context and on how much experience you have with it. Delegation works best when it's used in highly stylized ways—that is, in standard patterns.

Several design patterns use delegation. The State (305), Strategy (315), and Visitor (331) patterns depend on it. In the State pattern, an object delegates requests to a State object that represents its current state. In the Strategy pattern, an object delegates a specific request to an object that represents a strategy for carrying out the request. An object will only have one state, but it can have many strategies for different requests. The purpose of both patterns is to change the behavior of an object by changing the objects to which it delegates requests. In Visitor, the operation that gets performed on each element of an object structure is always delegated to the Visitor object.

Other patterns use delegation less heavily. Mediator (273) introduces an object to mediate communication between other objects. Sometimes the Mediator object implements operations simply by forwarding them to the other objects; other times it passes along a reference to itself and thus uses true delegation. Chain of Responsibility (223) handles requests by forwarding them from one object to another along a chain of objects. Sometimes this request carries with it a reference to the original object receiving the request, in which case the pattern is using delegation. Bridge (151) decouples an abstraction from its implementation. If the abstraction and a particular implementation are closely matched, then the abstraction may simply delegate operations to that implementation.

Delegation is an extreme example of object composition. It shows that you can always replace inheritance with object composition as a mechanism for code reuse.

Inheritance versus Parameterized Types

Another (not strictly object-oriented) technique for reusing functionality is through **parameterized types**, also known as **generics** (Ada, Eiffel) and **templates** (C++). This technique lets you define a type without specifying all the other types it uses. The unspecified types are supplied as *parameters* at the point of use. For example, a List class can be parameterized by the type of elements it contains. To declare a list of integers, you supply the type "integer" as a parameter to the List parameterized type.

To declare a list of String objects, you supply the "String" type as a parameter. The language implementation will create a customized version of the List class template for each type of element.

Parameterized types give us a third way (in addition to class inheritance and object composition) to compose behavior in object-oriented systems. Many designs can be implemented using any of these three techniques. To parameterize a sorting routine by the operation it uses to compare elements, we could make the comparison

1. an operation implemented by subclasses (an application of Template Method (325)),

2. the responsibility of an object that's passed to the sorting routine (Strategy (315)), or

3. an argument of a C++ template or Ada generic that specifies the name of the function to call to compare the elements.

There are important differences between these techniques. Object composition lets you change the behavior being composed at run-time, but it also requires indirection and can be less efficient. Inheritance lets you provide default implementations for operations and lets subclasses override them. Parameterized types let you change the types that a class can use. But neither inheritance nor parameterized types can change at run-time. Which approach is best depends on your design and implementation constraints.

None of the patterns in this book concerns parameterized types, though we use them on occasion to customize a pattern's C++ implementation. Parameterized types aren't needed at all in a language like Smalltalk that doesn't have compile-time type checking.

Relating Run-Time and Compile-Time Structures

An object-oriented program's run-time structure often bears little resemblance to its code structure. The code structure is frozen at compile-time; it consists of classes in fixed inheritance relationships. A program's run-time structure consists of rapidly changing networks of communicating objects. In fact, the two structures are largely independent. Trying to understand one from the other is like trying to understand the dynamism of living ecosystems from the static taxonomy of plants and animals, and vice versa.

Consider the distinction between object **aggregation** and **acquaintance** and how differently they manifest themselves at compile- and run-times. Aggregation implies that one object owns or is responsible for another object. Generally we speak of an object *having* or being *part of* another object. Aggregation implies that an aggregate object and its owner have identical lifetimes.

Acquaintance implies that an object merely *knows of* another object. Sometimes acquaintance is called "association" or the "using" relationship. Acquainted objects may request operations of each other, but they aren't responsible for each other. Acquaintance is a weaker relationship than aggregation and suggests much looser coupling between objects.

In our diagrams, a plain arrowhead line denotes acquaintance. An arrowhead line with a diamond at its base denotes aggregation:

It's easy to confuse aggregation and acquaintance, because they are often implemented in the same way. In Smalltalk, all variables are references to other objects. There's no distinction in the programming language between aggregation and acquaintance. In C++, aggregation can be implemented by defining member variables that are real instances, but it's more common to define them as pointers or references to instances. Acquaintance is implemented with pointers and references as well.

Ultimately, acquaintance and aggregation are determined more by intent than by explicit language mechanisms. The distinction may be hard to see in the compile-time structure, but it's significant. Aggregation relationships tend to be fewer and more permanent than acquaintance. Acquaintances, in contrast, are made and remade more frequently, sometimes existing only for the duration of an operation. Acquaintances are more dynamic as well, making them more difficult to discern in the source code.

With such disparity between a program's run-time and compile-time structures, it's clear that code won't reveal everything about how a system will work. The system's run-time structure must be imposed more by the designer than the language. The relationships between objects and their types must be designed with great care, because they determine how good or bad the run-time structure is.

Many design patterns (in particular those that have object scope) capture the distinction between compile-time and run-time structures explicitly. Composite (163) and Decorator (175) are especially useful for building complex run-time structures. Observer (293) involves run-time structures that are often hard to understand unless you know the pattern. Chain of Responsibility (223) also results in communication patterns that inheritance doesn't reveal. In general, the run-time structures aren't clear from the code until you understand the patterns.

Designing for Change

The key to maximizing reuse lies in anticipating new requirements and changes to existing requirements, and in designing your systems so that they can evolve accordingly.

To design the system so that it's robust to such changes, you must consider how the system might need to change over its lifetime. A design that doesn't take change into account risks major redesign in the future. Those changes might involve class redefinition and reimplementation, client modification, and retesting. Redesign affects many parts of the software system, and unanticipated changes are invariably expensive.

Design patterns help you avoid this by ensuring that a system can change in specific ways. Each design pattern lets some aspect of system structure vary independently of other aspects, thereby making a system more robust to a particular kind of change.

Here are some common causes of redesign along with the design pattern(s) that address them:

1. *Creating an object by specifying a class explicitly.* Specifying a class name when you create an object commits you to a particular implementation instead of a particular interface. This commitment can complicate future changes. To avoid it, create objects indirectly.

   Design patterns: Abstract Factory (87), Factory Method (107), Prototype (117).

2. *Dependence on specific operations.* When you specify a particular operation, you commit to one way of satisfying a request. By avoiding hard-coded requests, you make it easier to change the way a request gets satisfied both at compile-time and at run-time.

   Design patterns: Chain of Responsibility (223), Command (233).

3. *Dependence on hardware and software platform.* External operating system interfaces and application programming interfaces (APIs) are different on different hardware and software platforms. Software that depends on a particular platform will be harder to port to other platforms. It may even be difficult to keep it up to date on its native platform. It's important therefore to design your system to limit its platform dependencies.

   Design patterns: Abstract Factory (87), Bridge (151).

4. *Dependence on object representations or implementations.* Clients that know how an object is represented, stored, located, or implemented might need to be changed when the object changes. Hiding this information from clients keeps changes from cascading.

   Design patterns: Abstract Factory (87), Bridge (151), Memento (283), Proxy (207).

5. *Algorithmic dependencies.* Algorithms are often extended, optimized, and replaced during development and reuse. Objects that depend on an algorithm will have to change when the algorithm changes. Therefore algorithms that are likely to change should be isolated.

   Design patterns: Builder (97), Iterator (257), Strategy (315), Template Method (325), Visitor (331).

6. *Tight coupling.* Classes that are tightly coupled are hard to reuse in isolation, since they depend on each other. Tight coupling leads to monolithic systems, where you can't change or remove a class without understanding and changing many

other classes. The system becomes a dense mass that's hard to learn, port, and maintain.

Loose coupling increases the probability that a class can be reused by itself and that a system can be learned, ported, modified, and extended more easily. Design patterns use techniques such as abstract coupling and layering to promote loosely coupled systems.

Design patterns: Abstract Factory (87), Bridge (151), Chain of Responsibility (223), Command (233), Facade (185), Mediator (273), Observer (293).

7. *Extending functionality by subclassing.* Customizing an object by subclassing often isn't easy. Every new class has a fixed implementation overhead (initialization, finalization, etc.). Defining a subclass also requires an in-depth understanding of the parent class. For example, overriding one operation might require overriding another. An overridden operation might be required to call an inherited operation. And subclassing can lead to an explosion of classes, because you might have to introduce many new subclasses for even a simple extension.

   Object composition in general and delegation in particular provide flexible alternatives to inheritance for combining behavior. New functionality can be added to an application by composing existing objects in new ways rather than by defining new subclasses of existing classes. On the other hand, heavy use of object composition can make designs harder to understand. Many design patterns produce designs in which you can introduce customized functionality just by defining one subclass and composing its instances with existing ones.

   Design patterns: Bridge (151), Chain of Responsibility (223), Composite (163), Decorator (175), Observer (293), Strategy (315).

8. *Inability to alter classes conveniently.* Sometimes you have to modify a class that can't be modified conveniently. Perhaps you need the source code and don't have it (as may be the case with a commercial class library). Or maybe any change would require modifying lots of existing subclasses. Design patterns offer ways to modify classes in such circumstances.

   Design patterns: Adapter (139), Decorator (175), Visitor (331).

These examples reflect the flexibility that design patterns can help you build into your software. How crucial such flexibility is depends on the kind of software you're building. Let's look at the role design patterns play in the development of three broad classes of software: application programs, toolkits, and frameworks.

Application Programs

If you're building an application program such as a document editor or spreadsheet, then *internal* reuse, maintainability, and extension are high priorities. Internal reuse ensures that you don't design and implement any more than you have to. Design patterns that reduce dependencies can increase internal reuse. Looser coupling boosts the likelihood that one class of object can cooperate with several others. For example, when you eliminate dependencies on specific operations by isolating and encapsulating each operation, you make it easier to reuse an operation in different contexts. The same thing can happen when you remove algorithmic and representational dependencies too.

Design patterns also make an application more maintainable when they're used to limit platform dependencies and to layer a system. They enhance extensibility by showing you how to extend class hierarchies and how to exploit object composition. Reduced coupling also enhances extensibility. Extending a class in isolation is easier if the class doesn't depend on lots of other classes.

Toolkits

Often an application will incorporate classes from one or more libraries of predefined classes called **toolkits**. A toolkit is a set of related and reusable classes designed to provide useful, general-purpose functionality. An example of a toolkit is a set of collection classes for lists, associative tables, stacks, and the like. The C++ I/O stream library is another example. Toolkits don't impose a particular design on your application; they just provide functionality that can help your application do its job. They let you as an implementer avoid recoding common functionality. Toolkits emphasize *code reuse*. They are the object-oriented equivalent of subroutine libraries.

Toolkit design is arguably harder than application design, because toolkits have to work in many applications to be useful. Moreover, the toolkit writer isn't in a position to know what those applications will be or their special needs. That makes it all the more important to avoid assumptions and dependencies that can limit the toolkit's flexibility and consequently its applicability and effectiveness.

Frameworks

A **framework** is a set of cooperating classes that make up a reusable design for a specific class of software [Deu89, JF88]. For example, a framework can be geared toward building graphical editors for different domains like artistic drawing, music composition, and mechanical CAD [VL90, Joh92]. Another framework can help you build compilers for different programming languages and target machines [JML92]. Yet another might help you build financial modeling applications [BE93]. You customize a framework to a particular application by creating application-specific subclasses of abstract classes from the framework.

The framework dictates the architecture of your application. It will define the overall structure, its partitioning into classes and objects, the key responsibilities thereof, how the classes and objects collaborate, and the thread of control. A framework predefines these design parameters so that you, the application designer/implementer, can concentrate on the specifics of your application. The framework captures the design decisions that are common to its application domain. Frameworks thus emphasize *design reuse* over code reuse, though a framework will usually include concrete subclasses you can put to work immediately.

Reuse on this level leads to an inversion of control between the application and the software on which it's based. When you use a toolkit (or a conventional subroutine library for that matter), you write the main body of the application and call the code you want to reuse. When you use a framework, you reuse the main body and write the code *it* calls. You'll have to write operations with particular names and calling conventions, but that reduces the design decisions you have to make.

Not only can you build applications faster as a result, but the applications have similar structures. They are easier to maintain, and they seem more consistent to their users. On the other hand, you lose some creative freedom, since many design decisions have been made for you.

If applications are hard to design, and toolkits are harder, then frameworks are hardest of all. A framework designer gambles that one architecture will work for all applications in the domain. Any substantive change to the framework's design would reduce its benefits considerably, since the framework's main contribution to an application is the architecture it defines. Therefore it's imperative to design the framework to be as flexible and extensible as possible.

Furthermore, because applications are so dependent on the framework for their design, they are particularly sensitive to changes in framework interfaces. As a framework evolves, applications have to evolve with it. That makes loose coupling all the more important; otherwise even a minor change to the framework will have major repercussions.

The design issues just discussed are most critical to framework design. A framework that addresses them using design patterns is far more likely to achieve high levels of design and code reuse than one that doesn't. Mature frameworks usually incorporate several design patterns. The patterns help make the framework's architecture suitable to many different applications without redesign.

An added benefit comes when the framework is documented with the design patterns it uses [BJ94]. People who know the patterns gain insight into the framework faster. Even people who don't know the patterns can benefit from the structure they lend to the framework's documentation. Enhancing documentation is important for all types of software, but it's particularly important for frameworks. Frameworks often pose a steep learning curve that must be overcome before they're useful. While design patterns might not flatten the learning curve entirely, they can make it less steep by making key elements of the framework's design more explicit.

Because patterns and frameworks have some similarities, people often wonder how or even if they differ. They are different in three major ways:

1. *Design patterns are more abstract than frameworks.* Frameworks can be embodied in code, but only *examples* of patterns can be embodied in code. A strength of frameworks is that they can be written down in programming languages and not only studied but executed and reused directly. In contrast, the design patterns in this book have to be implemented each time they're used. Design patterns also explain the intent, trade-offs, and consequences of a design.

2. *Design patterns are smaller architectural elements than frameworks.* A typical framework contains several design patterns, but the reverse is never true.

3. *Design patterns are less specialized than frameworks.* Frameworks always have a particular application domain. A graphical editor framework might be used in a factory simulation, but it won't be mistaken for a simulation framework. In contrast, the design patterns in this catalog can be used in nearly any kind of application. While more specialized design patterns than ours are certainly possible (say, design patterns for distributed systems or concurrent programming), even these wouldn't dictate an application architecture like a framework would.

Frameworks are becoming increasingly common and important. They are the way that object-oriented systems achieve the most reuse. Larger object-oriented applications will end up consisting of layers of frameworks that cooperate with each other. Most of the design and code in the application will come from or be influenced by the frameworks it uses.

1.7   How to Select a Design Pattern

With more than 20 design patterns in the catalog to choose from, it might be hard to find the one that addresses a particular design problem, especially if the catalog is new and unfamiliar to you. Here are several different approaches to finding the design pattern that's right for your problem:

- *Consider how design patterns solve design problems.* Section 1.6 discusses how design patterns help you find appropriate objects, determine object granularity, specify object interfaces, and several other ways in which design patterns solve design problems. Referring to these discussions can help guide your search for the right pattern.

- *Scan Intent sections.* Section 1.4 (page 8) lists the Intent sections from all the patterns in the catalog. Read through each pattern's intent to find one or more that sound relevant to your problem. You can use the classification scheme presented in Table 1.1 (page 10) to narrow your search.

- *Study how patterns interrelate.* Figure 1.1 (page 12) shows relationships between design patterns graphically. Studying these relationships can help direct you to the right pattern or group of patterns.

- *Study patterns of like purpose.* The catalog (page 79) has three chapters, one for creational patterns, another for structural patterns, and a third for behavioral patterns. Each chapter starts off with introductory comments on the patterns and concludes with a section that compares and contrasts them. These sections give you insight into the similarities and differences between patterns of like purpose.

- *Examine a cause of redesign.* Look at the causes of redesign starting on page 24 to see if your problem involves one or more of them. Then look at the patterns that help you avoid the causes of redesign.

- *Consider what should be variable in your design.* This approach is the opposite of focusing on the causes of redesign. Instead of considering what might *force* a change to a design, consider what you want to be *able* to change without redesign. The focus here is on *encapsulating the concept that varies*, a theme of many design patterns. Table 1.2 lists the design aspect(s) that design patterns let you vary independently, thereby letting you change them without redesign.

1.8   How to Use a Design Pattern

Once you've picked a design pattern, how do you use it? Here's a step-by-step approach to applying a design pattern effectively:

1. *Read the pattern once through for an overview.* Pay particular attention to the Applicability and Consequences sections to ensure the pattern is right for your problem.

2. *Go back and study the Structure, Participants, and Collaborations sections.* Make sure you understand the classes and objects in the pattern and how they relate to one another.

3. *Look at the Sample Code section to see a concrete example of the pattern in code.* Studying the code helps you learn how to implement the pattern.

4. *Choose names for pattern participants that are meaningful in the application context.* The names for participants in design patterns are usually too abstract to appear directly in an application. Nevertheless, it's useful to incorporate the participant name into the name that appears in the application. That helps make the pattern more explicit in the implementation. For example, if you use the Strategy pattern for a text compositing algorithm, then you might have classes SimpleLayoutStrategy or TeXLayoutStrategy.

5. *Define the classes.* Declare their interfaces, establish their inheritance relationships, and define the instance variables that represent data and object references. Identify existing classes in your application that the pattern will affect, and modify them accordingly.

Purpose	Design Pattern	Aspect(s) That Can Vary
Creational	Abstract Factory (87)	families of product objects
	Builder (97)	how a composite object gets created
	Factory Method (107)	subclass of object that is instantiated
	Prototype (117)	class of object that is instantiated
	Singleton (127)	the sole instance of a class
Structural	Adapter (139)	interface to an object
	Bridge (151)	implementation of an object
	Composite (163)	structure and composition of an object
	Decorator (175)	responsibilities of an object without subclassing
	Facade (185)	interface to a subsystem
	Flyweight (195)	storage costs of objects
	Proxy (207)	how an object is accessed; its location
Behavioral	Chain of Responsibility (223)	object that can fulfill a request
	Command (233)	when and how a request is fulfilled
	Interpreter (243)	grammar and interpretation of a language
	Iterator (257)	how an aggregate's elements are accessed, traversed
	Mediator (273)	how and which objects interact with each other
	Memento (283)	what private information is stored outside an object, and when
	Observer (293)	number of objects that depend on another object; how the dependent objects stay up to date
	State (305)	states of an object
	Strategy (315)	an algorithm
	Template Method (325)	steps of an algorithm
	Visitor (331)	operations that can be applied to object(s) without changing their class(es)

Table 1.2: Design aspects that design patterns let you vary

6. *Define application-specific names for operations in the pattern.* Here again, the names generally depend on the application. Use the responsibilities and collaborations associated with each operation as a guide. Also, be consistent in your naming conventions. For example, you might use the "Create-" prefix consistently to denote a factory method.

7. *Implement the operations to carry out the responsibilities and collaborations in the pattern.* The Implementation section offers hints to guide you in the implementation. The examples in the Sample Code section can help as well.

These are just guidelines to get you started. Over time you'll develop your own way of working with design patterns.

No discussion of how to use design patterns would be complete without a few words on how *not* to use them. Design patterns should not be applied indiscriminately. Often they achieve flexibility and variability by introducing additional levels of indirection, and that can complicate a design and/or cost you some performance. A design pattern should only be applied when the flexibility it affords is actually needed. The Consequences sections are most helpful when evaluating a pattern's benefits and liabilities.

Chapter 2

A Case Study:
Designing a Document Editor

This chapter presents a case study in the design of a "What-You-See-Is-What-You-Get" (or "WYSIWYG") document editor called **Lexi**.[1] We'll see how design patterns capture solutions to design problems in Lexi and applications like it. By the end of this chapter you will have gained experience with eight patterns, learning them by example.

Figure 2.1 depicts Lexi's user interface. A WYSIWYG representation of the document occupies the large rectangular area in the center. The document can mix text and graphics freely in a variety of formatting styles. Surrounding the document are the usual pull-down menus and scroll bars, plus a collection of page icons for jumping to a particular page in the document.

2.1 Design Problems

We will examine seven problems in Lexi's design:

1. *Document structure.* The choice of internal representation for the document affects nearly every aspect of Lexi's design. All editing, formatting, displaying, and textual analysis will require traversing the representation. The way we organize this information will impact the design of the rest of the application.

2. *Formatting.* How does Lexi actually arrange text and graphics into lines and columns? What objects are responsible for carrying out different formatting policies? How do these policies interact with the document's internal representation?

---

[1] Lexi's design is based on Doc, a text editing application developed by Calder [CL92].

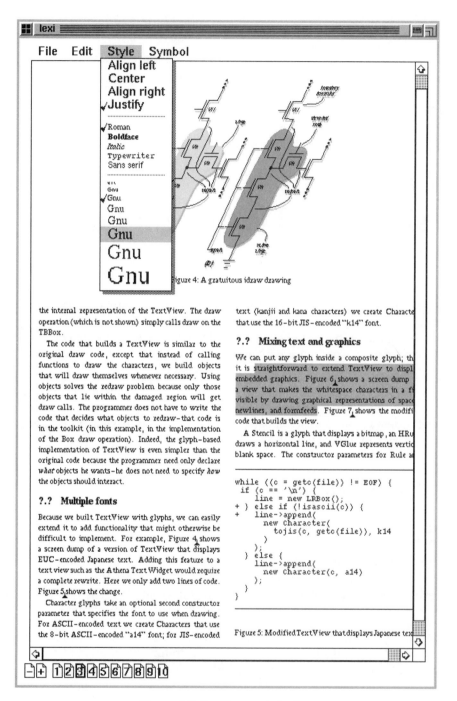

Figure 2.1: Lexi's user interface

3. *Embellishing the user interface.* Lexi's user interface includes scroll bars, borders, and drop shadows that embellish the WYSIWYG document interface. Such embellishments are likely to change as Lexi's user interface evolves. Hence it's important to be able to add and remove embellishments easily without affecting the rest of the application.

4. *Supporting multiple look-and-feel standards.* Lexi should adapt easily to different look-and-feel standards such as Motif and Presentation Manager (PM) without major modification.

5. *Supporting multiple window systems.* Different look-and-feel standards are usually implemented on different window systems. Lexi's design should be as independent of the window system as possible.

6. *User operations.* Users control Lexi through various user interfaces, including buttons and pull-down menus. The functionality behind these interfaces is scattered throughout the objects in the application. The challenge here is to provide a uniform mechanism both for accessing this scattered functionality and for undoing its effects.

7. *Spelling checking and hyphenation.* How does Lexi support analytical operations such as checking for misspelled words and determining hyphenation points? How can we minimize the number of classes we have to modify to add a new analytical operation?

We discuss these design problems in the sections that follow. Each problem has an associated set of goals plus constraints on how we achieve those goals. We explain the goals and constraints in detail before proposing a specific solution. The problem and its solution will illustrate one or more design patterns. The discussion for each problem will culminate in a brief introduction to the relevant patterns.

2.2 Document Structure

A document is ultimately just an arrangement of basic graphical elements such as characters, lines, polygons, and other shapes. These elements capture the total information content of the document. Yet an author often views these elements not in graphical terms but in terms of the document's physical structure—lines, columns, figures, tables, and other substructures.[2] In turn, these substructures have substructures of their own, and so on.

Lexi's user interface should let users manipulate these substructures directly. For example, a user should be able to treat a diagram as a unit rather than as a collection of

---

[2] Authors often view the document in terms of its *logical* structure as well, that is, in terms of sentences, paragraphs, sections, subsections, and chapters. To keep this example simple, our internal representation won't store information about the logical structure explicitly. But the design solution we describe works equally well for representing such information.

individual graphical primitives. The user should be able to refer to a table as a whole, not as an unstructured mass of text and graphics. That helps make the interface simple and intuitive. To give Lexi's implementation similar qualities, we'll choose an internal representation that matches the document's physical structure.

In particular, the internal representation should support the following:

- Maintaining the document's physical structure, that is, the arrangement of text and graphics into lines, columns, tables, etc.

- Generating and presenting the document visually.

- Mapping positions on the display to elements in the internal representation. This lets Lexi determine what the user is referring to when he points to something in the visual representation.

In addition to these goals are some constraints. First, we should treat text and graphics uniformly. The application's interface lets the user embed text within graphics freely and vice versa. We should avoid treating graphics as a special case of text or text as a special case of graphics; otherwise we'll end up with redundant formatting and manipulation mechanisms. One set of mechanisms should suffice for both text and graphics.

Second, our implementation shouldn't have to distinguish between single elements and groups of elements in the internal representation. Lexi should be able to treat simple and complex elements uniformly, thereby allowing arbitrarily complex documents. The tenth element in line five of column two, for instance, could be a single character or an intricate diagram with many subelements. As long as we know this element can draw itself and specify its dimensions, its complexity has no bearing on how and where it should appear on the page.

Opposing the second constraint, however, is the need to analyze the text for such things as spelling errors and potential hyphenation points. Often we don't care whether the element of a line is a simple or complex object. But sometimes an analysis depends on the objects being analyzed. It makes little sense, for example, to check the spelling of a polygon or to hyphenate it. The internal representation's design should take this and other potentially conflicting constraints into account.

Recursive Composition

A common way to represent hierarchically structured information is through a technique called **recursive composition**, which entails building increasingly complex elements out of simpler ones. Recursive composition gives us a way to compose a document out of simple graphical elements. As a first step, we can tile a set of characters and graphics from left to right to form a line in the document. Then multiple lines can be arranged to form a column, multiple columns can form a page, and so on (see Figure 2.2).

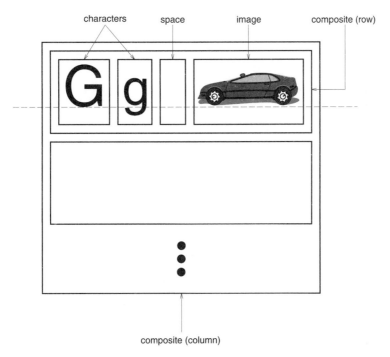

Figure 2.2: Recursive composition of text and graphics

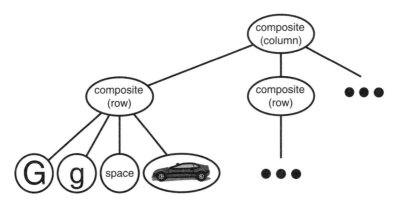

Figure 2.3: Object structure for recursive composition of text and graphics

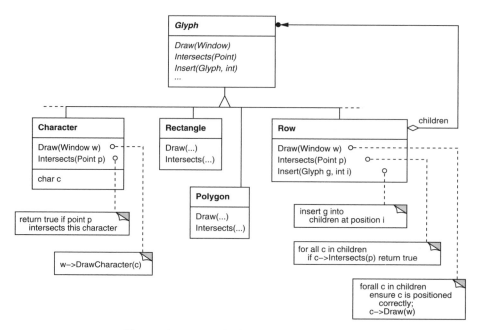

Figure 2.4: Partial Glyph class hierarchy

We can represent this physical structure by devoting an object to each important element. That includes not just the visible elements like the characters and graphics but the invisible, structural elements as well—the lines and the column. The result is the object structure shown in Figure 2.3.

By using an object for each character and graphical element in the document, we promote flexibility at the finest levels of Lexi's design. We can treat text and graphics uniformly with respect to how they are drawn, formatted, and embedded within each other. We can extend Lexi to support new character sets without disturbing other functionality. Lexi's object structure mimics the document's physical structure.

This approach has two important implications. The first is obvious: The objects need corresponding classes. The second implication, which may be less obvious, is that these classes must have compatible interfaces, because we want to treat the objects uniformly. The way to make interfaces compatible in a language like C++ is to relate the classes through inheritance.

Glyphs

We'll define a **Glyph** abstract class for all objects that can appear in a document structure.[3] Its subclasses define both primitive graphical elements (like characters and

---

[3] Calder was the first to use the term "glyph" in this context [CL90]. Most contemporary document editors don't use an object for every character, presumably for efficiency reasons. Calder demonstrated that this

Responsibility	Operations
appearance	`virtual void Draw(Window*)`
	`virtual void Bounds(Rect&)`
hit detection	`virtual bool Intersects(const Point&)`
structure	`virtual void Insert(Glyph*, int)`
	`virtual void Remove(Glyph*)`
	`virtual Glyph* Child(int)`
	`virtual Glyph* Parent()`

Table 2.1: Basic glyph interface

images) and structural elements (like rows and columns). Figure 2.4 depicts a representative part of the Glyph class hierarchy, and Table 2.1 presents the basic glyph interface in more detail using C++ notation.[4]

Glyphs have three basic responsibilities. They know (1) how to draw themselves, (2) what space they occupy, and (3) their children and parent.

Glyph subclasses redefine the `Draw` operation to render themselves onto a window. They are passed a reference to a `Window` object in the call to `Draw`. The **Window** class defines graphics operations for rendering text and basic shapes in a window on the screen. A **Rectangle** subclass of Glyph might redefine `Draw` as follows:

```
void Rectangle::Draw (Window* w) {
    w->DrawRect(_x0, _y0, _x1, _y1);
}
```

where _x0, _y0, _x1, and _y1 are data members of `Rectangle` that define two opposing corners of the rectangle. `DrawRect` is the Window operation that makes the rectangle appear on the screen.

A parent glyph often needs to know how much space a child glyph occupies, for example, to arrange it and other glyphs in a line so that none overlaps (as shown in Figure 2.2). The `Bounds` operation returns the rectangular area that the glyph occupies. It returns the opposite corners of the smallest rectangle that contains the glyph. Glyph subclasses redefine this operation to return the rectangular area in which they draw.

The `Intersects` operation returns whether a specified point intersects the glyph. Whenever the user clicks somewhere in the document, Lexi calls this operation to determine which glyph or glyph structure is under the mouse. The Rectangle class redefines this operation to compute the intersection of the rectangle and the given point.

---

approach is feasible in his thesis [Cal93]. Our glyphs are less sophisticated than his in that we have restricted ours to strict hierarchies for simplicity. Calder's glyphs can be shared to reduce storage costs, thereby forming directed-acyclic graph structures. We can apply the Flyweight (195) pattern to get the same effect, but we'll leave that as an exercise for the reader.

[4] The interface we describe here is purposely minimal to keep the discussion simple. A complete interface would include operations for managing graphical attributes such as color, font, and coordinate transformations, plus operations for more sophisticated child management.

Because glyphs can have children, we need a common interface to add, remove, and access those children. For example, a Row's children are the glyphs it arranges into a row. The `Insert` operation inserts a glyph at a position specified by an integer index.[5] The `Remove` operation removes a specified glyph if it is indeed a child.

The `Child` operation returns the child (if any) at the given index. Glyphs like Row that can have children should use `Child` internally instead of accessing the child data structure directly. That way you won't have to modify operations like `Draw` that iterate through the children when you change the data structure from, say, an array to a linked list. Similarly, `Parent` provides a standard interface to the glyph's parent, if any. Glyphs in Lexi store a reference to their parent, and their `Parent` operation simply returns this reference.

Composite Pattern

Recursive composition is good for more than just documents. We can use it to represent any potentially complex, hierarchical structure. The Composite (163) pattern captures the essence of recursive composition in object-oriented terms. Now would be a good time to turn to that pattern and study it, referring back to this scenario as needed.

2.3   Formatting

We've settled on a way to *represent* the document's physical structure. Next, we need to figure out how to construct a *particular* physical structure, one that corresponds to a properly formatted document. Representation and formatting are distinct: The ability to capture the document's physical structure doesn't tell us how to arrive at a particular structure. This responsibility rests mostly on Lexi. It must break text into lines, lines into columns, and so on, taking into account the user's higher-level desires. For example, the user might want to vary margin widths, indentation, and tabulation; single or double space; and probably many other formatting constraints.[6] Lexi's formatting algorithm must take all of these into account.

By the way, we'll restrict "formatting" to mean breaking a collection of glyphs into lines. In fact, we'll use the terms "formatting" and "linebreaking" interchangeably. The techniques we'll discuss apply equally well to breaking lines into columns and to breaking columns into pages.

---

[5] An integer index is probably not the best way to specify a glyph's children, depending on the data structure the glyph uses. If it stores its children in a linked list, then a pointer into the list would be more efficient. We'll see a better solution to the indexing problem in Section 2.8, when we discuss document analysis.

[6] The user will have even more to say about the document's *logical* structure—the sentences, paragraphs, sections, chapters, and so forth. The *physical* structure is less interesting by comparison. Most people don't care where the linebreaks in a paragraph occur as long as the paragraph is formatted properly. The same is true for formatting columns and pages. Thus users end up specifying only high-level constraints on the physical structure, leaving Lexi to do the hard work of satisfying them.

Responsibility	Operations
what to format	`void SetComposition(Composition*)`
when to format	`virtual void Compose()`

Table 2.2: Basic compositor interface

Encapsulating the Formatting Algorithm

The formatting process, with all its constraints and details, isn't easy to automate. There are many approaches to the problem, and people have come up with a variety of formatting algorithms with different strengths and weaknesses. Because Lexi is a WYSIWYG editor, an important trade-off to consider is the balance between formatting quality and formatting speed. We want generally good response from the editor without sacrificing how good the document looks. This trade-off is subject to many factors, not all of which can be ascertained at compile-time. For example, the user might tolerate slightly slower response in exchange for better formatting. That trade-off might make an entirely different formatting algorithm more appropriate than the current one. Another, more implementation-driven trade-off balances formatting speed and storage requirements: It may be possible to decrease formatting time by caching more information.

Because formatting algorithms tend to be complex, it's also desirable to keep them well-contained or—better yet—completely independent of the document structure. Ideally we could add a new kind of Glyph subclass without regard to the formatting algorithm. Conversely, adding a new formatting algorithm shouldn't require modifying existing glyphs.

These characteristics suggest we should design Lexi so that it's easy to change the formatting algorithm at least at compile-time, if not at run-time as well. We can isolate the algorithm and make it easily replaceable at the same time by encapsulating it in an object. More specifically, we'll define a separate class hierarchy for objects that encapsulate formatting algorithms. The root of the hierarchy will define an interface that supports a wide range of formatting algorithms, and each subclass will implement the interface to carry out a particular algorithm. Then we can introduce a Glyph subclass that will structure its children automatically using a given algorithm object.

Compositor and Composition

We'll define a **Compositor** class for objects that can encapsulate a formatting algorithm. The interface (Table 2.2) lets the compositor know *what* glyphs to format and *when* to do the formatting. The glyphs it formats are the children of a special Glyph subclass called **Composition**. A composition gets an instance of a Compositor subclass (specialized for a particular linebreaking algorithm) when it is created, and it tells the compositor to `Compose` its glyphs when necessary, for example, when the user changes a document. Figure 2.5 depicts the relationships between the Composition and Compositor classes.

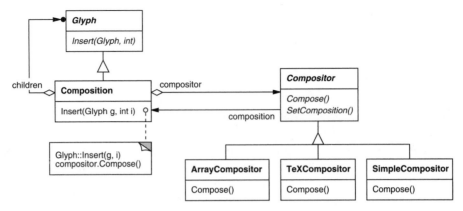

Figure 2.5: Composition and Compositor class relationships

An unformatted Composition object contains only the visible glyphs that make up the document's basic content. It doesn't contain glyphs that determine the document's physical structure, such as Row and Column. The composition is in this state just after it's created and initialized with the glyphs it should format. When the composition needs formatting, it calls its compositor's `Compose` operation. The compositor in turn iterates through the composition's children and inserts new Row and Column glyphs according to its linebreaking algorithm.[7] Figure 2.6 shows the resulting object structure. Glyphs that the compositor created and inserted into the object structure appear with gray backgrounds in the figure.

Each Compositor subclass can implement a different linebreaking algorithm. For example, a SimpleCompositor might do a quick pass without regard for such esoterica as the document's "color." Good color means having an even distribution of text and whitespace. A TeXCompositor would implement the full TeX algorithm [Knu84], which takes things like color into account in exchange for longer formatting times.

The Compositor-Composition class split ensures a strong separation between code that supports the document's physical structure and the code for different formatting algorithms. We can add new Compositor subclasses without touching the glyph classes, and vice versa. In fact, we can change the linebreaking algorithm at run-time by adding a single `SetCompositor` operation to Composition's basic glyph interface.

Strategy Pattern

Encapsulating an algorithm in an object is the intent of the Strategy (315) pattern. The key participants in the pattern are Strategy objects (which encapsulate different algorithms) and the context in which they operate. Compositors are strategies; they en-

---

[7] The compositor must get the character codes of Character glyphs in order to compute the linebreaks. In Section 2.8 we'll see how to get this information polymorphically without adding a character-specific operation to the Glyph interface.

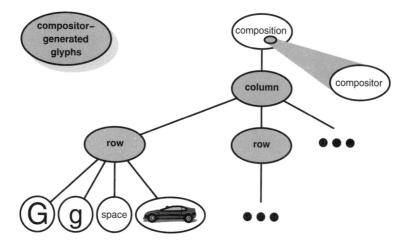

Figure 2.6: Object structure reflecting compositor-directed linebreaking

capsulate different formatting algorithms. A composition is the context for a compositor strategy.

The key to applying the Strategy pattern is designing interfaces for the strategy and its context that are general enough to support a range of algorithms. You shouldn't have to change the strategy or context interface to support a new algorithm. In our example, the basic Glyph interface's support for child access, insertion, and removal is general enough to let Compositor subclasses change the document's physical structure, regardless of the algorithm they use to do it. Likewise, the Compositor interface gives compositions whatever they need to initiate formatting.

2.4   Embellishing the User Interface

We consider two embellishments in Lexi's user interface. The first adds a border around the text editing area to demarcate the page of text. The second adds scroll bars that let the user view different parts of the page. To make it easy to add and remove these embellishments (especially at run-time), we shouldn't use inheritance to add them to the user interface. We achieve the most flexibility if other user interface objects don't even know the embellishments are there. That will let us add and remove the embellishments without changing other classes.

Transparent Enclosure

From a programming point of view, embellishing the user interface involves extending existing code. Using inheritance to do such extension precludes rearranging embellishments at run-time, but an equally serious problem is the explosion of classes that can result from an inheritance-based approach.

We could add a border to Composition by subclassing it to yield a BorderedComposition class. Or we could add a scrolling interface in the same way to yield a Scrollable-Composition. If we want both scroll bars and a border, we might produce a Bordered-ScrollableComposition, and so forth. In the extreme, we end up with a class for every possible combination of embellishments, a solution that quickly becomes unworkable as the variety of embellishments grows.

Object composition offers a potentially more workable and flexible extension mechanism. But what objects do we compose? Since we know we're embellishing an existing glyph, we could make the embellishment itself an object (say, an instance of class **Border**). That gives us two candidates for composition, the glyph and the border. The next step is to decide who composes whom. We could have the border contain the glyph, which makes sense given that the border will surround the glyph on the screen. Or we could do the opposite—put the border into the glyph—but then we must make modifications to the corresponding Glyph subclass to make it aware of the border. Our first choice, composing the glyph in the border, keeps the border-drawing code entirely in the Border class, leaving other classes alone.

What does the Border class look like? The fact that borders have an appearance suggests they should actually be glyphs; that is, Border should be a subclass of Glyph. But there's a more compelling reason for doing this: Clients shouldn't care whether glyphs have borders or not. They should treat glyphs uniformly. When clients tell a plain, unbordered glyph to draw itself, it should do so without embellishment. If that glyph is composed in a border, clients shouldn't have to treat the border containing the glyph any differently; they just tell it to draw itself as they told the plain glyph before. This implies that the Border interface matches the Glyph interface. We subclass Border from Glyph to guarantee this relationship.

All this leads us to the concept of **transparent enclosure**, which combines the notions of (1) single-child (or single-**component**) composition and (2) compatible interfaces. Clients generally can't tell whether they're dealing with the component or its **enclosure** (i.e., the child's parent), especially if the enclosure simply delegates all its operations to its component. But the enclosure can also *augment* the component's behavior by doing work of its own before and/or after delegating an operation. The enclosure can also effectively add state to the component. We'll see how next.

Monoglyph

We can apply the concept of transparent enclosure to all glyphs that embellish other glyphs. To make this concept concrete, we'll define a subclass of Glyph called **Mono-Glyph** to serve as an abstract class for "embellishment glyphs," like Border (see Figure 2.7). MonoGlyph stores a reference to a component and forwards all requests to it.

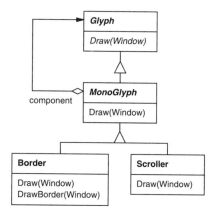

Figure 2.7: MonoGlyph class relationships

That makes MonoGlyph totally transparent to clients by default. For example, Mono-Glyph implements the `Draw` operation like this:

```
void MonoGlyph::Draw (Window* w) {
    _component->Draw(w);
}
```

MonoGlyph subclasses reimplement at least one of these forwarding operations. `Border::Draw`, for instance, first invokes the parent class operation `MonoGlyph::Draw` on the component to let the component do its part—that is, draw everything but the border. Then `Border::Draw` draws the border by calling a private operation called `DrawBorder`, the details of which we'll omit:

```
void Border::Draw (Window* w) {
    MonoGlyph::Draw(w);
    DrawBorder(w);
}
```

Notice how `Border::Draw` effectively *extends* the parent class operation to draw the border. This is in contrast to merely *replacing* the parent class operation, which would omit the call to `MonoGlyph::Draw`.

Another MonoGlyph subclass appears in Figure 2.7. **Scroller** is a MonoGlyph that draws its component in different locations based on the positions of two scroll bars, which it adds as embellishments. When Scroller draws its component, it tells the graphics system to clip to its bounds. Clipping parts of the component that are scrolled out of view keeps them from appearing on the screen.

Now we have all the pieces we need to add a border and a scrolling interface to Lexi's text editing area. We compose the existing Composition instance in a Scroller instance to add the scrolling interface, and we compose that in a Border instance. The resulting object structure appears in Figure 2.8.

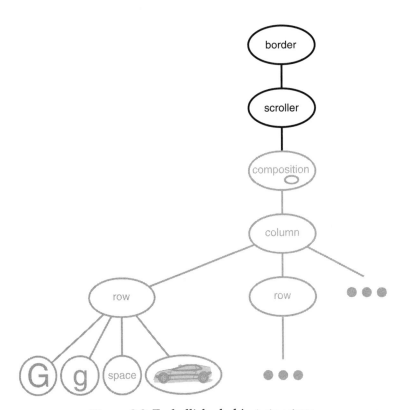

Figure 2.8: Embellished object structure

Note that we can reverse the order of composition, putting the bordered composition into the Scroller instance. In that case the border would be scrolled along with the text, which may or may not be desirable. The point is, transparent enclosure makes it easy to experiment with different alternatives, and it keeps clients free of embellishment code.

Note also how the border composes one glyph, not two or more. This is unlike compositions we've defined so far, in which parent objects were allowed to have arbitrarily many children. Here, putting a border around something implies that "something" is singular. We could assign a meaning to embellishing more than one object at a time, but then we'd have to mix many kinds of composition in with the notion of embellishment: row embellishment, column embellishment, and so forth. That won't help us, since we already have classes to do those kinds of compositions. So it's better to use existing classes for composition and add new classes to embellish the result. Keeping embellishment independent of other kinds of composition both simplifies the embellishment classes and reduces their number. It also keeps us from replicating existing composition functionality.

Decorator Pattern

The Decorator (175) pattern captures class and object relationships that support embellishment by transparent enclosure. The term "embellishment" actually has broader meaning than what we've considered here. In the Decorator pattern, embellishment refers to anything that adds responsibilities to an object. We can think for example of embellishing an abstract syntax tree with semantic actions, a finite state automaton with new transitions, or a network of persistent objects with attribute tags. Decorator generalizes the approach we've used in Lexi to make it more widely applicable.

2.5 Supporting Multiple Look-and-Feel Standards

Achieving portability across hardware and software platforms is a major problem in system design. Retargeting Lexi to a new platform shouldn't require a major overhaul, or it wouldn't be worth retargeting. We should make porting as easy as possible.

One obstacle to portability is the diversity of look-and-feel standards, which are intended to enforce uniformity between applications. These standards define guidelines for how applications appear and react to the user. While existing standards aren't that different from each other, people certainly won't confuse one for the other—Motif applications don't look and feel exactly like their counterparts on other platforms, and vice versa. An application that runs on more than one platform must conform to the user interface style guide on each platform.

Our design goals are to make Lexi conform to multiple existing look-and-feel standards and to make it easy to add support for new standards as they (invariably) emerge. We also want our design to support the ultimate in flexibility: changing Lexi's look and feel at run-time.

Abstracting Object Creation

Everything we see and interact with in Lexi's user interface is a glyph composed in other, invisible glyphs like Row and Column. The invisible glyphs compose visible ones like Button and Character and lay them out properly. Style guides have much to say about the look and feel of so-called "widgets," another term for visible glyphs like buttons, scroll bars, and menus that act as controlling elements in a user interface. Widgets might use simpler glyphs such as characters, circles, rectangles, and polygons to present data.

We'll assume we have two sets of widget glyph classes with which to implement multiple look-and-feel standards:

1. A set of abstract Glyph subclasses for each category of widget glyph. For example, an abstract class ScrollBar will augment the basic glyph interface to add general scrolling operations; Button is an abstract class that adds button-oriented operations; and so on.

2. A set of concrete subclasses for each abstract subclass that implement different look-and-feel standards. For example, ScrollBar might have MotifScrollBar and PMScrollBar subclasses that implement Motif and Presentation Manager-style scroll bars, respectively.

Lexi must distinguish between widget glyphs for different look-and-feel styles. For example, when Lexi needs to put a button in its interface, it must instantiate a Glyph subclass for the right style of button (MotifButton, PMButton, MacButton, etc.).

It's clear that Lexi's implementation can't do this directly, say, using a constructor call in C++. That would hard-code the button of a particular style, making it impossible to select the style at run-time. We'd also have to track down and change every such constructor call to port Lexi to another platform. And buttons are only one of a variety of widgets in Lexi's user interface. Littering our code with constructor calls to specific look-and-feel classes yields a maintenance nightmare—miss just one, and you could end up with a Motif menu in the middle of your Mac application.

Lexi needs a way to determine the look-and-feel standard that's being targeted in order to create the appropriate widgets. Not only must we avoid making explicit constructor calls; we must also be able to replace an entire widget set easily. We can achieve both by *abstracting the process of object creation*. An example will illustrate what we mean.

Factories and Product Classes

Normally we might create an instance of a Motif scroll bar glyph with the following C++ code:

```
ScrollBar* sb = new MotifScrollBar;
```

This is the kind of code to avoid if you want to minimize Lexi's look-and-feel dependencies. But suppose we initialize sb as follows:

```
ScrollBar* sb = guiFactory->CreateScrollBar();
```

where guiFactory is an instance of a **MotifFactory** class. CreateScrollBar returns a new instance of the proper ScrollBar subclass for the look and feel desired, Motif in this case. As far as clients are concerned, the effect is the same as calling the MotifScrollBar constructor directly. But there's a crucial difference: There's no longer anything in the code that mentions Motif by name. The guiFactory object abstracts the process of creating not just Motif scroll bars but scroll bars for *any* look-and-feel standard. And guiFactory isn't limited to producing scroll bars. It can manufacture a full range of widget glyphs, including scroll bars, buttons, entry fields, menus, and so forth.

All this is possible because MotifFactory is a subclass of **GUIFactory**, an abstract class that defines a general interface for creating widget glyphs. It includes operations like CreateScrollBar and CreateButton for instantiating different kinds of widget glyphs. Subclasses of GUIFactory implement these operations to return glyphs such as MotifScrollBar and PMButton that implement a particular look and feel. Figure 2.9 shows the resulting class hierarchy for guiFactory objects.

We say that factories create **product** objects. Moreover, the products that a factory produces are related to one another; in this case, the products are all widgets for the same look and feel. Figure 2.10 shows some of the product classes needed to make factories work for widget glyphs.

The last question we have to answer is, Where does the GUIFactory instance come from? The answer is, Anywhere that's convenient. The variable guiFactory could be a global, a static member of a well-known class, or even a local variable if the entire user interface is created within one class or function. There's even a design pattern, Singleton (127), for managing well-known, one-of-a-kind objects like this. The important thing, though, is to initialize guiFactory at a point in the program *before* it's ever used to create widgets but *after* it's clear which look and feel is desired.

If the look and feel is known at compile-time, then guiFactory can be initialized with a simple assignment of a new factory instance at the beginning of the program:

```
GUIFactory* guiFactory = new MotifFactory;
```

If the user can specify the look and feel with a string name at startup time, then the code to create the factory might be

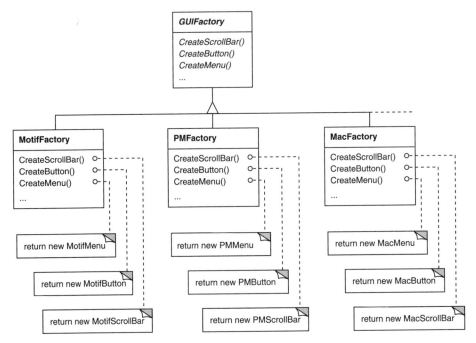

Figure 2.9: GUIFactory class hierarchy

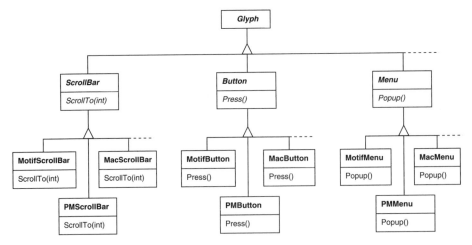

Figure 2.10: Abstract product classes and concrete subclasses

```
GUIFactory* guiFactory;
const char* styleName = getenv("LOOK_AND_FEEL");
    // user or environment supplies this at startup

if (strcmp(styleName, "Motif") == 0) {
    guiFactory = new MotifFactory;

} else if (strcmp(styleName, "Presentation_Manager") == 0) {
    guiFactory = new PMFactory;

} else {
    guiFactory = new DefaultGUIFactory;
}
```

There are more sophisticated ways to select the factory at run-time. For example, you could maintain a registry that maps strings to factory objects. That lets you register instances of new factory subclasses without modifying existing code, as the preceding approach requires. And you don't have to link all platform-specific factories into the application. That's important, because it might not be possible to link a MotifFactory on a platform that doesn't support Motif.

But the point is that once we've configured the application with the right factory object, its look and feel is set from then on. If we change our minds, we can reinitialize guiFactory with a factory for a different look and feel and then reconstruct the interface. Regardless of how and when we decide to initialize guiFactory, we know that once we do, the application can create the appropriate look and feel without modification.

Abstract Factory Pattern

Factories and products are the key participants in the Abstract Factory (87) pattern. This pattern captures how to create families of related product objects without instantiating classes directly. It's most appropriate when the number and general kinds of product objects stay constant, and there are differences in specific product families. We choose between families by instantiating a particular concrete factory and using it consistently to create products thereafter. We can also swap entire families of products by replacing the concrete factory with an instance of a different one. The Abstract Factory pattern's emphasis on *families* of products distinguishes it from other creational patterns, which involve only one kind of product object.

2.6   Supporting Multiple Window Systems

Look and feel is just one of many portability issues. Another is the windowing environment in which Lexi runs. A platform's window system creates the illusion of multiple overlapping windows on a bitmapped display. It manages screen space for windows and routes input to them from the keyboard and mouse. Several important and largely incompatible window systems exist today (e.g., Macintosh, Presentation Manager, Windows, X). We'd like Lexi to run on as many of them as possible for exactly the same reasons we support multiple look-and-feel standards.

Can We Use an Abstract Factory?

At first glance this may look like another opportunity to apply the Abstract Factory pattern. But the constraints for window system portability differ significantly from those for look-and-feel independence.

In applying the Abstract Factory pattern, we assumed we would define the concrete widget glyph classes for each look-and-feel standard. That meant we could derive each concrete product for a particular standard (e.g., MotifScrollBar and MacScrollBar) from an abstract product class (e.g., ScrollBar). But suppose we already have several class hierarchies from different vendors, one for each look-and-feel standard. Of course, it's highly unlikely these hierarchies are compatible in any way. Hence we won't have a common abstract product class for each kind of widget (ScrollBar, Button, Menu, etc.)—and the Abstract Factory pattern won't work without those crucial classes. We have to make the different widget hierarchies adhere to a common set of abstract product interfaces. Only then could we declare the Create... operations properly in our abstract factory's interface.

We solved this problem for widgets by developing our own abstract and concrete product classes. Now we're faced with a similar problem when we try to make Lexi work on existing window systems; namely, different window systems have incompatible programming interfaces. Things are a bit tougher this time, though, because we can't afford to implement our own nonstandard window system.

But there's a saving grace. Like look-and-feel standards, window system interfaces aren't radically different from one another, because all window systems do generally the same thing. We need a uniform set of windowing abstractions that lets us take different window system implementations and slide any one of them under a common interface.

Encapsulating Implementation Dependencies

In Section 2.2 we introduced a Window class for displaying a glyph or glyph structure on the display. We didn't specify the window system that this object worked with, because the truth is that it doesn't come from any particular window system. The Window class encapsulates the things windows tend to do across window systems:

- They provide operations for drawing basic geometric shapes.

- They can iconify and de-iconify themselves.

Responsibility	Operations

window management	`virtual void Redraw()`
	`virtual void Raise()`
	`virtual void Lower()`
	`virtual void Iconify()`
	`virtual void Deiconify()`
	`...`

graphics	`virtual void DrawLine(...)`
	`virtual void DrawRect(...)`
	`virtual void DrawPolygon(...)`
	`virtual void DrawText(...)`
	`...`

Table 2.3: Window class interface

- They can resize themselves.

- They can (re)draw their contents on demand, for example, when they are de-iconified or when an overlapped and obscured portion of their screen space is exposed.

The Window class must span the functionality of windows from different window systems. Let's consider two extreme philosophies:

1. *Intersection of functionality.* The Window class interface provides only functionality that's common to *all* window systems. The problem with this approach is that our Window interface winds up being only as powerful as the least capable window system. We can't take advantage of more advanced features even if most (but not all) window systems support them.

2. *Union of functionality.* Create an interface that incorporates the capabilities of *all* existing systems. The trouble here is that the resulting interface may well be huge and incoherent. Besides, we'll have to change it (and Lexi, which depends on it) anytime a vendor revises its window system interface.

Neither extreme is a viable solution, so our design will fall somewhere between the two. The Window class will provide a convenient interface that supports the most popular windowing features. Because Lexi will deal with this class directly, the Window class must also support the things Lexi knows about, namely, glyphs. That means Window's interface must include a basic set of graphics operations that lets glyphs draw themselves in the window. Table 2.3 gives a sampling of the operations in the Window class interface.

Window is an abstract class. Concrete subclasses of Window support the different kinds of windows that users deal with. For example, application windows, icons, and warning dialogs are all windows, but they have somewhat different behaviors. So we can define subclasses like ApplicationWindow, IconWindow, and DialogWindow to capture these differences. The resulting class hierarchy gives applications like Lexi a uniform and intuitive windowing abstraction, one that doesn't depend on any particular vendor's window system:

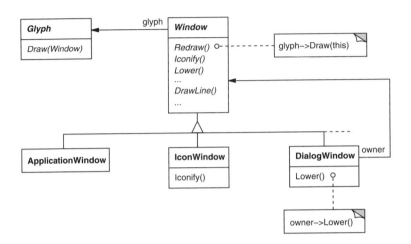

Now that we've defined a window interface for Lexi to work with, where does the real platform-specific window come in? If we're not implementing our own window system, then at some point our window abstraction must be implemented in terms of what the target window system provides. So where does that implementation live?

One approach is to implement multiple versions of the Window class and its subclasses, one version for each windowing platform. We'd have to choose the version to use when we build Lexi for a given platform. But imagine the maintenance headaches we'd have keeping track of multiple classes, all named "Window" but each implemented on a different window system. Alternatively, we could create implementation-specific subclasses of each class in the Window hierarchy—and end up with another subclass explosion problem like the one we had trying to add embellishments. Both of these alternatives have another drawback: Neither gives us the flexibility to change the window system we use after we've compiled the program. So we'll have to keep several different executables around as well.

Neither alternative is very appealing, but what else can we do? The same thing we did for formatting and embellishment, namely, *encapsulate the concept that varies*. What varies in this case is the window system implementation. If we encapsulate a window system's functionality in an object, then we can implement our Window class and subclasses in terms of that object's interface. Moreover, if that interface can serve all the window systems we're interested in, then we won't have to change Window or any of its subclasses to support different window systems. We can configure window objects to the window system we want simply by passing them the right window system-encapsulating object. We can even configure the window at run-time.

Window and WindowImp

We'll define a separate **WindowImp** class hierarchy in which to hide different window system implementations. WindowImp is an abstract class for objects that encapsulate window system-dependent code. To make Lexi work on a particular window system, we configure each window object with an instance of a WindowImp subclass for that system. The following diagram shows the relationship between the Window and WindowImp hierarchies:

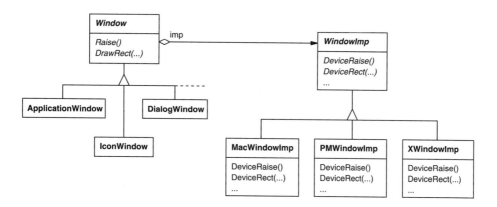

By hiding the implementations in WindowImp classes, we avoid polluting the Window classes with window system dependencies, which keeps the Window class hierarchy comparatively small and stable. Meanwhile we can easily extend the implementation hierarchy to support new window systems.

WindowImp Subclasses

Subclasses of WindowImp convert requests into window system-specific operations. Consider the example we used in Section 2.2. We defined the `Rectangle::Draw` in terms of the `DrawRect` operation on the Window instance:

```
void Rectangle::Draw (Window* w) {
    w->DrawRect(_x0, _y0, _x1, _y1);
}
```

The default implementation of `DrawRect` uses the abstract operation for drawing rectangles declared by WindowImp:

```
void Window::DrawRect (
    Coord x0, Coord y0, Coord x1, Coord y1
) {
    _imp->DeviceRect(x0, y0, x1, y1);
}
```

where _imp is a member variable of Window that stores the WindowImp with which the Window is configured. The window implementation is defined by the instance of the WindowImp subclass that _imp points to. For an XWindowImp (that is, a WindowImp subclass for the X Window System), the `DeviceRect`'s implementation might look like

```
void XWindowImp::DeviceRect (
    Coord x0, Coord y0, Coord x1, Coord y1
) {
    int x = round(min(x0, x1));
    int y = round(min(y0, y1));
    int w = round(abs(x0 - x1));
    int h = round(abs(y0 - y1));
    XDrawRectangle(_dpy, _winid, _gc, x, y, w, h);
}
```

`DeviceRect` is defined like this because `XDrawRectangle` (the X interface for drawing a rectangle) defines a rectangle in terms of its lower left corner, its width, and its height. `DeviceRect` must compute these values from those supplied. First it ascertains the lower left corner (since (x0, y0) might be any one of the rectangle's four corners) and then calculates the width and height.

PMWindowImp (a subclass of WindowImp for Presentation Manager) would define `DeviceRect` differently:

```
void PMWindowImp::DeviceRect (
    Coord x0, Coord y0, Coord x1, Coord y1
) {
    Coord left = min(x0, x1);
    Coord right = max(x0, x1);
    Coord bottom = min(y0, y1);
    Coord top = max(y0, y1);

    PPOINTL point[4];

    point[0].x = left;     point[0].y = top;
    point[1].x = right;    point[1].y = top;
    point[2].x = right;    point[2].y = bottom;
    point[3].x = left;     point[3].y = bottom;

    if (
        (GpiBeginPath(_hps, 1L) == false) ||
        (GpiSetCurrentPosition(_hps, &point[3]) == false) ||
        (GpiPolyLine(_hps, 4L, point) == GPI_ERROR)  ||
        (GpiEndPath(_hps) == false)
    ) {
        // report error

    } else {
        GpiStrokePath(_hps, 1L, 0L);
    }
}
```

Why is this so different from the X version? Well, PM doesn't have an operation for drawing rectangles explicitly as X does. Instead, PM has a more general interface for specifying vertices of multisegment shapes (called a **path**) and for outlining or filling the area they enclose.

PM's implementation of `DeviceRect` is obviously quite different from X's, but that doesn't matter. WindowImp hides variations in window system interfaces behind a potentially large but stable interface. That lets Window subclass writers focus on the window abstraction and not on window system details. It also lets us add support for new window systems without disturbing the Window classes.

Configuring Windows with WindowImps

A key issue we haven't addressed is how a window gets configured with the proper WindowImp subclass in the first place. Stated another way, when does _imp get initialized, and who knows what window system (and consequently which WindowImp subclass) is in use? The window will need some kind of WindowImp before it can do anything interesting.

There are several possibilities, but we'll focus on one that uses the Abstract Factory (87) pattern. We can define an abstract factory class WindowSystemFactory that provides an interface for creating different kinds of window system-dependent implementation objects:

```
class WindowSystemFactory {
public:
    virtual WindowImp* CreateWindowImp() = 0;
    virtual ColorImp* CreateColorImp() = 0;
    virtual FontImp* CreateFontImp() = 0;

    // a "Create..." operation for all window system resources
};
```

Now we can define a concrete factory for each window system:

```
class PMWindowSystemFactory : public WindowSystemFactory {
    virtual WindowImp* CreateWindowImp()
        { return new PMWindowImp; }
    // ...
};

class XWindowSystemFactory : public WindowSystemFactory {
    virtual WindowImp* CreateWindowImp()
        { return new XWindowImp; }
    // ...
};
```

The Window base class constructor can use the `WindowSystemFactory` interface to initialize the _imp member with the WindowImp that's right for the window system:

```
Window::Window () {
    _imp = windowSystemFactory->CreateWindowImp();
}
```

The windowSystemFactory variable is a well-known instance of a WindowSystem-Factory subclass, akin to the well-known guiFactory variable defining the look and feel. The windowSystemFactory variable can be initialized in the same way.

Bridge Pattern

The WindowImp class defines an interface to common window system facilities, but its design is driven by different constraints than Window's interface. Application programmers won't deal with WindowImp's interface directly; they only deal with Window objects. So WindowImp's interface needn't match the application programmer's view of the world, as was our concern in the design of the Window class hierarchy and interface. WindowImp's interface can more closely reflect what window systems actually provide, warts and all. It can be biased toward either an intersection or a union of functionality approach, whichever suits the target window systems best.

The important thing to realize is that Window's interface caters to the applications programmer, while WindowImp caters to window systems. Separating windowing functionality into Window and WindowImp hierarchies lets us implement and specialize these interfaces independently. Objects from these hierarchies cooperate to let Lexi work without modification on multiple window systems.

The relationship between Window and WindowImp is an example of the Bridge (151) pattern. The intent behind Bridge is to allow separate class hierarchies to work together even as they evolve independently. Our design criteria led us to create two separate class hierarchies, one that supports the logical notion of windows, and another for capturing different implementations of windows. The Bridge pattern lets us maintain and enhance our logical windowing abstractions without touching window system-dependent code, and vice versa.

2.7   User Operations

Some of Lexi's functionality is available through the document's WYSIWYG representation. You enter and delete text, move the insertion point, and select ranges of text by pointing, clicking, and typing directly in the document. Other functionality is accessed indirectly through user operations in Lexi's pull-down menus, buttons, and keyboard accelerators. The functionality includes operations for

- creating a new document,

- opening, saving, and printing an existing document,

- cutting selected text out of the document and pasting it back in,

- changing the font and style of selected text,

- changing the formatting of text, such as its alignment and justification,

- quitting the application,

- and on and on.

Lexi provides different user interfaces for these operations. But we don't want to associate a particular user operation with a particular user interface, because we may want multiple user interfaces to the same operation (you can turn the page using either a page button or a menu operation, for example). We may also want to change the interface in the future.

Furthermore, these operations are implemented in many different classes. We as implementors want to access their functionality without creating a lot of dependencies between implementation and user interface classes. Otherwise we'll end up with a tightly coupled implementation, which will be harder to understand, extend, and maintain.

To further complicate matters, we want Lexi to support undo and redo[8] of most *but not all* its functionality. Specifically, we want to be able to undo document-modifying operations like delete, with which a user can destroy lots of data inadvertently. But we shouldn't try to undo an operation like saving a drawing or quitting the application. These operations should have no effect on the undo process. We also don't want an arbitrary limit on the number of levels of undo and redo.

It's clear that support for user operations permeates the application. The challenge is to come up with a simple and extensible mechanism that satisfies all of these needs.

Encapsulating a Request

From our perspective as designers, a pull-down menu is just another kind of glyph that contains other glyphs. What distinguishes pull-down menus from other glyphs that have children is that most glyphs in menus do some work in response to an up-click.

Let's assume that these work-performing glyphs are instances of a Glyph subclass called **MenuItem** and that they do their work in response to a request from a client.[9] Carrying out the request might involve an operation on one object, or many operations on many objects, or something in between.

We could define a subclass of MenuItem for every user operation and then hard-code each subclass to carry out the request. But that's not really right; we don't need a subclass of MenuItem for each request any more than we need a subclass for each text

---

[8] That is, redoing an operation that was just undone.
[9] Conceptually, the client is Lexi's user, but in reality it's another object (such as an event dispatcher) that manages inputs from the user.

string in a pull-down menu. Moreover, this approach couples the request to a particular user interface, making it hard to fulfill the request through a different user interface.

To illustrate, suppose you could advance to the last page in the document both through a MenuItem in a pull-down menu *and* by pressing a page icon at the bottom of Lexi's interface (which might be more convenient for short documents). If we associate the request with a MenuItem through inheritance, then we must do the same for the page icon and any other kind of widget that might issue such a request. That can give rise to a number of classes approaching the product of the number of widget types and the number of requests.

What's missing is a mechanism that lets us parameterize menu items by the request they should fulfill. That way we avoid a proliferation of subclasses and allow for greater flexibility at run-time. We could parameterize MenuItem with a function to call, but that's not a complete solution for at least three reasons:

1. It doesn't address the undo/redo problem.

2. It's hard to associate state with a function. For example, a function that changes the font needs to know *which* font.

3. Functions are hard to extend, and it's hard to reuse parts of them.

These reasons suggest that we should parameterize MenuItems with an *object*, not a function. Then we can use inheritance to extend and reuse the request's implementation. We also have a place to store state and implement undo/redo functionality. Here we have another example of encapsulating the concept that varies, in this case a request. We'll encapsulate each request in a **command** object.

Command Class and Subclasses

First we define a **Command** abstract class to provide an interface for issuing a request. The basic interface consists of a single abstract operation called "Execute." Subclasses of Command implement Execute in different ways to fulfill different requests. Some subclasses may delegate part or all of the work to other objects. Other subclasses may be in a position to fulfill the request entirely on their own (see Figure 2.11). To the requester, however, a Command object is a Command object—they are treated uniformly.

Now MenuItem can store a Command object that encapsulates a request (Figure 2.12). We give each menu item object an instance of the Command subclass that's suitable for that menu item, just as we specify the text to appear in the menu item. When a user chooses a particular menu item, the MenuItem simply calls Execute on its Command object to carry out the request. Note that buttons and other widgets can use commands in the same way menu items do.

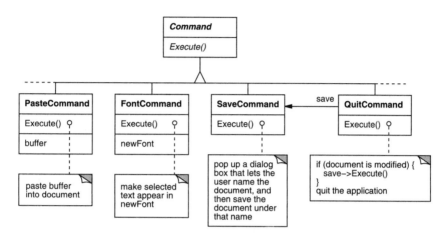

Figure 2.11: Partial Command class hierarchy

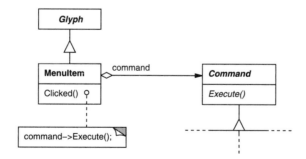

Figure 2.12: MenuItem-Command relationship

Undoability

Undo/redo is an important capability in interactive applications. To undo and redo commands, we add an Unexecute operation to Command's interface. Unexecute reverses the effects of a preceding Execute operation using whatever undo information Execute stored. In the case of a FontCommand, for example, the Execute operation would store the range of text affected by the font change along with the original font(s). FontCommand's Unexecute operation would restore the range of text to its original font(s).

Sometimes undoability must be determined at run-time. A request to change the font of a selection does nothing if the text already appears in that font. Suppose the user selects some text and then requests a spurious font change. What should be the result of a subsequent undo request? Should a meaningless change cause the undo request to do something equally meaningless? Probably not. If the user repeats the spurious font change several times, he shouldn't have to perform exactly the same number of undo operations to get back to the last meaningful operation. If the net effect of executing a command was nothing, then there's no need for a corresponding undo request.

So to determine if a command is undoable, we add an abstract Reversible operation to the Command interface. Reversible returns a Boolean value. Subclasses can redefine this operation to return true or false based on run-time criteria.

Command History

The final step in supporting arbitrary-level undo and redo is to define a **command history**, or list of commands that have been executed (or unexecuted, if some commands have been undone). Conceptually, the command history looks like this:

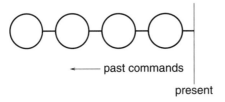

Each circle represents a Command object. In this case the user has issued four commands. The leftmost command was issued first, followed by the second-leftmost, and so on until the most recently issued command, which is rightmost. The line marked "present" keeps track of the most recently executed (and unexecuted) command.

To undo the last command, we simply call Unexecute on the most recent command:

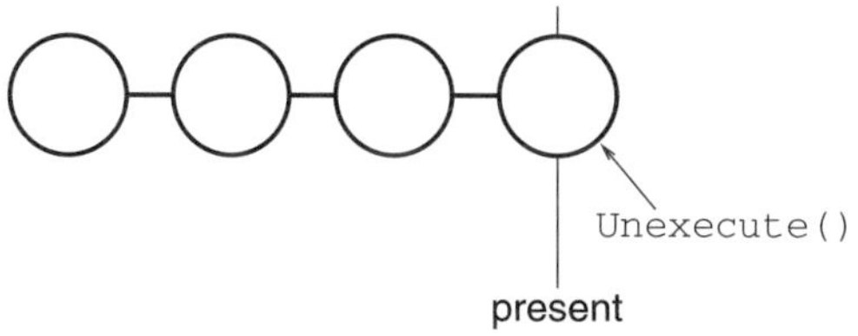

Unexecute()

present

After unexecuting the command, we move the "present" line one command to the left. If the user chooses undo again, the next-most recently issued command will be undone in the same way, and we're left in the state depicted here:

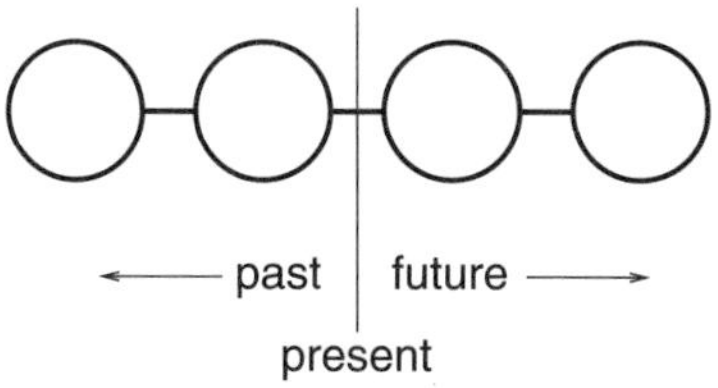

←——— past │ future ———→

present

You can see that by simply repeating this procedure we get multiple levels of undo. The number of levels is limited only by the length of the command history.

To redo a command that's just been undone, we do the same thing in reverse. Commands to the right of the present line are commands that may be redone in the future. To redo the last undone command, we call Execute on the command to the right of the present line:

Execute()

present

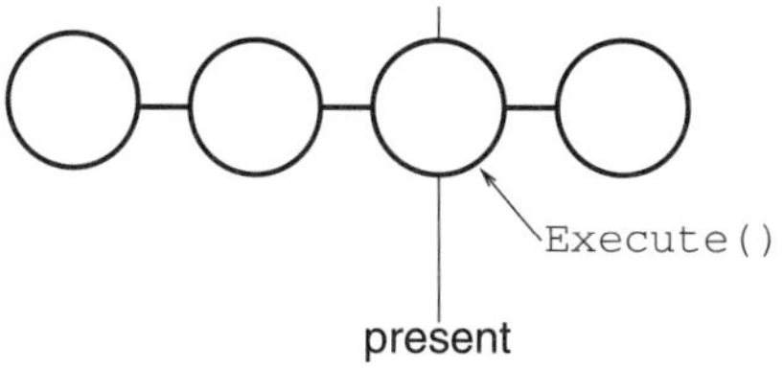

Then we advance the present line so that a subsequent redo will call redo on the following command in the future.

Of course, if the subsequent operation is not another redo but an undo, then the command to the left of the present line will be undone. Thus the user can effectively go back and forth in time as needed to recover from errors.

Command Pattern

Lexi's commands are an application of the Command (233) pattern, which describes how to encapsulate a request. The Command pattern prescribes a uniform interface for issuing requests that lets you configure clients to handle different requests. The interface shields clients from the request's implementation. A command may delegate all, part, or none of the request's implementation to other objects. This is perfect for applications like Lexi that must provide centralized access to functionality scattered throughout the application. The pattern also discusses undo and redo mechanisms built on the basic Command interface.

2.8   Spelling Checking and Hyphenation

The last design problem involves textual analysis, specifically checking for misspellings and introducing hyphenation points where needed for good formatting.

The constraints here are similar to those we had for the formatting design problem in Section 2.3. As was the case for linebreaking strategies, there's more than one way to check spelling and compute hyphenation points. So here too we want to support multiple algorithms. A diverse set of algorithms can provide a choice of space/time/quality trade-offs. We should make it easy to add new algorithms as well.

We also want to avoid wiring this functionality into the document structure. This goal is even more important here than it was in the formatting case, because spelling checking and hyphenation are just two of potentially many kinds of analyses we may want Lexi to support. Inevitably we'll want to expand Lexi's analytical abilities over time. We might add searching, word counting, a calculation facility for adding up tabular values, grammar checking, and so forth. But we don't want to change the Glyph class and all its subclasses every time we introduce new functionality of this sort.

There are actually two pieces to this puzzle: (1) accessing the information to be analyzed, which we have scattered over the glyphs in the document structure, and (2) doing the analysis. We'll look at these two pieces separately.

Accessing Scattered Information

Many kinds of analysis require examining the text character by character. The text we need to analyze is scattered throughout a hierarchical structure of glyph objects. To examine text in such a structure, we need an access mechanism that has knowledge about the data structures in which objects are stored. Some glyphs might store their children in linked lists, others might use arrays, and still others might use more esoteric data structures. Our access mechanism must be able to handle all of these possibilities.

An added complication is that different analyses access information in different ways. *Most* analyses will traverse the text from beginning to end. But some do the opposite—a reverse search, for example, needs to progress through the text backward rather than forward. Evaluating algebraic expressions could require an inorder traversal.

So our access mechanism must accommodate differing data structures, and we must support different kinds of traversals, such as preorder, postorder, and inorder.

Encapsulating Access and Traversal

Right now our glyph interface uses an integer index to let clients refer to children. Although that might be reasonable for glyph classes that store their children in an array, it may be inefficient for glyphs that use a linked list. An important role of the glyph abstraction is to hide the data structure in which children are stored. That way we can change the data structure a glyph class uses without affecting other classes.

Therefore only the glyph can know the data structure it uses. A corollary is that the glyph interface shouldn't be biased toward one data structure or another. It shouldn't be better suited to arrays than to linked lists, for example, as it is now.

We can solve this problem and support several different kinds of traversals at the same time. We can put multiple access and traversal capabilities directly in the glyph classes and provide a way to choose among them, perhaps by supplying an enumerated constant as a parameter. The classes pass this parameter around during a traversal to ensure they're all doing the same kind of traversal. They have to pass around any information they've accumulated during traversal.

We might add the following abstract operations to Glyph's interface to support this approach:

```
void First(Traversal kind)
void Next()
bool IsDone()
Glyph* GetCurrent()
void Insert(Glyph*)
```

Operations `First`, `Next`, and `IsDone` control the traversal. `First` initializes the traversal. It takes the kind of traversal as a parameter of type `Traversal`, an enumerated constant with values such as `CHILDREN` (to traverse the glyph's immediate children only), `PREORDER` (to traverse the entire structure in preorder), `POSTORDER`, and `INORDER`. `Next` advances to the next glyph in the traversal, and `IsDone` reports whether the traversal is over or not. `GetCurrent` replaces the `Child` operation; it accesses the current glyph in the traversal. `Insert` replaces the old operation; it inserts the given glyph at the current position.

An analysis would use the following C++ code to do a preorder traversal of a glyph structure rooted at g:

```
Glyph* g;

for (g->First(PREORDER); !g->IsDone(); g->Next()) {
    Glyph* current = g->GetCurrent();

    // do some analysis
}
```

Notice that we've banished the integer index from the glyph interface. There's no longer anything that biases the interface toward one kind of collection or another. We've also saved clients from having to implement common kinds of traversals themselves.

But this approach still has problems. For one thing, it can't support new traversals without either extending the set of enumerated values or adding new operations. Say we wanted to have a variation on preorder traversal that automatically skips non-textual glyphs. We'd have to change the `Traversal` enumeration to include something like `TEXTUAL_PREORDER`.

We'd like to avoid changing existing declarations. Putting the traversal mechanism entirely in the Glyph class hierarchy makes it hard to modify or extend without changing lots of classes. It's also difficult to reuse the mechanism to traverse other kinds of object structures. And we can't have more than one traversal in progress on a structure.

Once again, a better solution is to encapsulate the concept that varies, in this case the access and traversal mechanisms. We can introduce a class of objects called **iterators** whose sole purpose is to define different sets of these mechanisms. We can use inheritance to let us access different data structures uniformly and support new kinds of traversals as well. And we won't have to change glyph interfaces or disturb existing glyph implementations to do it.

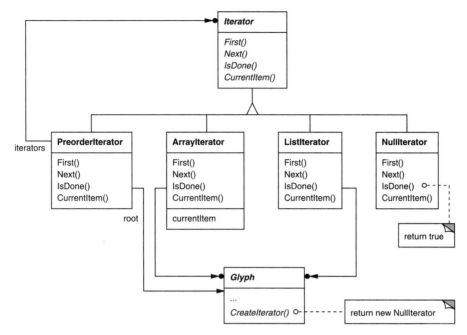

Figure 2.13: Iterator class and subclasses

Iterator Class and Subclasses

We'll use an abstract class called **Iterator** to define a general interface for access and traversal. Concrete subclasses like **ArrayIterator** and **ListIterator** implement the interface to provide access to arrays and lists, while **PreorderIterator**, **PostorderIterator**, and the like implement different traversals on specific structures. Each Iterator subclass has a reference to the structure it traverses. Subclass instances are initialized with this reference when they are created. Figure 2.13 illustrates the Iterator class along with several subclasses. Notice that we've added a CreateIterator abstract operation to the Glyph class interface to support iterators.

The Iterator interface provides operations First, Next, and IsDone for controlling the traversal. The ListIterator class implements First to point to the first element in the list, and Next advances the iterator to the next item in the list. IsDone returns whether or not the list pointer points beyond the last element in the list. CurrentItem dereferences the iterator to return the glyph it points to. An `ArrayIterator` class would do similar things but on an array of glyphs.

Now we can access the children of a glyph structure without knowing its representation:

```
Glyph* g;
Iterator<Glyph*>* i = g->CreateIterator();

for (i->First(); !i->IsDone(); i->Next()) {
    Glyph* child = i->CurrentItem();

    // do something with current child
}
```

CreateIterator returns a NullIterator instance by default. A NullIterator is a degenerate iterator for glyphs that have no children, that is, leaf glyphs. NullIterator's IsDone operation always returns true.

A glyph subclass that has children will override CreateIterator to return an instance of a different Iterator subclass. *Which* subclass depends on the structure that stores the children. If the Row subclass of Glyph stores its children in a list _children, then its CreateIterator operation would look like this:

```
Iterator<Glyph*>* Row::CreateIterator () {
    return new ListIterator<Glyph*>(_children);
}
```

Iterators for preorder and inorder traversals implement their traversals in terms of glyph-specific iterators. The iterators for these traversals are supplied the root glyph in the structure they traverse. They call CreateIterator on the glyphs in the structure and use a stack to keep track of the resulting iterators.

For example, class `PreorderIterator` gets the iterator from the root glyph, initializes it to point to its first element, and then pushes it onto the stack:

```
void PreorderIterator::First () {
    Iterator<Glyph*>* i = _root->CreateIterator();

    if (i) {
        i->First();
        _iterators.RemoveAll();
        _iterators.Push(i);
    }
}
```

`CurrentItem` would simply call `CurrentItem` on the iterator at the top of the stack:

```
Glyph* PreorderIterator::CurrentItem () const {
    return
        _iterators.Size() > 0 ?
        _iterators.Top()->CurrentItem() : 0;
}
```

The `Next` operation gets the top iterator on the stack and asks its current item to create an iterator, in an effort to descend the glyph structure as far as possible (this is a preorder traversal, after all). `Next` sets the new iterator to the first item in the traversal and pushes it on the stack. Then `Next` tests the latest iterator; if its `IsDone` operation returns true, then we've finished traversing the current subtree (or leaf) in the traversal. In that case, `Next` pops the top iterator off the stack and repeats this process until it finds the next incomplete traversal, if there is one; if not, then we have finished traversing the structure.

```
void PreorderIterator::Next () {
    Iterator<Glyph*>* i =
        _iterators.Top()->CurrentItem()->CreateIterator();

    i->First();
    _iterators.Push(i);

    while (
        _iterators.Size() > 0 && _iterators.Top()->IsDone()
    ) {
        delete _iterators.Pop();
        _iterators.Top()->Next();
    }
}
```

Notice how the Iterator class hierarchy lets us add new kinds of traversals without modifying glyph classes—we simply subclass `Iterator` and add a new traversal as we have with `PreorderIterator`. Glyph subclasses use the same interface to give clients access to their children without revealing the underlying data structure they use to store them. Because iterators store their own copy of the state of a traversal, we can carry on multiple traversals simultaneously, even on the same structure. And though our traversals have been over glyph structures in this example, there's no reason we can't parameterize a class like `PreorderIterator` by the type of object in the structure. We'd use templates to do that in C++. Then we can reuse the machinery in `PreorderIterator` to traverse other structures.

Iterator Pattern

The Iterator (257) pattern captures these techniques for supporting access and traversal over object structures. It's applicable not only to composite structures but to collections as well. It abstracts the traversal algorithm and shields clients from the internal structure of the objects they traverse. The Iterator pattern illustrates once more how encapsulating the concept that varies helps us gain flexibility and reusability. Even so, the problem of iteration has surprising depth, and the Iterator pattern covers many more nuances and trade-offs than we've considered here.

Traversal versus Traversal Actions

Now that we have a way of traversing the glyph structure, we need to check the spelling and do the hyphenation. Both analyses involve accumulating information during the traversal.

First we have to decide where to put the responsibility for analysis. We could put it in the Iterator classes, thereby making analysis an integral part of traversal. But we get more flexibility and potential for reuse if we distinguish between the traversal and the actions performed during traversal. That's because different analyses often require the same kind of traversal. Hence we can reuse the same set of iterators for different analyses. For example, preorder traversal is common to many analyses, including spelling checking, hyphenation, forward search, and word count.

So analysis and traversal should be separate. Where else can we put the responsibility for analysis? We know there are many kinds of analyses we might want to do. Each analysis will do different things at different points in the traversal. Some glyphs are more significant than others depending on the kind of analysis. If we're checking spelling or hyphenating, we want to consider character glyphs and not graphical ones like lines and bitmapped images. If we're making color separations, we'd want to consider visible glyphs and not invisible ones. Inevitably, different analyses will analyze different glyphs.

Therefore a given analysis must be able to distinguish different kinds of glyphs. An obvious approach is to put the analytical capability into the glyph classes themselves. For each analysis we can add one or more abstract operations to the Glyph class and have subclasses implement them in accordance with the role they play in the analysis.

But the trouble with that approach is that we'll have to change every glyph class whenever we add a new kind of analysis. We can ease this problem in some cases: If only a few classes participate in the analysis, or if most classes do the analysis the same way, then we can supply a default implementation for the abstract operation in the Glyph class. The default operation would cover the common case. Thus we'd limit changes to just the Glyph class and those subclasses that deviate from the norm.

Yet even if a default implementation reduces the number of changes, an insidious problem remains: Glyph's interface expands with every new analytical capability. Over time the analytical operations will start to obscure the basic Glyph interface. It becomes hard to see that a glyph's main purpose is to define and structure objects that have appearance and shape—that interface gets lost in the noise.

Encapsulating the Analysis

From all indications, we need to encapsulate the analysis in a separate object, much like we've done many times before. We could put the machinery for a given analysis into its own class. We could use an instance of this class in conjunction with an appropriate iterator. The iterator would "carry" the instance to each glyph in the structure. The analysis object could then perform a piece of the analysis at each point in the traversal. The analyzer accumulates information of interest (characters in this case) as the traversal proceeds:

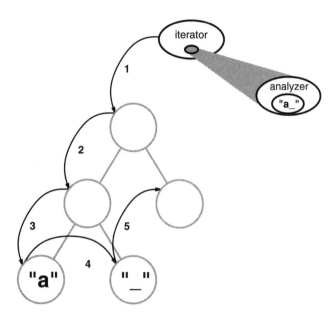

The fundamental question with this approach is how the analysis object distinguishes different kinds of glyphs without resorting to type tests or downcasts. We don't want a SpellingChecker class to include (pseudo)code like

```
void SpellingChecker::Check (Glyph* glyph) {
    Character* c;
    Row* r;
    Image* i;

    if (c = dynamic_cast<Character*>(glyph)) {
        // analyze the character

    } else if (r = dynamic_cast<Row*>(glyph)) {
        // prepare to analyze r's children
```

```
    } else if (i = dynamic_cast<Image*>(glyph)) {
        // do nothing
    }
}
```

This code is pretty ugly. It relies on fairly esoteric capabilities like type-safe casts. It's hard to extend as well. We'll have to remember to change the body of this function whenever we change the Glyph class hierarchy. In fact, this is the kind of code that object-oriented languages were intended to eliminate.

We want to avoid such a brute-force approach, but how? Let's consider what happens when we add the following abstract operation to the Glyph class:

```
void CheckMe(SpellingChecker&)
```

We define CheckMe in every Glyph subclass as follows:

```
void GlyphSubclass::CheckMe (SpellingChecker& checker) {
    checker.CheckGlyphSubclass(this);
}
```

where GlyphSubclass would be replaced by the name of the glyph subclass. Note that when CheckMe is called, the specific Glyph subclass is known—after all, we're in one of its operations. In turn, the SpellingChecker class interface includes an operation like CheckGlyphSubclass for every Glyph subclass[10]:

```
class SpellingChecker {
public:
    SpellingChecker();

    virtual void CheckCharacter(Character*);
    virtual void CheckRow(Row*);
    virtual void CheckImage(Image*);

    // ... and so forth

    List<char*>& GetMisspellings();

protected:
    virtual bool IsMisspelled(const char*);

private:
    char _currentWord[MAX_WORD_SIZE];
    List<char*> _misspellings;
};
```

SpellingChecker's checking operation for Character glyphs might look something like this:

---

[10] We could use function overloading to give each of these member functions the same name, since their parameters already differentiate them. We've given them different names here to emphasize their differences, especially when they're called.

```
void SpellingChecker::CheckCharacter (Character* c) {
    const char ch = c->GetCharCode();

    if (isalpha(ch)) {
        // append alphabetic character to _currentWord

    } else {
        // we hit a nonalphabetic character

        if (IsMisspelled(_currentWord)) {
            // add _currentWord to _misspellings
            _misspellings.Append(strdup(_currentWord));
        }

        _currentWord[0] = '\0';
            // reset _currentWord to check next word
    }
}
```

Notice we've defined a special `GetCharCode` operation on just the `Character` class. The spelling checker can deal with subclass-specific operations without resorting to type tests or casts——it lets us treat objects specially.

`CheckCharacter` accumulates alphabetic characters into the _currentWord buffer. When it encounters a nonalphabetic character, such as an underscore, it uses the `IsMisspelled` operation to check the spelling of the word in _currentWord.[11] If the word is misspelled, then `CheckCharacter` adds the word to the list of misspelled words. Then it must clear out the _currentWord buffer to ready it for the next word. When the traversal is over, you can retrieve the list of misspelled words with the `GetMisspellings` operation.

Now we can traverse the glyph structure, calling `CheckMe` on each glyph with the spelling checker as an argument. This effectively identifies each glyph to the SpellingChecker and prompts the checker to do the next increment in the spelling check.

```
SpellingChecker spellingChecker;
Composition* c;

// ...

Glyph* g;
PreorderIterator i(c);
```

---

[11] `IsMisspelled` implements the spelling algorithm, which we won't detail here because we've made it independent of Lexi's design. We can support different algorithms by subclassing `SpellingChecker`; alternatively, we can apply the Strategy (315) pattern (as we did for formatting in Section 2.3) to support different spelling checking algorithms.

```
for (i.First(); !i.IsDone(); i.Next()) {
    g = i.CurrentItem();
    g->CheckMe(spellingChecker);
}
```

The following interaction diagram illustrates how `Character` glyphs and the `SpellingChecker` object work together:

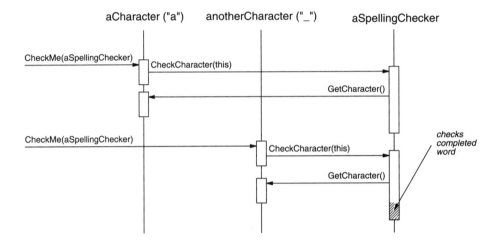

This approach works for finding spelling errors, but how does it help us support multiple kinds of analysis? It looks like we have to add an operation like `CheckMe(SpellingChecker&)` to Glyph and its subclasses whenever we add a new kind of analysis. That's true if we insist on an *independent* class for every analysis. But there's no reason why we can't give *all* analysis classes the same interface. Doing so lets us use them polymorphically. That means we can replace analysis-specific operations like `CheckMe(SpellingChecker&)` with an analysis-independent operation that takes a more general parameter.

Visitor Class and Subclasses

We'll use the term **visitor** to refer generally to classes of objects that "visit" other objects during a traversal and do something appropriate.[12] In this case we can define a `Visitor` class that defines an abstract interface for visiting glyphs in a structure.

---

[12] "Visit" is just a slightly more general term for "analyze." It foreshadows the terminology we use in the design pattern we're leading to.

```
class Visitor {
public:
    virtual void VisitCharacter(Character*) { }
    virtual void VisitRow(Row*) { }
    virtual void VisitImage(Image*) { }

    // ... and so forth
};
```

Concrete subclasses of `Visitor` perform different analyses. For example, we could have a `SpellingCheckingVisitor` subclass for checking spelling, and a `HyphenationVisitor` subclass for hyphenation. `SpellingCheckingVisitor` would be implemented exactly as we implemented `SpellingChecker` above, except the operation names would reflect the more general `Visitor` interface. For example, `CheckCharacter` would be called `VisitCharacter`.

Since `CheckMe` isn't appropriate for visitors that don't check anything, we'll give it a more general name: `Accept`. Its argument must also change to take a `Visitor&`, reflecting the fact that it can accept any visitor. Now adding a new analysis requires just defining a new subclass of `Visitor`—we don't have to touch any of the glyph classes. We support all future analyses by adding this one operation to `Glyph` and its subclasses.

We've already seen how spelling checking works. We use a similar approach in `HyphenationVisitor` to accumulate text. But once `HyphenationVisitor`'s `VisitCharacter` operation has assembled an entire word, it works a little differently. Instead of checking the word for misspelling, it applies a hyphenation algorithm to determine the potential hyphenation points in the word, if any. Then at each hyphenation point, it inserts a **discretionary** glyph into the composition. Discretionary glyphs are instances of `Discretionary`, a subclass of `Glyph`.

A discretionary glyph has one of two possible appearances depending on whether or not it is the last character on a line. If it's the last character, then the discretionary looks like a hyphen; if it's not at the end of a line, then the discretionary has no appearance whatsoever. The discretionary checks its parent (a Row object) to see if it is the last child. The discretionary makes this check whenever it's called on to draw itself or calculate its boundaries. The formatting strategy treats discretionaries the same as whitespace, making them candidates for ending a line. The following diagram shows how an embedded discretionary can appear.

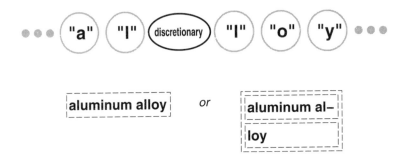

Visitor Pattern

What we've described here is an application of the Visitor (331) pattern. The Visitor class and its subclasses described earlier are the key participants in the pattern. The Visitor pattern captures the technique we've used to allow an open-ended number of analyses of glyph structures without having to change the glyph classes themselves. Another nice feature of visitors is that they can be applied not just to composites like our glyph structures but to *any* object structure. That includes sets, lists, even directed-acyclic graphs. Furthermore, the classes that a visitor can visit needn't be related to each other through a common parent class. That means visitors can work across class hierarchies.

An important question to ask yourself before applying the Visitor pattern is, Which class hierarchies change most often? The pattern is most suitable when you want to be able to do a variety of different things to objects that have a stable class structure. Adding a new kind of visitor requires no change to that class structure, which is especially important when the class structure is large. But whenever you add a subclass to the structure, you'll also have to update all your visitor interfaces to include a `Visit...` operation for that subclass. In our example that means adding a new `Glyph` subclass called `Foo` will require changing `Visitor` and all its subclasses to include a `VisitFoo` operation. But given our design constraints, we're much more likely to add a new kind of analysis to Lexi than a new kind of Glyph. So the Visitor pattern is well-suited to our needs.

2.9   Summary

We've applied eight different patterns to Lexi's design:

1. Composite (163) to represent the document's physical structure,

2. Strategy (315) to allow different formatting algorithms,

3. Decorator (175) for embellishing the user interface,

4. Abstract Factory (87) for supporting multiple look-and-feel standards,

5. Bridge (151) to allow multiple windowing platforms,

6. Command (233) for undoable user operations,

7. Iterator (257) for accessing and traversing object structures, and

8. Visitor (331) for allowing an open-ended number of analytical capabilities without complicating the document structure's implementation.

None of these design issues is limited to document editing applications like Lexi. Indeed, most nontrivial applications will have occasion to use many of these patterns, though perhaps to do different things. A financial analysis application might use Composite to define investment portfolios made up of subportfolios and accounts of different sorts. A compiler might use the Strategy pattern to allow different register allocation schemes for different target machines. Applications with a graphical user interface will probably apply at least Decorator and Command just as we have here.

While we've covered several major problems in Lexi's design, there are lots of others we haven't discussed. Then again, this book describes more than just the eight patterns we've used here. So as you study the remaining patterns, think about how you might use each one in Lexi. Or better yet, think about using them in your own designs!

Design Pattern Catalog

Chapter 3

Creational Patterns

Creational design patterns abstract the instantiation process. They help make a system independent of how its objects are created, composed, and represented. A class creational pattern uses inheritance to vary the class that's instantiated, whereas an object creational pattern will delegate instantiation to another object.

Creational patterns become important as systems evolve to depend more on object composition than class inheritance. As that happens, emphasis shifts away from hardcoding a fixed set of behaviors toward defining a smaller set of fundamental behaviors that can be composed into any number of more complex ones. Thus creating objects with particular behaviors requires more than simply instantiating a class.

There are two recurring themes in these patterns. First, they all encapsulate knowledge about which concrete classes the system uses. Second, they hide how instances of these classes are created and put together. All the system at large knows about the objects is their interfaces as defined by abstract classes. Consequently, the creational patterns give you a lot of flexibility in *what* gets created, *who* creates it, *how* it gets created, and *when*. They let you configure a system with "product" objects that vary widely in structure and functionality. Configuration can be static (that is, specified at compile-time) or dynamic (at run-time).

Sometimes creational patterns are competitors. For example, there are cases when either Prototype (117) or Abstract Factory (87) could be used profitably. At other times they are complementary: Builder (97) can use one of the other patterns to implement which components get built. Prototype (117) can use Singleton (127) in its implementation.

Because the creational patterns are closely related, we'll study all five of them together to highlight their similarities and differences. We'll also use a common example—building a maze for a computer game—to illustrate their implementations. The maze and the game will vary slightly from pattern to pattern. Sometimes the game will be simply to find your way out of a maze; in that case the player will probably only have a local view of the maze. Sometimes mazes contain problems to solve and dangers to

81

overcome, and these games may provide a map of the part of the maze that has been explored.

We'll ignore many details of what can be in a maze and whether a maze game has a single or multiple players. Instead, we'll just focus on how mazes get created. We define a maze as a set of rooms. A room knows its neighbors; possible neighbors are another room, a wall, or a door to another room.

The classes Room, Door, and Wall define the components of the maze used in all our examples. We define only the parts of these classes that are important for creating a maze. We'll ignore players, operations for displaying and wandering around in a maze, and other important functionality that isn't relevant to building the maze.

The following diagram shows the relationships between these classes:

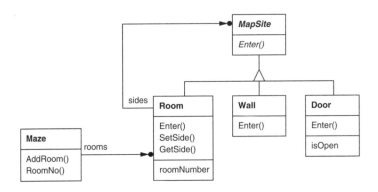

Each room has four sides. We use an enumeration Direction in C++ implementations to specify the north, south, east, and west sides of a room:

```
enum Direction {North, South, East, West};
```

The Smalltalk implementations use corresponding symbols to represent these directions.

The class MapSite is the common abstract class for all the components of a maze. To simplify the example, MapSite defines only one operation, Enter. Its meaning depends on what you're entering. If you enter a room, then your location changes. If you try to enter a door, then one of two things happen: If the door is open, you go into the next room. If the door is closed, then you hurt your nose.

```
class MapSite {
public:
    virtual void Enter() = 0;
};
```

Enter provides a simple basis for more sophisticated game operations. For example, if you are in a room and say "Go East," the game can simply determine which MapSite is immediately to the east and then call Enter on it. The subclass-specific Enter operation will figure out whether your location changed or your nose got hurt. In a real game, `Enter` could take the player object that's moving about as an argument.

`Room` is the concrete subclass of `MapSite` that defines the key relationships between components in the maze. It maintains references to other `MapSite` objects and stores a room number. The number will identify rooms in the maze.

```
class Room : public MapSite {
public:
    Room(int roomNo);

    MapSite* GetSide(Direction) const;
    void SetSide(Direction, MapSite*);

    virtual void Enter();

private:
    MapSite* _sides[4];
    int _roomNumber;
};
```

The following classes represent the wall or door that occurs on each side of a room.

```
class Wall : public MapSite {
public:
    Wall();

    virtual void Enter();
};

class Door : public MapSite {
public:
    Door(Room* = 0, Room* = 0);

    virtual void Enter();
    Room* OtherSideFrom(Room*);

private:
    Room* _room1;
    Room* _room2;
    bool _isOpen;
};
```

We need to know about more than just the parts of a maze. We'll also define a `Maze` class to represent a collection of rooms. `Maze` can also find a particular room given a room number using its `RoomNo` operation.

```
class Maze {
public:
    Maze();

    void AddRoom(Room*);
    Room* RoomNo(int) const;
private:
    // ...
};
```

RoomNo could do a look-up using a linear search, a hash table, or even a simple array. But we won't worry about such details here. Instead, we'll focus on how to specify the components of a maze object.

Another class we define is MazeGame, which creates the maze. One straightforward way to create a maze is with a series of operations that add components to a maze and then interconnect them. For example, the following member function will create a maze consisting of two rooms with a door between them:

```
Maze* MazeGame::CreateMaze () {
    Maze* aMaze = new Maze;
    Room* r1 = new Room(1);
    Room* r2 = new Room(2);
    Door* theDoor = new Door(r1, r2);

    aMaze->AddRoom(r1);
    aMaze->AddRoom(r2);

    r1->SetSide(North, new Wall);
    r1->SetSide(East, theDoor);
    r1->SetSide(South, new Wall);
    r1->SetSide(West, new Wall);

    r2->SetSide(North, new Wall);
    r2->SetSide(East, new Wall);
    r2->SetSide(South, new Wall);
    r2->SetSide(West, theDoor);

    return aMaze;
}
```

This function is pretty complicated, considering that all it does is create a maze with two rooms. There are obvious ways to make it simpler. For example, the Room constructor could initialize the sides with walls ahead of time. But that just moves the code somewhere else. The real problem with this member function isn't its size but its *inflexibility*. It hard-codes the maze layout. Changing the layout means changing this member function, either by overriding it—which means reimplementing the whole thing—or by changing parts of it—which is error-prone and doesn't promote reuse.

The creational patterns show how to make this design more *flexible*, not necessarily smaller. In particular, they will make it easy to change the classes that define the components of a maze.

Suppose you wanted to reuse an existing maze layout for a new game containing (of all things) enchanted mazes. The enchanted maze game has new kinds of components, like `DoorNeedingSpell`, a door that can be locked and opened subsequently only with a spell; and `EnchantedRoom`, a room that can have unconventional items in it, like magic keys or spells. How can you change `CreateMaze` easily so that it creates mazes with these new classes of objects?

In this case, the biggest barrier to change lies in hard-coding the classes that get instantiated. The creational patterns provide different ways to remove explicit references to concrete classes from code that needs to instantiate them:

- If `CreateMaze` calls virtual functions instead of constructor calls to create the rooms, walls, and doors it requires, then you can change the classes that get instantiated by making a subclass of `MazeGame` and redefining those virtual functions. This approach is an example of the Factory Method (107) pattern.

- If `CreateMaze` is passed an object as a parameter to use to create rooms, walls, and doors, then you can change the classes of rooms, walls, and doors by passing a different parameter. This is an example of the Abstract Factory (87) pattern.

- If `CreateMaze` is passed an object that can create a new maze in its entirety using operations for adding rooms, doors, and walls to the maze it builds, then you can use inheritance to change parts of the maze or the way the maze is built. This is an example of the Builder (97) pattern.

- If `CreateMaze` is parameterized by various prototypical room, door, and wall objects, which it then copies and adds to the maze, then you can change the maze's composition by replacing these prototypical objects with different ones. This is an example of the Prototype (117) pattern.

The remaining creational pattern, Singleton (127), can ensure there's only one maze per game and that all game objects have ready access to it—without resorting to global variables or functions. Singleton also makes it easy to extend or replace the maze without touching existing code.

ABSTRACT FACTORY

Object Creational

Intent

Provide an interface for creating families of related or dependent objects without specifying their concrete classes.

Also Known As

Kit

Motivation

Consider a user interface toolkit that supports multiple look-and-feel standards, such as Motif and Presentation Manager. Different look-and-feels define different appearances and behaviors for user interface "widgets" like scroll bars, windows, and buttons. To be portable across look-and-feel standards, an application should not hard-code its widgets for a particular look and feel. Instantiating look-and-feel-specific classes of widgets throughout the application makes it hard to change the look and feel later.

We can solve this problem by defining an abstract WidgetFactory class that declares an interface for creating each basic kind of widget. There's also an abstract class for each kind of widget, and concrete subclasses implement widgets for specific look-and-feel standards. WidgetFactory's interface has an operation that returns a new widget object for each abstract widget class. Clients call these operations to obtain widget instances, but clients aren't aware of the concrete classes they're using. Thus clients stay independent of the prevailing look and feel.

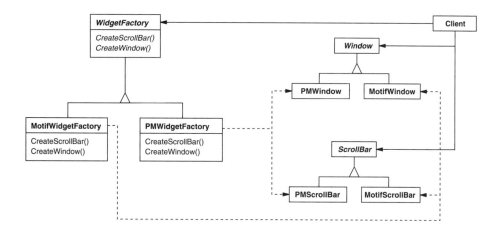

There is a concrete subclass of WidgetFactory for each look-and-feel standard. Each subclass implements the operations to create the appropriate widget for the look and feel. For example, the CreateScrollBar operation on the MotifWidgetFactory instantiates and returns a Motif scroll bar, while the corresponding operation on the PMWidgetFactory returns a scroll bar for Presentation Manager. Clients create widgets solely through the WidgetFactory interface and have no knowledge of the classes that implement widgets for a particular look and feel. In other words, clients only have to commit to an interface defined by an abstract class, not a particular concrete class.

A WidgetFactory also enforces dependencies between the concrete widget classes. A Motif scroll bar should be used with a Motif button and a Motif text editor, and that constraint is enforced automatically as a consequence of using a MotifWidgetFactory.

Applicability

Use the Abstract Factory pattern when

- a system should be independent of how its products are created, composed, and represented.

- a system should be configured with one of multiple families of products.

- a family of related product objects is designed to be used together, and you need to enforce this constraint.

- you want to provide a class library of products, and you want to reveal just their interfaces, not their implementations.

Structure

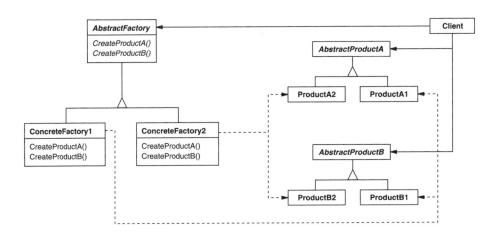

Participants

- **AbstractFactory** (WidgetFactory)
  - declares an interface for operations that create abstract product objects.
- **ConcreteFactory** (MotifWidgetFactory, PMWidgetFactory)
  - implements the operations to create concrete product objects.
- **AbstractProduct** (Window, ScrollBar)
  - declares an interface for a type of product object.
- **ConcreteProduct** (MotifWindow, MotifScrollBar)
  - defines a product object to be created by the corresponding concrete factory.
  - implements the AbstractProduct interface.
- **Client**
  - uses only interfaces declared by AbstractFactory and AbstractProduct classes.

Collaborations

- Normally a single instance of a ConcreteFactory class is created at run-time. This concrete factory creates product objects having a particular implementation. To create different product objects, clients should use a different concrete factory.
- AbstractFactory defers creation of product objects to its ConcreteFactory subclass.

Consequences

The Abstract Factory pattern has the following benefits and liabilities:

1. *It isolates concrete classes*. The Abstract Factory pattern helps you control the classes of objects that an application creates. Because a factory encapsulates the responsibility and the process of creating product objects, it isolates clients from implementation classes. Clients manipulate instances through their abstract interfaces. Product class names are isolated in the implementation of the concrete factory; they do not appear in client code.

2. *It makes exchanging product families easy*. The class of a concrete factory appears only once in an application—that is, where it's instantiated. This makes it easy to change the concrete factory an application uses. It can use different product configurations simply by changing the concrete factory. Because an abstract factory creates a complete family of products, the whole product family changes at once. In our user interface example, we can switch from Motif widgets to Presentation Manager widgets simply by switching the corresponding factory objects and recreating the interface.

3. *It promotes consistency among products.* When product objects in a family are designed to work together, it's important that an application use objects from only one family at a time. AbstractFactory makes this easy to enforce.

4. *Supporting new kinds of products is difficult.* Extending abstract factories to produce new kinds of Products isn't easy. That's because the AbstractFactory interface fixes the set of products that can be created. Supporting new kinds of products requires extending the factory interface, which involves changing the AbstractFactory class and all of its subclasses. We discuss one solution to this problem in the Implementation section.

Implementation

Here are some useful techniques for implementing the Abstract Factory pattern.

1. *Factories as singletons.* An application typically needs only one instance of a ConcreteFactory per product family. So it's usually best implemented as a Singleton (127).

2. *Creating the products.* AbstractFactory only declares an *interface* for creating products. It's up to ConcreteProduct subclasses to actually create them. The most common way to do this is to define a factory method (see Factory Method (107)) for each product. A concrete factory will specify its products by overriding the factory method for each. While this implementation is simple, it requires a new concrete factory subclass for each product family, even if the product families differ only slightly.

   If many product families are possible, the concrete factory can be implemented using the Prototype (117) pattern. The concrete factory is initialized with a prototypical instance of each product in the family, and it creates a new product by cloning its prototype. The Prototype-based approach eliminates the need for a new concrete factory class for each new product family.

   Here's a way to implement a Prototype-based factory in Smalltalk. The concrete factory stores the prototypes to be cloned in a dictionary called `partCatalog`. The method `make:` retrieves the prototype and clones it:

   ```
   make: partName
       ^ (partCatalog at: partName) copy
   ```

   The concrete factory has a method for adding parts to the catalog.

   ```
   addPart: partTemplate named: partName
       partCatalog at: partName put: partTemplate
   ```

   Prototypes are added to the factory by identifying them with a symbol:

   ```
   aFactory addPart: aPrototype named: #ACMEWidget
   ```

   A variation on the Prototype-based approach is possible in languages that treat classes as first-class objects (Smalltalk and Objective C, for example). You can think of a class in these languages as a degenerate factory that creates only one kind of product. You can store *classes* inside a concrete factory that create the various concrete products in variables, much like prototypes. These classes create new instances on behalf of the concrete factory. You define a new factory by initializing an instance of a concrete factory with *classes* of products rather than by subclassing. This approach takes advantage of language characteristics, whereas the pure Prototype-based approach is language-independent.

Like the Prototype-based factory in Smalltalk just discussed, the class-based version will have a single instance variable partCatalog, which is a dictionary whose key is the name of the part. Instead of storing prototypes to be cloned, partCatalog stores the classes of the products. The method make: now looks like this:

```
make: partName
    ^ (partCatalog at: partName) new
```

3. *Defining extensible factories.* AbstractFactory usually defines a different operation for each kind of product it can produce. The kinds of products are encoded in the operation signatures. Adding a new kind of product requires changing the AbstractFactory interface and all the classes that depend on it.

A more flexible but less safe design is to add a parameter to operations that create objects. This parameter specifies the kind of object to be created. It could be a class identifier, an integer, a string, or anything else that identifies the kind of product. In fact with this approach, AbstractFactory only needs a single "Make" operation with a parameter indicating the kind of object to create. This is the technique used in the Prototype- and the class-based abstract factories discussed earlier.

This variation is easier to use in a dynamically typed language like Smalltalk than in a statically typed language like C++. You can use it in C++ only when all objects have the same abstract base class or when the product objects can be safely coerced to the correct type by the client that requested them. The implementation section of Factory Method (107) shows how to implement such parameterized operations in C++.

But even when no coercion is needed, an inherent problem remains: All products are returned to the client with the *same* abstract interface as given by the return type. The client will not be able to differentiate or make safe assumptions about the class of a product. If clients need to perform subclass-specific operations, they won't be accessible through the abstract interface. Although the client could perform a downcast (e.g., with dynamic_cast in C++), that's not always feasible or safe, because the downcast can fail. This is the classic trade-off for a highly flexible and extensible interface.

Sample Code

We'll apply the Abstract Factory pattern to creating the mazes we discussed at the beginning of this chapter.

Class MazeFactory can create components of mazes. It builds rooms, walls, and doors between rooms. It might be used by a program that reads plans for mazes from a file and builds the corresponding maze. Or it might be used by a program that builds mazes randomly. Programs that build mazes take a MazeFactory as an argument so that the programmer can specify the classes of rooms, walls, and doors to construct.

```
class MazeFactory {
public:
    MazeFactory();

    virtual Maze* MakeMaze() const
        { return new Maze; }
    virtual Wall* MakeWall() const
        { return new Wall; }
    virtual Room* MakeRoom(int n) const
        { return new Room(n); }
    virtual Door* MakeDoor(Room* r1, Room* r2) const
        { return new Door(r1, r2); }
};
```

Recall that the member function CreateMaze (page 84) builds a small maze consisting of two rooms with a door between them. CreateMaze hard-codes the class names, making it difficult to create mazes with different components.

Here's a version of CreateMaze that remedies that shortcoming by taking a MazeFactory as a parameter:

```
Maze* MazeGame::CreateMaze (MazeFactory& factory) {
    Maze* aMaze = factory.MakeMaze();
    Room* r1 = factory.MakeRoom(1);
    Room* r2 = factory.MakeRoom(2);
    Door* aDoor = factory.MakeDoor(r1, r2);

    aMaze->AddRoom(r1);
    aMaze->AddRoom(r2);

    r1->SetSide(North, factory.MakeWall());
    r1->SetSide(East, aDoor);
    r1->SetSide(South, factory.MakeWall());
    r1->SetSide(West, factory.MakeWall());
```

```
    r2->SetSide(North, factory.MakeWall());
    r2->SetSide(East, factory.MakeWall());
    r2->SetSide(South, factory.MakeWall());
    r2->SetSide(West, aDoor);

    return aMaze;
}
```

We can create EnchantedMazeFactory, a factory for enchanted mazes, by sub-classing MazeFactory. EnchantedMazeFactory will override different member functions and return different subclasses of Room, Wall, etc.

```
class EnchantedMazeFactory : public MazeFactory {
public:
    EnchantedMazeFactory();

    virtual Room* MakeRoom(int n)  const
        { return new EnchantedRoom(n, CastSpell()); }

    virtual Door* MakeDoor(Room* r1, Room* r2)  const
        { return new DoorNeedingSpell(r1, r2); }

protected:
    Spell* CastSpell() const;
};
```

Now suppose we want to make a maze game in which a room can have a bomb set in it. If the bomb goes off, it will damage the walls (at least). We can make a subclass of Room keep track of whether the room has a bomb in it and whether the bomb has gone off. We'll also need a subclass of Wall to keep track of the damage done to the wall. We'll call these classes RoomWithABomb and BombedWall.

The last class we'll define is BombedMazeFactory, a subclass of MazeFactory that ensures walls are of class BombedWall and rooms are of class RoomWithABomb. BombedMazeFactory only needs to override two functions:

```
Wall* BombedMazeFactory::MakeWall () const {
    return new BombedWall;
}

Room* BombedMazeFactory::MakeRoom(int n) const {
    return new RoomWithABomb(n);
}
```

To build a simple maze that can contain bombs, we simply call CreateMaze with a BombedMazeFactory.

```
MazeGame game;
BombedMazeFactory factory;

game.CreateMaze(factory);
```

`CreateMaze` can take an instance of `EnchantedMazeFactory` just as well to build enchanted mazes.

Notice that the `MazeFactory` is just a collection of factory methods. This is the most common way to implement the Abstract Factory pattern. Also note that `MazeFactory` is not an abstract class; thus it acts as both the AbstractFactory *and* the ConcreteFactory. This is another common implementation for simple applications of the Abstract Factory pattern. Because the `MazeFactory` is a concrete class consisting entirely of factory methods, it's easy to make a new `MazeFactory` by making a subclass and overriding the operations that need to change.

`CreateMaze` used the `SetSide` operation on rooms to specify their sides. If it creates rooms with a `BombedMazeFactory`, then the maze will be made up of `RoomWithABomb` objects with `BombedWall` sides. If `RoomWithABomb` had to access a subclass-specific member of `BombedWall`, then it would have to cast a reference to its walls from `Wall*` to `BombedWall*`. This downcasting is safe as long as the argument *is* in fact a `BombedWall`, which is guaranteed to be true if walls are built solely with a `BombedMazeFactory`.

Dynamically typed languages such as Smalltalk don't require downcasting, of course, but they might produce run-time errors if they encounter a `Wall` where they expect a *subclass* of `Wall`. Using Abstract Factory to build walls helps prevent these run-time errors by ensuring that only certain kinds of walls can be created.

Let's consider a Smalltalk version of `MazeFactory`, one with a single `make` operation that takes the kind of object to make as a parameter. Moreover, the concrete factory stores the classes of the products it creates.

First, we'll write an equivalent of `CreateMaze` in Smalltalk:

```
createMaze: aFactory
    | room1 room2 aDoor |
    room1 := (aFactory make: #room) number: 1.
    room2 := (aFactory make: #room) number: 2.
    aDoor := (aFactory make: #door) from: room1 to: room2.
    room1 atSide: #north put: (aFactory make: #wall).
    room1 atSide: #east put: aDoor.
    room1 atSide: #south put: (aFactory make: #wall).
    room1 atSide: #west put: (aFactory make: #wall).
    room2 atSide: #north put: (aFactory make: #wall).
    room2 atSide: #east put: (aFactory make: #wall).
    room2 atSide: #south put: (aFactory make: #wall).
    room2 atSide: #west put: aDoor.
    ^ Maze new addRoom: room1; addRoom: room2; yourself
```

As we discussed in the Implementation section, `MazeFactory` needs only a single instance variable `partCatalog` to provide a dictionary whose key is the class of the component. Also recall how we implemented the `make:` method:

```
make: partName
    ^ (partCatalog at: partName) new
```

Now we can create a `MazeFactory` and use it to implement `createMaze`. We'll create the factory using a method `createMazeFactory` of class `MazeGame`.

```
createMazeFactory
    ^ (MazeFactory new
        addPart: Wall named: #wall;
        addPart: Room named: #room;
        addPart: Door named: #door;
        yourself)
```

A `BombedMazeFactory` or `EnchantedMazeFactory` is created by associating different classes with the keys. For example, an `EnchantedMazeFactory` could be created like this:

```
createMazeFactory
    ^ (MazeFactory new
        addPart: Wall named: #wall;
        addPart: EnchantedRoom named: #room;
        addPart: DoorNeedingSpell named: #door;
        yourself)
```

Known Uses

InterViews uses the "Kit" suffix [Lin92] to denote AbstractFactory classes. It defines WidgetKit and DialogKit abstract factories for generating look-and-feel-specific user interface objects. InterViews also includes a LayoutKit that generates different composition objects depending on the layout desired. For example, a layout that is conceptually horizontal may require different composition objects depending on the document's orientation (portrait or landscape).

ET++ [WGM88] uses the Abstract Factory pattern to achieve portability across different window systems (X Windows and SunView, for example). The WindowSystem abstract base class defines the interface for creating objects that represent window system resources (MakeWindow, MakeFont, MakeColor, for example). Concrete subclasses implement the interfaces for a specific window system. At run-time, ET++ creates an instance of a concrete WindowSystem subclass that creates concrete system resource objects.

Related Patterns

AbstractFactory classes are often implemented with factory methods (Factory Method (107)), but they can also be implemented using Prototype (117).

A concrete factory is often a singleton (Singleton (127)).

BUILDER   Object Creational

Intent

Separate the construction of a complex object from its representation so that the same construction process can create different representations.

Motivation

A reader for the RTF (Rich Text Format) document exchange format should be able to convert RTF to many text formats. The reader might convert RTF documents into plain ASCII text or into a text widget that can be edited interactively. The problem, however, is that the number of possible conversions is open-ended. So it should be easy to add a new conversion without modifying the reader.

A solution is to configure the RTFReader class with a TextConverter object that converts RTF to another textual representation. As the RTFReader parses the RTF document, it uses the TextConverter to perform the conversion. Whenever the RTFReader recognizes an RTF token (either plain text or an RTF control word), it issues a request to the TextConverter to convert the token. TextConverter objects are responsible both for performing the data conversion and for representing the token in a particular format.

Subclasses of TextConverter specialize in different conversions and formats. For example, an ASCIIConverter ignores requests to convert anything except plain text. A TeXConverter, on the other hand, will implement operations for all requests in order to produce a TeX representation that captures all the stylistic information in the text. A TextWidgetConverter will produce a complex user interface object that lets the user see and edit the text.

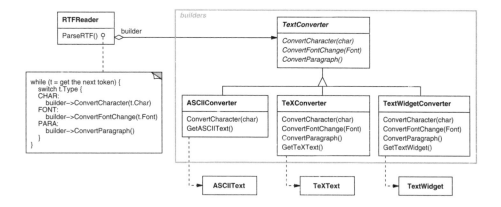

Each kind of converter class takes the mechanism for creating and assembling a complex object and puts it behind an abstract interface. The converter is separate from the reader, which is responsible for parsing an RTF document.

The Builder pattern captures all these relationships. Each converter class is called a **builder** in the pattern, and the reader is called the **director**. Applied to this example, the Builder pattern separates the algorithm for interpreting a textual format (that is, the parser for RTF documents) from how a converted format gets created and represented. This lets us reuse the RTFReader's parsing algorithm to create different text representations from RTF documents—just configure the RTFReader with different subclasses of TextConverter.

Applicability

Use the Builder pattern when

- the algorithm for creating a complex object should be independent of the parts that make up the object and how they're assembled.

- the construction process must allow different representations for the object that's constructed.

Structure

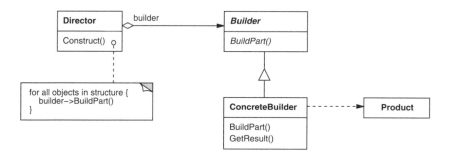

Participants

- **Builder** (TextConverter)

  - specifies an abstract interface for creating parts of a Product object.

- **ConcreteBuilder** (ASCIIConverter, TeXConverter, TextWidgetConverter)
  - constructs and assembles parts of the product by implementing the Builder interface.
  - defines and keeps track of the representation it creates.
  - provides an interface for retrieving the product (e.g., GetASCIIText, GetTextWidget).
- **Director** (RTFReader)
  - constructs an object using the Builder interface.
- **Product** (ASCIIText, TeXText, TextWidget)
  - represents the complex object under construction. ConcreteBuilder builds the product's internal representation and defines the process by which it's assembled.
  - includes classes that define the constituent parts, including interfaces for assembling the parts into the final result.

Collaborations

- The client creates the Director object and configures it with the desired Builder object.
- Director notifies the builder whenever a part of the product should be built.
- Builder handles requests from the director and adds parts to the product.
- The client retrieves the product from the builder.

The following interaction diagram illustrates how Builder and Director cooperate with a client.

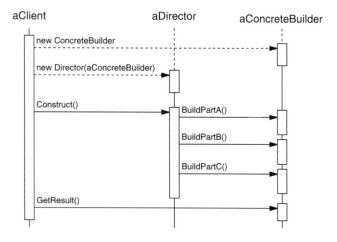

Consequences

Here are key consequences of the Builder pattern:

1. *It lets you vary a product's internal representation.* The Builder object provides the director with an abstract interface for constructing the product. The interface lets the builder hide the representation and internal structure of the product. It also hides how the product gets assembled. Because the product is constructed through an abstract interface, all you have to do to change the product's internal representation is define a new kind of builder.

2. *It isolates code for construction and representation.* The Builder pattern improves modularity by encapsulating the way a complex object is constructed and represented. Clients needn't know anything about the classes that define the product's internal structure; such classes don't appear in Builder's interface.

   Each ConcreteBuilder contains all the code to create and assemble a particular kind of product. The code is written once; then different Directors can reuse it to build Product variants from the same set of parts. In the earlier RTF example, we could define a reader for a format other than RTF, say, an SGMLReader, and use the same TextConverters to generate ASCIIText, TeXText, and TextWidget renditions of SGML documents.

3. *It gives you finer control over the construction process.* Unlike creational patterns that construct products in one shot, the Builder pattern constructs the product step by step under the director's control. Only when the product is finished does the director retrieve it from the builder. Hence the Builder interface reflects the process of constructing the product more than other creational patterns. This gives you finer control over the construction process and consequently the internal structure of the resulting product.

Implementation

Typically there's an abstract Builder class that defines an operation for each component that a director may ask it to create. The operations do nothing by default. A ConcreteBuilder class overrides operations for components it's interested in creating.

Here are other implementation issues to consider:

1. *Assembly and construction interface.* Builders construct their products in step-by-step fashion. Therefore the Builder class interface must be general enough to allow the construction of products for all kinds of concrete builders.

   A key design issue concerns the model for the construction and assembly process. A model where the results of construction requests are simply appended to the product is usually sufficient. In the RTF example, the builder converts and appends the next token to the text it has converted so far.

   But sometimes you might need access to parts of the product constructed earlier. In the Maze example we present in the Sample Code, the MazeBuilder interface lets you add a door between existing rooms. Tree structures such as parse trees that are built bottom-up are another example. In that case, the builder would return child nodes to the director, which then would pass them back to the builder to build the parent nodes.

2. *Why no abstract class for products?* In the common case, the products produced by the concrete builders differ so greatly in their representation that there is little to gain from giving different products a common parent class. In the RTF example, the ASCIIText and the TextWidget objects are unlikely to have a common interface, nor do they need one. Because the client usually configures the director with the proper concrete builder, the client is in a position to know which concrete subclass of Builder is in use and can handle its products accordingly.

3. *Empty methods as default in Builder.* In C++, the build methods are intentionally not declared pure virtual member functions. They're defined as empty methods instead, letting clients override only the operations they're interested in.

Sample Code

We'll define a variant of the `CreateMaze` member function (page 84) that takes a builder of class `MazeBuilder` as an argument.

The `MazeBuilder` class defines the following interface for building mazes:

```
class MazeBuilder {
public:
    virtual void BuildMaze() { }
    virtual void BuildRoom(int room) { }
    virtual void BuildDoor(int roomFrom, int roomTo) { }

    virtual Maze* GetMaze() { return 0; }
protected:
    MazeBuilder();
};
```

This interface can create three things: (1) the maze, (2) rooms with a particular room number, and (3) doors between numbered rooms. The `GetMaze` operation returns the maze to the client. Subclasses of `MazeBuilder` will override this operation to return the maze that they build.

All the maze-building operations of `MazeBuilder` do nothing by default. They're not declared pure virtual to let derived classes override only those methods in which they're interested.

Given the `MazeBuilder` interface, we can change the `CreateMaze` member function to take this builder as a parameter.

```
Maze* MazeGame::CreateMaze (MazeBuilder& builder) {
    builder.BuildMaze();

    builder.BuildRoom(1);
    builder.BuildRoom(2);
    builder.BuildDoor(1, 2);

    return builder.GetMaze();
}
```

Compare this version of `CreateMaze` with the original. Notice how the builder hides the internal representation of the Maze—that is, the classes that define rooms, doors, and walls—and how these parts are assembled to complete the final maze. Someone might guess that there are classes for representing rooms and doors, but there is no hint of one for walls. This makes it easier to change the way a maze is represented, since none of the clients of `MazeBuilder` has to be changed.

Like the other creational patterns, the Builder pattern encapsulates how objects get created, in this case through the interface defined by `MazeBuilder`. That means we can reuse `MazeBuilder` to build different kinds of mazes. The `CreateComplexMaze` operation gives an example:

```
Maze* MazeGame::CreateComplexMaze (MazeBuilder& builder) {
    builder.BuildRoom(1);
    // ...
    builder.BuildRoom(1001);

    return builder.GetMaze();
}
```

Note that `MazeBuilder` does not create mazes itself; its main purpose is just to define an interface for creating mazes. It defines empty implementations primarily for convenience. Subclasses of `MazeBuilder` do the actual work.

The subclass `StandardMazeBuilder` is an implementation that builds simple mazes. It keeps track of the maze it's building in the variable `_currentMaze`.

```
class StandardMazeBuilder : public MazeBuilder {
public:
    StandardMazeBuilder();

    virtual void BuildMaze();
    virtual void BuildRoom(int);
    virtual void BuildDoor(int, int);

    virtual Maze* GetMaze();
private:
    Direction CommonWall(Room*, Room*);
    Maze* _currentMaze;
};
```

`CommonWall` is a utility operation that determines the direction of the common wall between two rooms.

The `StandardMazeBuilder` constructor simply initializes `_currentMaze`.

```
StandardMazeBuilder::StandardMazeBuilder () {
    _currentMaze = 0;
}
```

`BuildMaze` instantiates a `Maze` that other operations will assemble and eventually return to the client (with `GetMaze`).

```
void StandardMazeBuilder::BuildMaze () {
    _currentMaze = new Maze;
}


Maze* StandardMazeBuilder::GetMaze () {
    return _currentMaze;
}
```

The `BuildRoom` operation creates a room and builds the walls around it:

```
void StandardMazeBuilder::BuildRoom (int n) {
    if (!_currentMaze->RoomNo(n)) {
        Room* room = new Room(n);
        _currentMaze->AddRoom(room);

        room->SetSide(North, new Wall);
        room->SetSide(South, new Wall);
        room->SetSide(East, new Wall);
        room->SetSide(West, new Wall);
    }
}
```

To build a door between two rooms, `StandardMazeBuilder` looks up both rooms in the maze and finds their adjoining wall:

```
void StandardMazeBuilder::BuildDoor (int n1, int n2) {
    Room* r1 = _currentMaze->RoomNo(n1);
    Room* r2 = _currentMaze->RoomNo(n2);
    Door* d = new Door(r1, r2);

    r1->SetSide(CommonWall(r1,r2), d);
    r2->SetSide(CommonWall(r2,r1), d);
}
```

Clients can now use `CreateMaze` in conjunction with `StandardMazeBuilder` to create a maze:

```
Maze* maze;
MazeGame game;
StandardMazeBuilder builder;

game.CreateMaze(builder);
maze = builder.GetMaze();
```

We could have put all the `StandardMazeBuilder` operations in `Maze` and let each `Maze` build itself. But making `Maze` smaller makes it easier to understand and modify, and `StandardMazeBuilder` is easy to separate from `Maze`. Most importantly, separating the two lets you have a variety of `MazeBuilders`, each using different classes for rooms, walls, and doors.

A more exotic `MazeBuilder` is `CountingMazeBuilder`. This builder doesn't create a maze at all; it just counts the different kinds of components that would have been created.

```cpp
class CountingMazeBuilder : public MazeBuilder {
public:
    CountingMazeBuilder();

    virtual void BuildMaze();
    virtual void BuildRoom(int);
    virtual void BuildDoor(int, int);
    virtual void AddWall(int, Direction);

    void GetCounts(int&, int&) const;
private:
    int _doors;
    int _rooms;
};
```

The constructor initializes the counters, and the overridden `MazeBuilder` operations increment them accordingly.

```cpp
CountingMazeBuilder::CountingMazeBuilder () {
    _rooms = _doors = 0;
}

void CountingMazeBuilder::BuildRoom (int) {
    _rooms++;
}

void CountingMazeBuilder::BuildDoor (int, int) {
    _doors++;
}

void CountingMazeBuilder::GetCounts (
    int& rooms, int& doors
) const {
    rooms = _rooms;
    doors = _doors;
}
```

Here's how a client might use a `CountingMazeBuilder`:

```
int rooms, doors;
MazeGame game;
CountingMazeBuilder builder;

game.CreateMaze(builder);
builder.GetCounts(rooms, doors);

cout << "The maze has "
     << rooms << " rooms and "
     << doors << " doors" << endl;
```

Known Uses

The RTF converter application is from ET++ [WGM88]. Its text building block uses a builder to process text stored in the RTF format.

Builder is a common pattern in Smalltalk-80 [Par90]:

- The Parser class in the compiler subsystem is a Director that takes a ProgramNodeBuilder object as an argument. A Parser object notifies its ProgramNodeBuilder object each time it recognizes a syntactic construct. When the parser is done, it asks the builder for the parse tree it built and returns it to the client.

- ClassBuilder is a builder that Classes use to create subclasses for themselves. In this case a Class is both the Director and the Product.

- ByteCodeStream is a builder that creates a compiled method as a byte array. ByteCodeStream is a nonstandard use of the Builder pattern, because the complex object it builds is encoded as a byte array, not as a normal Smalltalk object. But the interface to ByteCodeStream is typical of a builder, and it would be easy to replace ByteCodeStream with a different class that represented programs as a composite object.

The Service Configurator framework from the Adaptive Communications Environment uses a builder to construct network service components that are linked into a server at run-time [SS94]. The components are described with a configuration language that's parsed by an LALR(1) parser. The semantic actions of the parser perform operations on the builder that add information to the service component. In this case, the parser is the Director.

Related Patterns

Abstract Factory (87) is similar to Builder in that it too may construct complex objects. The primary difference is that the Builder pattern focuses on constructing a complex object step by step. Abstract Factory's emphasis is on families of product objects (either simple or complex). Builder returns the product as a final step, but as far as the Abstract Factory pattern is concerned, the product gets returned immediately.

A Composite (163) is what the builder often builds.

FACTORY METHOD   Class Creational

Intent

Define an interface for creating an object, but let subclasses decide which class to instantiate. Factory Method lets a class defer instantiation to subclasses.

Also Known As

Virtual Constructor

Motivation

Frameworks use abstract classes to define and maintain relationships between objects. A framework is often responsible for creating these objects as well.

Consider a framework for applications that can present multiple documents to the user. Two key abstractions in this framework are the classes Application and Document. Both classes are abstract, and clients have to subclass them to realize their application-specific implementations. To create a drawing application, for example, we define the classes DrawingApplication and DrawingDocument. The Application class is responsible for managing Documents and will create them as required—when the user selects Open or New from a menu, for example.

Because the particular Document subclass to instantiate is application-specific, the Application class can't predict the subclass of Document to instantiate—the Application class only knows *when* a new document should be created, not *what kind* of Document to create. This creates a dilemma: The framework must instantiate classes, but it only knows about abstract classes, which it cannot instantiate.

The Factory Method pattern offers a solution. It encapsulates the knowledge of which Document subclass to create and moves this knowledge out of the framework.

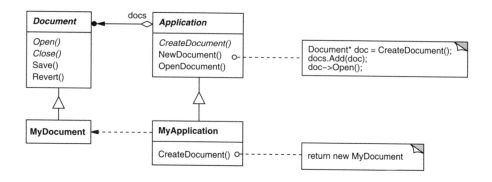

Application subclasses redefine an abstract CreateDocument operation on Application to return the appropriate Document subclass. Once an Application subclass is instantiated, it can then instantiate application-specific Documents without knowing their class. We call CreateDocument a **factory method** because it's responsible for "manufacturing" an object.

Applicability

Use the Factory Method pattern when

- a class can't anticipate the class of objects it must create.
- a class wants its subclasses to specify the objects it creates.
- classes delegate responsibility to one of several helper subclasses, and you want to localize the knowledge of which helper subclass is the delegate.

Structure

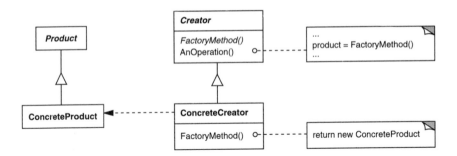

Participants

- **Product** (Document)
  - defines the interface of objects the factory method creates.
- **ConcreteProduct** (MyDocument)
  - implements the Product interface.
- **Creator** (Application)
  - declares the factory method, which returns an object of type Product. Creator may also define a default implementation of the factory method that returns a default ConcreteProduct object.
  - may call the factory method to create a Product object.

- **ConcreteCreator** (MyApplication)
  - – overrides the factory method to return an instance of a ConcreteProduct.

Collaborations

- Creator relies on its subclasses to define the factory method so that it returns an instance of the appropriate ConcreteProduct.

Consequences

Factory methods eliminate the need to bind application-specific classes into your code. The code only deals with the Product interface; therefore it can work with any user-defined ConcreteProduct classes.

A potential disadvantage of factory methods is that clients might have to subclass the Creator class just to create a particular ConcreteProduct object. Subclassing is fine when the client has to subclass the Creator class anyway, but otherwise the client now must deal with another point of evolution.

Here are two additional consequences of the Factory Method pattern:

1. *Provides hooks for subclasses.* Creating objects inside a class with a factory method is always more flexible than creating an object directly. Factory Method gives subclasses a hook for providing an extended version of an object.

   In the Document example, the Document class could define a factory method called CreateFileDialog that creates a default file dialog object for opening an existing document. A Document subclass can define an application-specific file dialog by overriding this factory method. In this case the factory method is not abstract but provides a reasonable default implementation.

2. *Connects parallel class hierarchies.* In the examples we've considered so far, the factory method is only called by Creators. But this doesn't have to be the case; clients can find factory methods useful, especially in the case of parallel class hierarchies.

   Parallel class hierarchies result when a class delegates some of its responsibilities to a separate class. Consider graphical figures that can be manipulated interactively; that is, they can be stretched, moved, or rotated using the mouse. Implementing such interactions isn't always easy. It often requires storing and updating information that records the state of the manipulation at a given time. This state is needed only during manipulation; therefore it needn't be kept in the figure object. Moreover, different figures behave differently when the user manipulates them. For example, stretching a line figure might have the effect of moving an endpoint, whereas stretching a text figure may change its line spacing.

   With these constraints, it's better to use a separate Manipulator object that implements the interaction and keeps track of any manipulation-specific state that's needed. Different figures will use different Manipulator subclasses to handle particular interactions. The resulting Manipulator class hierarchy parallels (at least partially) the Figure class hierarchy:

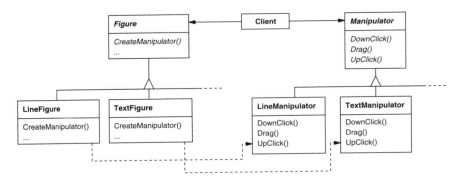

The Figure class provides a CreateManipulator factory method that lets clients create a Figure's corresponding Manipulator. Figure subclasses override this method to return an instance of the Manipulator subclass that's right for them. Alternatively, the Figure class may implement CreateManipulator to return a default Manipulator instance, and Figure subclasses may simply inherit that default. The Figure classes that do so need no corresponding Manipulator subclass—hence the hierarchies are only partially parallel.

Notice how the factory method defines the connection between the two class hierarchies. It localizes knowledge of which classes belong together.

Implementation

Consider the following issues when applying the Factory Method pattern:

1. *Two major varieties.* The two main variations of the Factory Method pattern are (1) the case when the Creator class is an abstract class and does not provide an implementation for the factory method it declares, and (2) the case when the Creator is a concrete class and provides a default implementation for the factory method. It's also possible to have an abstract class that defines a default implementation, but this is less common.

   The first case *requires* subclasses to define an implementation, because there's no reasonable default. It gets around the dilemma of having to instantiate unforeseeable classes. In the second case, the concrete Creator uses the factory method primarily for flexibility. It's following a rule that says, "Create objects in a separate operation so that subclasses can override the way they're created." This rule ensures that designers of subclasses can change the class of objects their parent class instantiates if necessary.

2. *Parameterized factory methods.* Another variation on the pattern lets the factory method create *multiple* kinds of products. The factory method takes a

parameter that identifies the kind of object to create. All objects the factory method creates will share the Product interface. In the Document example, Application might support different kinds of Documents. You pass Create-Document an extra parameter to specify the kind of document to create.

The Unidraw graphical editing framework [VL90] uses this approach for reconstructing objects saved on disk. Unidraw defines a `Creator` class with a factory method `Create` that takes a class identifier as an argument. The class identifier specifies the class to instantiate. When Unidraw saves an object to disk, it writes out the class identifier first and then its instance variables. When it reconstructs the object from disk, it reads the class identifier first.

Once the class identifier is read, the framework calls `Create`, passing the identifier as the parameter. `Create` looks up the constructor for the corresponding class and uses it to instantiate the object. Last, `Create` calls the object's `Read` operation, which reads the remaining information on the disk and initializes the object's instance variables.

A parameterized factory method has the following general form, where `MyProduct` and `YourProduct` are subclasses of `Product`:

```
class Creator {
public:
    virtual Product* Create(ProductId);
};

Product* Creator::Create (ProductId id) {
    if (id == MINE)  return new MyProduct;
    if (id == YOURS) return new YourProduct;
    // repeat for remaining products...

    return 0;
}
```

Overriding a parameterized factory method lets you easily and selectively extend or change the products that a Creator produces. You can introduce new identifiers for new kinds of products, or you can associate existing identifiers with different products.

For example, a subclass `MyCreator` could swap MyProduct and YourProduct and support a new `TheirProduct` subclass:

```
Product* MyCreator::Create (ProductId id) {
    if (id == YOURS)  return new MyProduct;
    if (id == MINE)   return new YourProduct;
        // N.B.: switched YOURS and MINE

    if (id == THEIRS) return new TheirProduct;

    return Creator::Create(id); // called if all others fail
}
```

Notice that the last thing this operation does is call `Create` on the parent class. That's because `MyCreator::Create` handles only YOURS, MINE, and

THEIRS differently than the parent class. It isn't interested in other classes. Hence MyCreator *extends* the kinds of products created, and it defers responsibility for creating all but a few products to its parent.

3. *Language-specific variants and issues.* Different languages lend themselves to other interesting variations and caveats.

Smalltalk programs often use a method that returns the class of the object to be instantiated. A Creator factory method can use this value to create a product, and a ConcreteCreator may store or even compute this value. The result is an even later binding for the type of ConcreteProduct to be instantiated.

A Smalltalk version of the Document example can define a documentClass method on Application. The documentClass method returns the proper Document class for instantiating documents. The implementation of documentClass in MyApplication returns the MyDocument class. Thus in class Application we have

```
clientMethod
    document := self documentClass new.

documentClass
    self subclassResponsibility
```

In class MyApplication we have

```
documentClass
    ^ MyDocument
```

which returns the class MyDocument to be instantiated to Application.

An even more flexible approach akin to parameterized factory methods is to store the class to be created as a class variable of Application. That way you don't have to subclass Application to vary the product.

Factory methods in C++ are always virtual functions and are often pure virtual. Just be careful not to call factory methods in the Creator's constructor— the factory method in the ConcreteCreator won't be available yet.

You can avoid this by being careful to access products solely through accessor operations that create the product on demand. Instead of creating the concrete product in the constructor, the constructor merely initializes it to 0. The accessor returns the product. But first it checks to make sure the product exists, and if it doesn't, the accessor creates it. This technique is sometimes called **lazy initialization**. The following code shows a typical implementation:

```
class Creator {
public:
    Product* GetProduct();
protected:
    virtual Product* CreateProduct();
private:
    Product* _product;
};

Product* Creator::GetProduct () {
    if (_product == 0) {
        _product = CreateProduct();
    }
    return _product;
}
```

4. *Using templates to avoid subclassing.* As we've mentioned, another potential problem with factory methods is that they might force you to subclass just to create the appropriate Product objects. Another way to get around this in C++ is to provide a template subclass of Creator that's parameterized by the Product class:

```
class Creator {
public:
    virtual Product* CreateProduct() = 0;
};

template <class TheProduct>
class StandardCreator: public Creator {
public:
    virtual Product* CreateProduct();
};

template <class TheProduct>
Product* StandardCreator<TheProduct>::CreateProduct () {
    return new TheProduct;
}
```

With this template, the client supplies just the product class—no subclassing of Creator is required.

```
class MyProduct : public Product {
public:
    MyProduct();
    // ...
};

StandardCreator<MyProduct> myCreator;
```

5. *Naming conventions.* It's good practice to use naming conventions that make it clear you're using factory methods. For example, the MacApp Macintosh application framework [App89] always declares the abstract operation that defines the factory method as Class* DoMakeClass(), where Class is the Product class.

Sample Code

The function `CreateMaze` (page 84) builds and returns a maze. One problem with this function is that it hard-codes the classes of maze, rooms, doors, and walls. We'll introduce factory methods to let subclasses choose these components.

First we'll define factory methods in `MazeGame` for creating the maze, room, wall, and door objects:

```
class MazeGame {
public:
    Maze* CreateMaze();

// factory methods:

    virtual Maze* MakeMaze() const
        { return new Maze; }
    virtual Room* MakeRoom(int n) const
        { return new Room(n); }
    virtual Wall* MakeWall() const
        { return new Wall; }
    virtual Door* MakeDoor(Room* r1, Room* r2) const
        { return new Door(r1, r2); }
};
```

Each factory method returns a maze component of a given type. `MazeGame` provides default implementations that return the simplest kinds of maze, rooms, walls, and doors.

Now we can rewrite `CreateMaze` to use these factory methods:

```
Maze* MazeGame::CreateMaze () {
    Maze* aMaze = MakeMaze();

    Room* r1 = MakeRoom(1);
    Room* r2 = MakeRoom(2);
    Door* theDoor = MakeDoor(r1, r2);

    aMaze->AddRoom(r1);
    aMaze->AddRoom(r2);

    r1->SetSide(North, MakeWall());
    r1->SetSide(East, theDoor);
    r1->SetSide(South, MakeWall());
    r1->SetSide(West, MakeWall());

    r2->SetSide(North, MakeWall());
    r2->SetSide(East, MakeWall());
    r2->SetSide(South, MakeWall());
    r2->SetSide(West, theDoor);
```

```
        return aMaze;
    }
```

Different games can subclass MazeGame to specialize parts of the maze. MazeGame subclasses can redefine some or all of the factory methods to specify variations in products. For example, a BombedMazeGame can redefine the Room and Wall products to return the bombed varieties:

```
class BombedMazeGame : public MazeGame {
public:
    BombedMazeGame();

    virtual Wall* MakeWall() const
        { return new BombedWall; }

    virtual Room* MakeRoom(int n) const
        { return new RoomWithABomb(n); }
};
```

An EnchantedMazeGame variant might be defined like this:

```
class EnchantedMazeGame : public MazeGame {
public:
    EnchantedMazeGame();

    virtual Room* MakeRoom(int n) const
        { return new EnchantedRoom(n, CastSpell()); }

    virtual Door* MakeDoor(Room* r1, Room* r2) const
        { return new DoorNeedingSpell(r1, r2); }
protected:
    Spell* CastSpell() const;
};
```

Known Uses

Factory methods pervade toolkits and frameworks. The preceding document example is a typical use in MacApp and ET++ [WGM88]. The manipulator example is from Unidraw.

Class View in the Smalltalk-80 Model/View/Controller framework has a method defaultController that creates a controller, and this might appear to be a factory method [Par90]. But subclasses of View specify the class of their default controller by defining defaultControllerClass, which returns the class from which default-Controller creates instances. So defaultControllerClass is the real factory method, that is, the method that subclasses should override.

A more esoteric example in Smalltalk-80 is the factory method parserClass defined by Behavior (a superclass of all objects representing classes). This enables a class to use a customized parser for its source code. For example, a client can define a class SQLParser to analyze the source code of a class with embedded SQL statements. The Behavior class implements parserClass to return the standard Smalltalk Parser class. A class that includes embedded SQL statements overrides this method (as a class method) and returns the SQLParser class.

The Orbix ORB system from IONA Technologies [ION94] uses Factory Method to generate an appropriate type of proxy (see Proxy (207)) when an object requests a reference to a remote object. Factory Method makes it easy to replace the default proxy with one that uses client-side caching, for example.

Related Patterns

Abstract Factory (87) is often implemented with factory methods. The Motivation example in the Abstract Factory pattern illustrates Factory Method as well.

Factory methods are usually called within Template Methods (325). In the document example above, NewDocument is a template method.

Prototypes (117) don't require subclassing Creator. However, they often require an Initialize operation on the Product class. Creator uses Initialize to initialize the object. Factory Method doesn't require such an operation.

PROTOTYPE
Object Creational

Intent

Specify the kinds of objects to create using a prototypical instance, and create new objects by copying this prototype.

Motivation

You could build an editor for music scores by customizing a general framework for graphical editors and adding new objects that represent notes, rests, and staves. The editor framework may have a palette of tools for adding these music objects to the score. The palette would also include tools for selecting, moving, and otherwise manipulating music objects. Users will click on the quarter-note tool and use it to add quarter notes to the score. Or they can use the move tool to move a note up or down on the staff, thereby changing its pitch.

Let's assume the framework provides an abstract Graphic class for graphical components, like notes and staves. Moreover, it'll provide an abstract Tool class for defining tools like those in the palette. The framework also predefines a Graphic-Tool subclass for tools that create instances of graphical objects and add them to the document.

But GraphicTool presents a problem to the framework designer. The classes for notes and staves are specific to our application, but the GraphicTool class belongs to the framework. GraphicTool doesn't know how to create instances of our music classes to add to the score. We could subclass GraphicTool for each kind of music object, but that would produce lots of subclasses that differ only in the kind of music object they instantiate. We know object composition is a flexible alternative to subclassing. The question is, how can the framework use it to parameterize instances of GraphicTool by the *class* of Graphic they're supposed to create?

The solution lies in making GraphicTool create a new Graphic by copying or "cloning" an instance of a Graphic subclass. We call this instance a **prototype**. GraphicTool is parameterized by the prototype it should clone and add to the document. If all Graphic subclasses support a Clone operation, then the Graphic-Tool can clone any kind of Graphic.

So in our music editor, each tool for creating a music object is an instance of GraphicTool that's initialized with a different prototype. Each GraphicTool instance will produce a music object by cloning its prototype and adding the clone to the score.

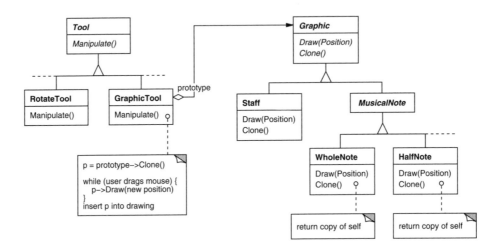

We can use the Prototype pattern to reduce the number of classes even further. We have separate classes for whole notes and half notes, but that's probably unnecessary. Instead they could be instances of the same class initialized with different bitmaps and durations. A tool for creating whole notes becomes just a GraphicTool whose prototype is a MusicalNote initialized to be a whole note. This can reduce the number of classes in the system dramatically. It also makes it easier to add a new kind of note to the music editor.

Applicability

Use the Prototype pattern when a system should be independent of how its products are created, composed, and represented; *and*

- when the classes to instantiate are specified at run-time, for example, by dynamic loading; *or*

- to avoid building a class hierarchy of factories that parallels the class hierarchy of products; *or*

- when instances of a class can have one of only a few different combinations of state. It may be more convenient to install a corresponding number of prototypes and clone them rather than instantiating the class manually, each time with the appropriate state.

Structure

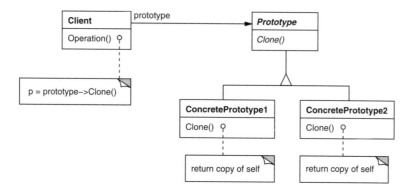

Participants

- **Prototype** (Graphic)
  - declares an interface for cloning itself.
- **ConcretePrototype** (Staff, WholeNote, HalfNote)
  - implements an operation for cloning itself.
- **Client** (GraphicTool)
  - creates a new object by asking a prototype to clone itself.

Collaborations

- A client asks a prototype to clone itself.

Consequences

Prototype has many of the same consequences that Abstract Factory (87) and Builder (97) have: It hides the concrete product classes from the client, thereby reducing the number of names clients know about. Moreover, these patterns let a client work with application-specific classes without modification.

Additional benefits of the Prototype pattern are listed below.

1. *Adding and removing products at run-time.* Prototypes let you incorporate a new concrete product class into a system simply by registering a prototypical instance with the client. That's a bit more flexible than other creational patterns, because a client can install and remove prototypes at run-time.

2. *Specifying new objects by varying values.* Highly dynamic systems let you define new behavior through object composition—by specifying values for an

object's variables, for example—and not by defining new classes. You effectively define new kinds of objects by instantiating existing classes and registering the instances as prototypes of client objects. A client can exhibit new behavior by delegating responsibility to the prototype.

This kind of design lets users define new "classes" without programming. In fact, cloning a prototype is similar to instantiating a class. The Prototype pattern can greatly reduce the number of classes a system needs. In our music editor, one GraphicTool class can create a limitless variety of music objects.

3. *Specifying new objects by varying structure.* Many applications build objects from parts and subparts. Editors for circuit design, for example, build circuits out of subcircuits.[1] For convenience, such applications often let you instantiate complex, user-defined structures, say, to use a specific subcircuit again and again.

The Prototype pattern supports this as well. We simply add this subcircuit as a prototype to the palette of available circuit elements. As long as the composite circuit object implements Clone as a deep copy, circuits with different structures can be prototypes.

4. *Reduced subclassing.* Factory Method (107) often produces a hierarchy of Creator classes that parallels the product class hierarchy. The Prototype pattern lets you clone a prototype instead of asking a factory method to make a new object. Hence you don't need a Creator class hierarchy at all. This benefit applies primarily to languages like C++ that don't treat classes as first-class objects. Languages that do, like Smalltalk and Objective C, derive less benefit, since you can always use a class object as a creator. Class objects already act like prototypes in these languages.

5. *Configuring an application with classes dynamically.* Some run-time environments let you load classes into an application dynamically. The Prototype pattern is the key to exploiting such facilities in a language like C++.

An application that wants to create instances of a dynamically loaded class won't be able to reference its constructor statically. Instead, the run-time environment creates an instance of each class automatically when it's loaded, and it registers the instance with a prototype manager (see the Implementation section). Then the application can ask the prototype manager for instances of newly loaded classes, classes that weren't linked with the program originally. The ET++ application framework [WGM88] has a run-time system that uses this scheme.

The main liability of the Prototype pattern is that each subclass of Prototype must implement the Clone operation, which may be difficult. For example, adding Clone is difficult when the classes under consideration already exist. Implementing Clone can be difficult when their internals include objects that don't support copying or have circular references.

[1] Such applications reflect the Composite (163) and Decorator (175) patterns.

Implementation

Prototype is particularly useful with static languages like C++, where classes are not objects, and little or no type information is available at run-time. It's less important in languages like Smalltalk or Objective C that provide what amounts to a prototype (i.e., a class object) for creating instances of each class. This pattern is built into prototype-based languages like Self [US87], in which all object creation happens by cloning a prototype.

Consider the following issues when implementing prototypes:

1. *Using a prototype manager.* When the number of prototypes in a system isn't fixed (that is, they can be created and destroyed dynamically), keep a registry of available prototypes. Clients won't manage prototypes themselves but will store and retrieve them from the registry. A client will ask the registry for a prototype before cloning it. We call this registry a **prototype manager**.

   A prototype manager is an associative store that returns the prototype matching a given key. It has operations for registering a prototype under a key and for unregistering it. Clients can change or even browse through the registry at run-time. This lets clients extend and take inventory on the system without writing code.

2. *Implementing the Clone operation.* The hardest part of the Prototype pattern is implementing the Clone operation correctly. It's particularly tricky when object structures contain circular references.

   Most languages provide some support for cloning objects. For example, Smalltalk provides an implementation of copy that's inherited by all subclasses of Object. C++ provides a copy constructor. But these facilities don't solve the "shallow copy versus deep copy" problem [GR83]. That is, does cloning an object in turn clone its instance variables, or do the clone and original just share the variables?

   A shallow copy is simple and often sufficient, and that's what Smalltalk provides by default. The default copy constructor in C++ does a member-wise copy, which means pointers will be shared between the copy and the original. But cloning prototypes with complex structures usually requires a deep copy, because the clone and the original must be independent. Therefore you must ensure that the clone's components are clones of the prototype's components. Cloning forces you to decide what if anything will be shared.

   If objects in the system provide Save and Load operations, then you can use them to provide a default implementation of Clone simply by saving the object and loading it back immediately. The Save operation saves the object into a memory buffer, and Load creates a duplicate by reconstructing the object from the buffer.

3. *Initializing clones.* While some clients are perfectly happy with the clone as is, others will want to initialize some or all of its internal state to values

of their choosing. You generally can't pass these values in the Clone operation, because their number will vary between classes of prototypes. Some prototypes might need multiple initialization parameters; others won't need any. Passing parameters in the Clone operation precludes a uniform cloning interface.

It might be the case that your prototype classes already define operations for (re)setting key pieces of state. If so, clients may use these operations immediately after cloning. If not, then you may have to introduce an Initialize operation (see the Sample Code section) that takes initialization parameters as arguments and sets the clone's internal state accordingly. Beware of deep-copying Clone operations—the copies may have to be deleted (either explicitly or within Initialize) before you reinitialize them.

Sample Code

We'll define a MazePrototypeFactory subclass of the MazeFactory class (page 92). MazePrototypeFactory will be initialized with prototypes of the objects it will create so that we don't have to subclass it just to change the classes of walls or rooms it creates.

MazePrototypeFactory augments the MazeFactory interface with a constructor that takes the prototypes as arguments:

```
class MazePrototypeFactory : public MazeFactory {
public:
    MazePrototypeFactory(Maze*, Wall*, Room*, Door*);

    virtual Maze* MakeMaze() const;
    virtual Room* MakeRoom(int) const;
    virtual Wall* MakeWall() const;
    virtual Door* MakeDoor(Room*, Room*) const;

private:
    Maze* _prototypeMaze;
    Room* _prototypeRoom;
    Wall* _prototypeWall;
    Door* _prototypeDoor;
};
```

The new constructor simply initializes its prototypes:

```
MazePrototypeFactory::MazePrototypeFactory (
    Maze* m, Wall* w, Room* r, Door* d
) {
    _prototypeMaze = m;
    _prototypeWall = w;
    _prototypeRoom = r;
    _prototypeDoor = d;
}
```

The member functions for creating walls, rooms, and doors are similar: Each clones a prototype and then initializes it. Here are the definitions of MakeWall and MakeDoor:

```
Wall* MazePrototypeFactory::MakeWall () const {
    return _prototypeWall->Clone();
}


Door* MazePrototypeFactory::MakeDoor (Room* r1, Room *r2) const {
    Door* door = _prototypeDoor->Clone();
    door->Initialize(r1, r2);
    return door;
}
```

We can use MazePrototypeFactory to create a prototypical or default maze just by initializing it with prototypes of basic maze components:

```
MazeGame game;
MazePrototypeFactory simpleMazeFactory(
    new Maze, new Wall, new Room, new Door
);

Maze* maze = game.CreateMaze(simpleMazeFactory);
```

To change the type of maze, we initialize MazePrototypeFactory with a different set of prototypes. The following call creates a maze with a BombedDoor and a RoomWithABomb:

```
MazePrototypeFactory bombedMazeFactory(
    new Maze, new BombedWall,
    new RoomWithABomb, new Door
);
```

An object that can be used as a prototype, such as an instance of Wall, must support the Clone operation. It must also have a copy constructor for cloning. It may also need a separate operation for reinitializing internal state. We'll add the Initialize operation to Door to let clients initialize the clone's rooms.

Compare the following definition of Door to the one on page 83:

```
class Door : public MapSite {
public:
    Door();
    Door(const Door&);

    virtual void Initialize(Room*, Room*);
    virtual Door* Clone() const;
```

```
        virtual void Enter();
        Room* OtherSideFrom(Room*);
    private:
        Room* _room1;
        Room* _room2;
    };


    Door::Door (const Door& other) {
        _room1 = other._room1;
        _room2 = other._room2;
    }

    void Door::Initialize (Room* r1, Room* r2) {
        _room1 = r1;
        _room2 = r2;
    }


    Door* Door::Clone () const {
        return new Door(*this);
    }
```

The BombedWall subclass must override Clone and implement a corresponding copy constructor.

```
    class BombedWall : public Wall {
    public:
        BombedWall();
        BombedWall(const BombedWall&);

        virtual Wall* Clone() const;
        bool HasBomb();
    private:
        bool _bomb;
    };

    BombedWall::BombedWall (const BombedWall& other) : Wall(other) {
        _bomb = other._bomb;
    }


    Wall* BombedWall::Clone () const {
        return new BombedWall(*this);
    }
```

Although BombedWall::Clone returns a Wall*, its implementation returns a pointer to a new instance of a subclass, that is, a BombedWall*. We define Clone like this in the base class to ensure that clients that clone the prototype don't have to know about their concrete subclasses. Clients should never need to downcast the return value of Clone to the desired type.

In Smalltalk, you can reuse the standard copy method inherited from Object to clone any MapSite. You can use MazeFactory to produce the prototypes you'll need; for example, you can create a room by supplying the name #room. The MazeFactory has a dictionary that maps names to prototypes. Its make: method looks like this:

```
make: partName
    ^ (partCatalog at: partName) copy
```

Given appropriate methods for initializing the MazeFactory with prototypes, you could create a simple maze with the following code:

```
CreateMaze
    on: (MazeFactory new
        with: Door new named: #door;
        with: Wall new named: #wall;
        with: Room new named: #room;
        yourself)
```

where the definition of the on: class method for CreateMaze would be

```
on: aFactory
    | room1 room2 |
    room1 := (aFactory make: #room) location: 1@1.
    room2 := (aFactory make: #room) location: 2@1.
    door := (aFactory make: #door) from: room1 to: room2.

    room1
        atSide: #north put: (aFactory make: #wall);
        atSide: #east put: door;
        atSide: #south put: (aFactory make: #wall);
        atSide: #west put: (aFactory make: #wall).
    room2
        atSide: #north put: (aFactory make: #wall);
        atSide: #east put: (aFactory make: #wall);
        atSide: #south put: (aFactory make: #wall);
        atSide: #west put: door.
    ^ Maze new
        addRoom: room1;
        addRoom: room2;
        yourself
```

Known Uses

Perhaps the first example of the Prototype pattern was in Ivan Sutherland's Sketch-pad system [Sut63]. The first widely known application of the pattern in an object-oriented language was in ThingLab, where users could form a composite object and then promote it to a prototype by installing it in a library of reusable objects [Bor81]. Goldberg and Robson mention prototypes as a pattern [GR83], but Coplien [Cop92] gives a much more complete description. He describes idioms related to the Prototype pattern for C++ and gives many examples and variations.

Etgdb is a debugger front-end based on ET++ that provides a point-and-click interface to different line-oriented debuggers. Each debugger has a corresponding DebuggerAdaptor subclass. For example, GdbAdaptor adapts etgdb to the command syntax of GNU gdb, while SunDbxAdaptor adapts etgdb to Sun's dbx debugger. Etgdb does not have a set of DebuggerAdaptor classes hard-coded into it. Instead, it reads the name of the adaptor to use from an environment variable, looks for a prototype with the specified name in a global table, and then clones the prototype. New debuggers can be added to etgdb by linking it with the DebuggerAdaptor that works for that debugger.

The "interaction technique library" in Mode Composer stores prototypes of objects that support various interaction techniques [Sha90]. Any interaction technique created by the Mode Composer can be used as a prototype by placing it in this library. The Prototype pattern lets Mode Composer support an unlimited set of interaction techniques.

The music editor example discussed earlier is based on the Unidraw drawing framework [VL90].

Related Patterns

Prototype and Abstract Factory (87) are competing patterns in some ways, as we discuss at the end of this chapter. They can also be used together, however. An Abstract Factory might store a set of prototypes from which to clone and return product objects.

Designs that make heavy use of the Composite (163) and Decorator (175) patterns often can benefit from Prototype as well.

SINGLETON

Object Creational

Intent

Ensure a class only has one instance, and provide a global point of access to it.

Motivation

It's important for some classes to have exactly one instance. Although there can be many printers in a system, there should be only one printer spooler. There should be only one file system and one window manager. A digital filter will have one A/D converter. An accounting system will be dedicated to serving one company.

How do we ensure that a class has only one instance and that the instance is easily accessible? A global variable makes an object accessible, but it doesn't keep you from instantiating multiple objects.

A better solution is to make the class itself responsible for keeping track of its sole instance. The class can ensure that no other instance can be created (by intercepting requests to create new objects), and it can provide a way to access the instance. This is the Singleton pattern.

Applicability

Use the Singleton pattern when

- there must be exactly one instance of a class, and it must be accessible to clients from a well-known access point.
- when the sole instance should be extensible by subclassing, and clients should be able to use an extended instance without modifying their code.

Structure

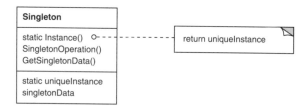

Participants

- **Singleton**
  - defines an Instance operation that lets clients access its unique instance. Instance is a class operation (that is, a class method in Smalltalk and a static member function in C++).
  - may be responsible for creating its own unique instance.

Collaborations

- Clients access a Singleton instance solely through Singleton's Instance operation.

Consequences

The Singleton pattern has several benefits:

1. *Controlled access to sole instance.* Because the Singleton class encapsulates its sole instance, it can have strict control over how and when clients access it.

2. *Reduced name space.* The Singleton pattern is an improvement over global variables. It avoids polluting the name space with global variables that store sole instances.

3. *Permits refinement of operations and representation.* The Singleton class may be subclassed, and it's easy to configure an application with an instance of this extended class. You can configure the application with an instance of the class you need at run-time.

4. *Permits a variable number of instances.* The pattern makes it easy to change your mind and allow more than one instance of the Singleton class. Moreover, you can use the same approach to control the number of instances that the application uses. Only the operation that grants access to the Singleton instance needs to change.

5. *More flexible than class operations.* Another way to package a singleton's functionality is to use class operations (that is, static member functions in C++ or class methods in Smalltalk). But both of these language techniques make it hard to change a design to allow more than one instance of a class. Moreover, static member functions in C++ are never virtual, so subclasses can't override them polymorphically.

Implementation

Here are implementation issues to consider when using the Singleton pattern:

1. *Ensuring a unique instance.* The Singleton pattern makes the sole instance a normal instance of a class, but that class is written so that only one instance

can ever be created. A common way to do this is to hide the operation that creates the instance behind a class operation (that is, either a static member function or a class method) that guarantees only one instance is created. This operation has access to the variable that holds the unique instance, and it ensures the variable is initialized with the unique instance before returning its value. This approach ensures that a singleton is created and initialized before its first use.

You can define the class operation in C++ with a static member function Instance of the Singleton class. Singleton also defines a static member variable _instance that contains a pointer to its unique instance.

The Singleton class is declared as

```
class Singleton {
public:
    static Singleton* Instance();
protected:
    Singleton();
private:
    static Singleton* _instance;
};
```

The corresponding implementation is

```
Singleton* Singleton::_instance = 0;

Singleton* Singleton::Instance () {
    if (_instance == 0) {
        _instance = new Singleton;
    }
    return _instance;
}
```

Clients access the singleton exclusively through the Instance member function. The variable _instance is initialized to 0, and the static member function Instance returns its value, initializing it with the unique instance if it is 0. Instance uses lazy initialization; the value it returns isn't created and stored until it's first accessed.

Notice that the constructor is protected. A client that tries to instantiate Singleton directly will get an error at compile-time. This ensures that only one instance can ever get created.

Moreover, since the _instance is a pointer to a Singleton object, the Instance member function can assign a pointer to a subclass of Singleton to this variable. We'll give an example of this in the Sample Code.

There's another thing to note about the C++ implementation. It isn't enough to define the singleton as a global or static object and then rely on automatic initialization. There are three reasons for this:

(a) We can't guarantee that only one instance of a static object will ever be declared.

(b) We might not have enough information to instantiate every singleton at static initialization time. A singleton might require values that are computed later in the program's execution.

(c) C++ doesn't define the order in which constructors for global objects are called across translation units [ES90]. This means that no dependencies can exist between singletons; if any do, then errors are inevitable.

An added (albeit small) liability of the global/static object approach is that it forces all singletons to be created whether they are used or not. Using a static member function avoids all of these problems.

In Smalltalk, the function that returns the unique instance is implemented as a class method on the Singleton class. To ensure that only one instance is created, override the new operation. The resulting Singleton class might have the following two class methods, where SoleInstance is a class variable that is not used anywhere else:

```
new
    self error: 'cannot create new object'

default
    SoleInstance isNil ifTrue: [SoleInstance := super new].
    ^ SoleInstance
```

2. *Subclassing the Singleton class.* The main issue is not so much defining the subclass but installing its unique instance so that clients will be able to use it. In essence, the variable that refers to the singleton instance must get initialized with an instance of the subclass. The simplest technique is to determine which singleton you want to use in the Singleton's Instance operation. An example in the Sample Code shows how to implement this technique with environment variables.

Another way to choose the subclass of Singleton is to take the implementation of Instance out of the parent class (e.g., MazeFactory) and put it in the subclass. That lets a C++ programmer decide the class of singleton at link-time (e.g., by linking in an object file containing a different implementation) but keeps it hidden from the clients of the singleton.

The link approach fixes the choice of singleton class at link-time, which makes it hard to choose the singleton class at run-time. Using conditional statements to determine the subclass is more flexible, but it hard-wires the set of possible Singleton classes. Neither approach is flexible enough in all cases.

A more flexible approach uses a **registry of singletons**. Instead of having Instance define the set of possible Singleton classes, the Singleton classes can register their singleton instance by name in a well-known registry.

The registry maps between string names and singletons. When Instance needs a singleton, it consults the registry, asking for the singleton by name.

The registry looks up the corresponding singleton (if it exists) and returns it. This approach frees `Instance` from knowing all possible Singleton classes or instances. All it requires is a common interface for all Singleton classes that includes operations for the registry:

```
class Singleton {
public:
    static void Register(const char* name, Singleton*);
    static Singleton* Instance();
protected:
    static Singleton* Lookup(const char* name);
private:
    static Singleton* _instance;
    static List<NameSingletonPair>* _registry;
};
```

`Register` registers the Singleton instance under the given name. To keep the registry simple, we'll have it store a list of `NameSingletonPair` objects. Each `NameSingletonPair` maps a name to a singleton. The `Lookup` operation finds a singleton given its name. We'll assume that an environment variable specifies the name of the singleton desired.

```
Singleton* Singleton::Instance () {
    if (_instance == 0) {
        const char* singletonName = getenv("SINGLETON");
        // user or environment supplies this at startup

        _instance = Lookup(singletonName);
        // Lookup returns 0 if there's no such singleton
    }
    return _instance;
}
```

Where do Singleton classes register themselves? One possibility is in their constructor. For example, a `MySingleton` subclass could do the following:

```
MySingleton::MySingleton() {
    // ...
    Singleton::Register("MySingleton", this);
}
```

Of course, the constructor won't get called unless someone instantiates the class, which echoes the problem the Singleton pattern is trying to solve! We can get around this problem in C++ by defining a static instance of `MySingleton`. For example, we can define

```
static MySingleton theSingleton;
```

in the file that contains `MySingleton`'s implementation.

No longer is the Singleton class responsible for creating the singleton. Instead, its primary responsibility is to make the singleton object of choice accessible in the system. The static object approach still has a potential drawback—namely that instances of all possible Singleton subclasses must be created, or else they won't get registered.

Sample Code

Suppose we define a `MazeFactory` class for building mazes as described on page 92. `MazeFactory` defines an interface for building different parts of a maze. Subclasses can redefine the operations to return instances of specialized product classes, like `BombedWall` objects instead of plain `Wall` objects.

What's relevant here is that the Maze application needs only one instance of a maze factory, and that instance should be available to code that builds any part of the maze. This is where the Singleton pattern comes in. By making the `MazeFactory` a singleton, we make the maze object globally accessible without resorting to global variables.

For simplicity, let's assume we'll never subclass `MazeFactory`. (We'll consider the alternative in a moment.) We make it a Singleton class in C++ by adding a static `Instance` operation and a static `_instance` member to hold the one and only instance. We must also protect the constructor to prevent accidental instantiation, which might lead to more than one instance.

```
class MazeFactory {
public:
    static MazeFactory* Instance();

    // existing interface goes here
protected:
    MazeFactory();
private:
    static MazeFactory* _instance;
};
```

The corresponding implementation is

```
MazeFactory* MazeFactory::_instance = 0;

MazeFactory* MazeFactory::Instance () {
    if (_instance == 0) {
        _instance = new MazeFactory;
    }
    return _instance;
}
```

Now let's consider what happens when there are subclasses of `MazeFactory`, and the application must decide which one to use. We'll select the kind of maze through an environment variable and add code that instantiates the proper `MazeFactory` subclass based on the environment variable's value. The `Instance` operation is a good place to put this code, because it already instantiates `MazeFactory`:

```
MazeFactory* MazeFactory::Instance () {
    if (_instance == 0) {
        const char* mazeStyle = getenv("MAZESTYLE");

        if (strcmp(mazeStyle, "bombed") == 0) {
            _instance = new BombedMazeFactory;

        } else if (strcmp(mazeStyle, "enchanted") == 0) {
            _instance = new EnchantedMazeFactory;

        // ... other possible subclasses

        } else {          // default
            _instance = new MazeFactory;
        }
    }
    return _instance;
}
```

Note that `Instance` must be modified whenever you define a new subclass of `MazeFactory`. That might not be a problem in this application, but it might be for abstract factories defined in a framework.

A possible solution would be to use the registry approach described in the Implementation section. Dynamic linking could be useful here as well—it would keep the application from having to load all the subclasses that are not used.

Known Uses

An example of the Singleton pattern in Smalltalk-80 [Par90] is the set of changes to the code, which is `ChangeSet current`. A more subtle example is the relationship between classes and their **metaclasses**. A metaclass is the class of a class, and each metaclass has one instance. Metaclasses do not have names (except indirectly through their sole instance), but they keep track of their sole instance and will not normally create another.

The InterViews user interface toolkit [LCI+92] uses the Singleton pattern to access the unique instance of its Session and WidgetKit classes, among others. Session defines the application's main event dispatch loop, stores the user's database of stylistic preferences, and manages connections to one or more physical displays. WidgetKit is an Abstract Factory (87) for defining the look and feel of user interface widgets. The `WidgetKit::instance()` operation determines the particular WidgetKit subclass that's instantiated based on an environment variable that Session defines. A similar operation on Session determines whether monochrome or color displays are supported and configures the singleton Session instance accordingly.

Related Patterns

Many patterns can be implemented using the Singleton pattern. See Abstract
Factory (87), Builder (97), and Prototype (117).

Discussion of Creational Patterns

There are two common ways to parameterize a system by the classes of objects it creates. One way is to subclass the class that creates the objects; this corresponds to using the Factory Method (107) pattern. The main drawback of this approach is that it can require creating a new subclass just to change the class of the product. Such changes can cascade. For example, when the product creator is itself created by a factory method, then you have to override its creator as well.

The other way to parameterize a system relies more on object composition: Define an object that's responsible for knowing the class of the product objects, and make it a parameter of the system. This is a key aspect of the Abstract Factory (87), Builder (97), and Prototype (117) patterns. All three involve creating a new "factory object" whose responsibility is to create product objects. Abstract Factory has the factory object producing objects of several classes. Builder has the factory object building a complex product incrementally using a correspondingly complex protocol. Prototype has the factory object building a product by copying a prototype object. In this case, the factory object and the prototype are the same object, because the prototype is responsible for returning the product.

Consider the drawing editor framework described in the Prototype pattern. There are several ways to parameterize a GraphicTool by the class of product:

- By applying the Factory Method pattern, a subclass of GraphicTool will be created for each subclass of Graphic in the palette. GraphicTool will have a NewGraphic operation that each GraphicTool subclass will redefine.

- By applying the Abstract Factory pattern, there will be a class hierarchy of GraphicsFactories, one for each Graphic subclass. Each factory creates just one product in this case: CircleFactory will create Circles, LineFactory will create Lines, and so on. A GraphicTool will be parameterized with a factory for creating the appropriate kind of Graphics.

- By applying the Prototype pattern, each subclass of Graphics will implement the Clone operation, and a GraphicTool will be parameterized with a prototype of the Graphic it creates.

Which pattern is best depends on many factors. In our drawing editor framework, the Factory Method pattern is easiest to use at first. It's easy to define a new subclass of GraphicTool, and the instances of GraphicTool are created only when the palette is defined. The main disadvantage here is that GraphicTool subclasses proliferate, and none of them does very much.

Abstract Factory doesn't offer much of an improvement, because it requires an equally large GraphicsFactory class hierarchy. Abstract Factory would be preferable to Factory Method only if there were already a GraphicsFactory class hierarchy—either because the compiler provides it automatically (as in Smalltalk or Objective C) or because it's needed in another part of the system.

Overall, the Prototype pattern is probably the best for the drawing editor framework, because it only requires implementing a Clone operation on each Graphics class. That reduces the number of classes, and Clone can be used for purposes other than pure instantiation (e.g., a Duplicate menu operation).

Factory Method makes a design more customizable and only a little more complicated. Other design patterns require new classes, whereas Factory Method only requires a new operation. People often use Factory Method as the standard way to create objects, but it isn't necessary when the class that's instantiated never changes or when instantiation takes place in an operation that subclasses can easily override, such as an initialization operation.

Designs that use Abstract Factory, Prototype, or Builder are even more flexible than those that use Factory Method, but they're also more complex. Often, designs start out using Factory Method and evolve toward the other creational patterns as the designer discovers where more flexibility is needed. Knowing many design patterns gives you more choices when trading off one design criterion against another.

Chapter 4

Structural Patterns

Structural patterns are concerned with how classes and objects are composed to form larger structures. Structural *class* patterns use inheritance to compose interfaces or implementations. As a simple example, consider how multiple inheritance mixes two or more classes into one. The result is a class that combines the properties of its parent classes. This pattern is particularly useful for making independently developed class libraries work together. Another example is the class form of the Adapter (139) pattern. In general, an adapter makes one interface (the adaptee's) conform to another, thereby providing a uniform abstraction of different interfaces. A class adapter accomplishes this by inheriting privately from an adaptee class. The adapter then expresses its interface in terms of the adaptee's.

Rather than composing interfaces or implementations, structural *object* patterns describe ways to compose objects to realize new functionality. The added flexibility of object composition comes from the ability to change the composition at run-time, which is impossible with static class composition.

Composite (163) is an example of a structural object pattern. It describes how to build a class hierarchy made up of classes for two kinds of objects: primitive and composite. The composite objects let you compose primitive and other composite objects into arbitrarily complex structures. In the Proxy (207) pattern, a proxy acts as a convenient surrogate or placeholder for another object. A proxy can be used in many ways. It can act as a local representative for an object in a remote address space. It can represent a large object that should be loaded on demand. It might protect access to a sensitive object. Proxies provide a level of indirection to specific properties of objects. Hence they can restrict, enhance, or alter these properties.

The Flyweight (195) pattern defines a structure for sharing objects. Objects are shared for at least two reasons: efficiency and consistency. Flyweight focuses on sharing for space efficiency. Applications that use lots of objects must pay careful attention to the cost of each object. Substantial savings can be had by sharing objects instead of replicating them. But objects can be shared only if they don't define context-dependent state. Flyweight objects have no such state. Any additional information they need to perform their task is passed to them when needed. With no context-dependent state, Flyweight objects may be shared freely.

Whereas Flyweight shows how to make lots of little objects, Facade (185) shows how to make a single object represent an entire subsystem. A facade is a representative for a set of objects. The facade carries out its responsibilities by forwarding messages to the objects it represents. The Bridge (151) pattern separates an object's abstraction from its implementation so that you can vary them independently.

Decorator (175) describes how to add responsibilities to objects dynamically. Decorator is a structural pattern that composes objects recursively to allow an open-ended number of additional responsibilities. For example, a Decorator object containing a user interface component can add a decoration like a border or shadow to the component, or it can add functionality like scrolling and zooming. We can add two decorations simply by nesting one Decorator object within another, and so on for additional decorations. To accomplish this, each Decorator object must conform to the interface of its component and must forward messages to it. The Decorator can do its job (such as drawing a border around the component) either before or after forwarding a message.

Many structural patterns are related to some degree. We'll discuss these relationships at the end of the chapter.

ADAPTER   Class, Object Structural

Intent

Convert the interface of a class into another interface clients expect. Adapter lets classes work together that couldn't otherwise because of incompatible interfaces.

Also Known As

Wrapper

Motivation

Sometimes a toolkit class that's designed for reuse isn't reusable only because its interface doesn't match the domain-specific interface an application requires.

Consider for example a drawing editor that lets users draw and arrange graphical elements (lines, polygons, text, etc.) into pictures and diagrams. The drawing editor's key abstraction is the graphical object, which has an editable shape and can draw itself. The interface for graphical objects is defined by an abstract class called Shape. The editor defines a subclass of Shape for each kind of graphical object: a LineShape class for lines, a PolygonShape class for polygons, and so forth.

Classes for elementary geometric shapes like LineShape and PolygonShape are rather easy to implement, because their drawing and editing capabilities are inherently limited. But a TextShape subclass that can display and edit text is considerably more difficult to implement, since even basic text editing involves complicated screen update and buffer management. Meanwhile, an off-the-shelf user interface toolkit might already provide a sophisticated TextView class for displaying and editing text. Ideally we'd like to reuse TextView to implement TextShape, but the toolkit wasn't designed with Shape classes in mind. So we can't use TextView and Shape objects interchangeably.

How can existing and unrelated classes like TextView work in an application that expects classes with a different and incompatible interface? We could change the TextView class so that it conforms to the Shape interface, but that isn't an option unless we have the toolkit's source code. Even if we did, it wouldn't make sense to change TextView; the toolkit shouldn't have to adopt domain-specific interfaces just to make one application work.

Instead, we could define TextShape so that it *adapts* the TextView interface to Shape's. We can do this in one of two ways: (1) by inheriting Shape's interface and TextView's implementation or (2) by composing a TextView instance within a TextShape and implementing TextShape in terms of TextView's interface. These two approaches correspond to the class and object versions of the Adapter pattern. We call TextShape an **adapter**.

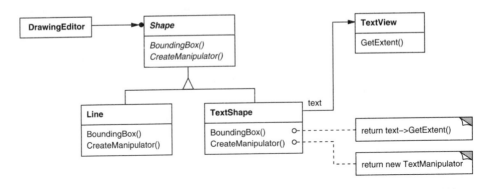

This diagram illustrates the object adapter case. It shows how BoundingBox requests, declared in class Shape, are converted to GetExtent requests defined in TextView. Since TextShape adapts TextView to the Shape interface, the drawing editor can reuse the otherwise incompatible TextView class.

Often the adapter is responsible for functionality the adapted class doesn't provide. The diagram shows how an adapter can fulfill such responsibilities. The user should be able to "drag" every Shape object to a new location interactively, but TextView isn't designed to do that. TextShape can add this missing functionality by implementing Shape's CreateManipulator operation, which returns an instance of the appropriate Manipulator subclass.

Manipulator is an abstract class for objects that know how to animate a Shape in response to user input, like dragging the shape to a new location. There are subclasses of Manipulator for different shapes; TextManipulator, for example, is the corresponding subclass for TextShape. By returning a TextManipulator instance, TextShape adds the functionality that TextView lacks but Shape requires.

Applicability

Use the Adapter pattern when

- you want to use an existing class, and its interface does not match the one you need.

- you want to create a reusable class that cooperates with unrelated or unforeseen classes, that is, classes that don't necessarily have compatible interfaces.

- (object adapter only) you need to use several existing subclasses, but it's impractical to adapt their interface by subclassing every one. An object adapter can adapt the interface of its parent class.

Structure

A class adapter uses multiple inheritance to adapt one interface to another:

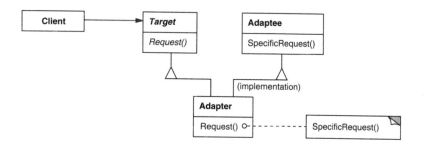

An object adapter relies on object composition:

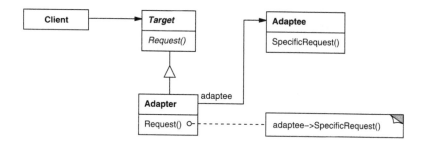

Participants

- **Target** (Shape)

  - defines the domain-specific interface that Client uses.

- **Client** (DrawingEditor)

  - collaborates with objects conforming to the Target interface.

- **Adaptee** (TextView)

  - defines an existing interface that needs adapting.

- **Adapter** (TextShape)

  - adapts the interface of Adaptee to the Target interface.

Collaborations

- Clients call operations on an Adapter instance. In turn, the adapter calls Adaptee operations that carry out the request.

Consequences

Class and object adapters have different trade-offs. A class adapter

- adapts Adaptee to Target by committing to a concrete Adaptee class. As a consequence, a class adapter won't work when we want to adapt a class *and* all its subclasses.

- lets Adapter override some of Adaptee's behavior, since Adapter is a subclass of Adaptee.

- introduces only one object, and no additional pointer indirection is needed to get to the adaptee.

An object adapter

- lets a single Adapter work with many Adaptees—that is, the Adaptee itself and all of its subclasses (if any). The Adapter can also add functionality to all Adaptees at once.

- makes it harder to override Adaptee behavior. It will require subclassing Adaptee and making Adapter refer to the subclass rather than the Adaptee itself.

Here are other issues to consider when using the Adapter pattern:

1. *How much adapting does Adapter do?* Adapters vary in the amount of work they do to adapt Adaptee to the Target interface. There is a spectrum of possible work, from simple interface conversion—for example, changing the names of operations—to supporting an entirely different set of operations. The amount of work Adapter does depends on how similar the Target interface is to Adaptee's.

2. *Pluggable adapters.* A class is more reusable when you minimize the assumptions other classes must make to use it. By building interface adaptation into a class, you eliminate the assumption that other classes see the same interface. Put another way, interface adaptation lets us incorporate our class into existing systems that might expect different interfaces to the class. Object-Works\Smalltalk [Par90] uses the term **pluggable adapter** to describe classes with built-in interface adaptation.

   Consider a TreeDisplay widget that can display tree structures graphically. If this were a special-purpose widget for use in just one application, then we might require the objects that it displays to have a specific interface; that is, all must descend from a Tree abstract class. But if we wanted to make TreeDisplay more reusable (say we wanted to make it part of a toolkit of useful widgets), then that requirement would be unreasonable. Applications will define their own classes for tree structures. They shouldn't be forced to use our Tree abstract class. Different tree structures will have different interfaces.

In a directory hierarchy, for example, children might be accessed with a GetSubdirectories operation, whereas in an inheritance hierarchy, the corresponding operation might be called GetSubclasses. A reusable TreeDisplay widget must be able to display both kinds of hierarchies even if they use different interfaces. In other words, the TreeDisplay should have interface adaptation built into it.

We'll look at different ways to build interface adaptation into classes in the Implementation section.

3. *Using two-way adapters to provide transparency.* A potential problem with adapters is that they aren't transparent to all clients. An adapted object no longer conforms to the Adaptee interface, so it can't be used as is wherever an Adaptee object can. **Two-way adapters** can provide such transparency. Specifically, they're useful when two different clients need to view an object differently.

Consider the two-way adapter that integrates Unidraw, a graphical editor framework [VL90], and QOCA, a constraint-solving toolkit [HHMV92]. Both systems have classes that represent variables explicitly: Unidraw has StateVariable, and QOCA has ConstraintVariable. To make Unidraw work with QOCA, ConstraintVariable must be adapted to StateVariable; to let QOCA propagate solutions to Unidraw, StateVariable must be adapted to ConstraintVariable.

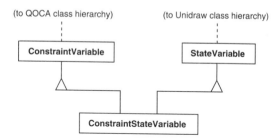

The solution involves a two-way class adapter ConstraintStateVariable, a subclass of both StateVariable and ConstraintVariable, that adapts the two interfaces to each other. Multiple inheritance is a viable solution in this case because the interfaces of the adapted classes are substantially different. The two-way class adapter conforms to both of the adapted classes and can work in either system.

Implementation

Although the implementation of Adapter is usually straightforward, here are some issues to keep in mind:

1. *Implementing class adapters in C++.* In a C++ implementation of a class adapter, Adapter would inherit publicly from Target and privately from Adaptee. Thus Adapter would be a subtype of Target but not of Adaptee.

2. *Pluggable adapters.* Let's look at three ways to implement pluggable adapters for the TreeDisplay widget described earlier, which can lay out and display a hierarchical structure automatically.

   The first step, which is common to all three of the implementations discussed here, is to find a "narrow" interface for Adaptee, that is, the smallest subset of operations that lets us do the adaptation. A narrow interface consisting of only a couple of operations is easier to adapt than an interface with dozens of operations. For TreeDisplay, the adaptee is any hierarchical structure. A minimalist interface might include two operations, one that defines how to present a node in the hierarchical structure graphically, and another that retrieves the node's children.

   The narrow interface leads to three implementation approaches:

   (a) *Using abstract operations.* Define corresponding abstract operations for the narrow Adaptee interface in the TreeDisplay class. Subclasses must implement the abstract operations and adapt the hierarchically structured object. For example, a DirectoryTreeDisplay subclass will implement these operations by accessing the directory structure.

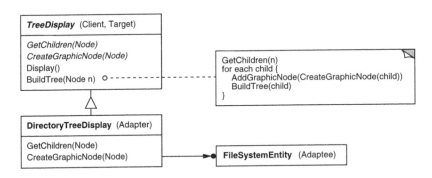

   DirectoryTreeDisplay specializes the narrow interface so that it can display directory structures made up of FileSystemEntity objects.

   (b) *Using delegate objects.* In this approach, TreeDisplay forwards requests for accessing the hierarchical structure to a **delegate** object. TreeDisplay can use a different adaptation strategy by substituting a different delegate.

   For example, suppose there exists a DirectoryBrowser that uses a Tree-Display. DirectoryBrowser might make a good delegate for adapting TreeDisplay to the hierarchical directory structure. In dynamically typed languages like Smalltalk or Objective C, this approach only requires an interface for registering the delegate with the adapter. Then TreeDisplay simply forwards the requests to the delegate. NEXTSTEP [Add94] uses this approach heavily to reduce subclassing.

Statically typed languages like C++ require an explicit interface definition for the delegate. We can specify such an interface by putting the narrow interface that TreeDisplay requires into an abstract TreeAccessorDelegate class. Then we can mix this interface into the delegate of our choice—DirectoryBrowser in this case—using inheritance. We use single inheritance if the DirectoryBrowser has no existing parent class, multiple inheritance if it does. Mixing classes together like this is easier than introducing a new TreeDisplay subclass and implementing its operations individually.

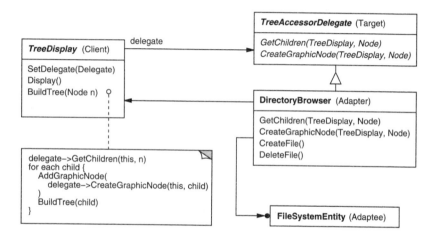

(c) *Parameterized adapters.* The usual way to support pluggable adapters in Smalltalk is to parameterize an adapter with one or more blocks. The block construct supports adaptation without subclassing. A block can adapt a request, and the adapter can store a block for each individual request. In our example, this means TreeDisplay stores one block for converting a node into a GraphicNode and another block for accessing a node's children.

For example, to create TreeDisplay on a directory hierarchy, we write

```
directoryDisplay :=
    (TreeDisplay on: treeRoot)
        getChildrenBlock:
            [:node | node getSubdirectories]
        createGraphicNodeBlock:
            [:node | node createGraphicNode].
```

If you're building interface adaptation into a class, this approach offers a convenient alternative to subclassing.

Sample Code

We'll give a brief sketch of the implementation of class and object adapters for the Motivation example beginning with the classes Shape and TextView.

```
class Shape {
public:
    Shape();
    virtual void BoundingBox(
        Point& bottomLeft, Point& topRight
    ) const;
    virtual Manipulator* CreateManipulator() const;
};

class TextView {
public:
    TextView();
    void GetOrigin(Coord& x, Coord& y) const;
    void GetExtent(Coord& width, Coord& height) const;
    virtual bool IsEmpty() const;
};
```

Shape assumes a bounding box defined by its opposing corners. In contrast, TextView is defined by an origin, height, and width. Shape also defines a CreateManipulator operation for creating a Manipulator object, which knows how to animate a shape when the user manipulates it.[1] TextView has no equivalent operation. The class TextShape is an adapter between these different interfaces.

A class adapter uses multiple inheritance to adapt interfaces. The key to class adapters is to use one inheritance branch to inherit the interface and another branch to inherit the implementation. The usual way to make this distinction in C++ is to inherit the interface publicly and inherit the implementation privately. We'll use this convention to define the TextShape adapter.

```
class TextShape : public Shape, private TextView {
public:
    TextShape();

    virtual void BoundingBox(
        Point& bottomLeft, Point& topRight
    ) const;
    virtual bool IsEmpty() const;
    virtual Manipulator* CreateManipulator() const;
};
```

The BoundingBox operation converts TextView's interface to conform to Shape's.

---

[1] CreateManipulator is an example of a Factory Method (107).

```
void TextShape::BoundingBox (
    Point& bottomLeft, Point& topRight
) const {
    Coord bottom, left, width, height;

    GetOrigin(bottom, left);
    GetExtent(width, height);

    bottomLeft = Point(bottom, left);
    topRight = Point(bottom + height, left + width);
}
```

The `IsEmpty` operation demonstrates the direct forwarding of requests common in adapter implementations:

```
bool TextShape::IsEmpty () const {
    return TextView::IsEmpty();
}
```

Finally, we define `CreateManipulator` (which isn't supported by `TextView`) from scratch. Assume we've already implemented a `TextManipulator` class that supports manipulation of a `TextShape`.

```
Manipulator* TextShape::CreateManipulator () const {
    return new TextManipulator(this);
}
```

The object adapter uses object composition to combine classes with different interfaces. In this approach, the adapter `TextShape` maintains a pointer to `TextView`.

```
class TextShape : public Shape {
public:
    TextShape(TextView*);

    virtual void BoundingBox(
        Point& bottomLeft, Point& topRight
    ) const;
    virtual bool IsEmpty() const;
    virtual Manipulator* CreateManipulator() const;
private:
    TextView* _text;
};
```

`TextShape` must initialize the pointer to the `TextView` instance, and it does so in the constructor. It must also call operations on its `TextView` object whenever its own operations are called. In this example, assume that the client creates the `TextView` object and passes it to the `TextShape` constructor:

```
TextShape::TextShape (TextView* t) {
    _text = t;
}
```

```
void TextShape::BoundingBox (
    Point& bottomLeft, Point& topRight
) const {
    Coord bottom, left, width, height;

    _text->GetOrigin(bottom, left);
    _text->GetExtent(width, height);

    bottomLeft = Point(bottom, left);
    topRight = Point(bottom + height, left + width);
}

bool TextShape::IsEmpty () const {
    return _text->IsEmpty();
}
```

`CreateManipulator`'s implementation doesn't change from the class adapter version, since it's implemented from scratch and doesn't reuse any existing `TextView` functionality.

```
Manipulator* TextShape::CreateManipulator () const {
    return new TextManipulator(this);
}
```

Compare this code to the class adapter case. The object adapter requires a little more effort to write, but it's more flexible. For example, the object adapter version of `TextShape` will work equally well with subclasses of `TextView`—the client simply passes an instance of a `TextView` subclass to the `TextShape` constructor.

Known Uses

The Motivation example comes from ET++Draw, a drawing application based on ET++ [WGM88]. ET++Draw reuses the ET++ classes for text editing by using a TextShape adapter class.

InterViews 2.6 defines an Interactor abstract class for user interface elements such as scroll bars, buttons, and menus [VL88]. It also defines a Graphic abstract class for structured graphic objects such as lines, circles, polygons, and splines. Both Interactors and Graphics have graphical appearances, but they have different interfaces and implementations (they share no common parent class) and are therefore incompatible—you can't embed a structured graphic object in, say, a dialog box directly.

Instead, InterViews 2.6 defines an object adapter called GraphicBlock, a subclass of Interactor that contains a Graphic instance. The GraphicBlock adapts the interface of the Graphic class to that of Interactor. The GraphicBlock lets a Graphic instance be displayed, scrolled, and zoomed within an Interactor structure.

Pluggable adapters are common in ObjectWorks\Smalltalk [Par90]. Standard Smalltalk defines a ValueModel class for views that display a single value. ValueModel defines a `value`, `value:` interface for accessing the value. These are abstract methods. Application writers access the value with more domain-specific names like `width` and `width:`, but they shouldn't have to subclass ValueModel to adapt such application-specific names to the ValueModel interface.

Instead, ObjectWorks\Smalltalk includes a subclass of ValueModel called PluggableAdaptor. A PluggableAdaptor object adapts other objects to the ValueModel interface (`value`, `value:`). It can be parameterized with blocks for getting and setting the desired value. PluggableAdaptor uses these blocks internally to implement the `value, value:` interface. PluggableAdaptor also lets you pass in the selector names (e.g., `width`, `width:`) directly for syntactic convenience. It converts these selectors into the corresponding blocks automatically.

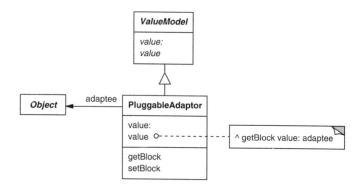

Another example from ObjectWorks\Smalltalk is the TableAdaptor class. A TableAdaptor can adapt a sequence of objects to a tabular presentation. The table displays one object per row. The client parameterizes TableAdaptor with the set of messages that a table can use to get the column values from an object.

Some classes in NeXT's AppKit [Add94] use delegate objects to perform interface adaptation. An example is the NXBrowser class that can display hierarchical lists of data. NXBrowser uses a delegate object for accessing and adapting the data.

Meyer's "Marriage of Convenience" [Mey88] is a form of class adapter. Meyer describes how a FixedStack class adapts the implementation of an Array class to the interface of a Stack class. The result is a stack containing a fixed number of entries.

Related Patterns

Bridge (151) has a structure similar to an object adapter, but Bridge has a different intent: It is meant to separate an interface from its implementation so that they can be varied easily and independently. An adapter is meant to change the interface of an *existing* object.

Decorator (175) enhances another object without changing its interface. A decorator is thus more transparent to the application than an adapter is. As a consequence, Decorator supports recursive composition, which isn't possible with pure adapters.

Proxy (207) defines a representative or surrogate for another object and does not change its interface.

BRIDGE   Object Structural

Intent

Decouple an abstraction from its implementation so that the two can vary independently.

Also Known As

Handle/Body

Motivation

When an abstraction can have one of several possible implementations, the usual way to accommodate them is to use inheritance. An abstract class defines the interface to the abstraction, and concrete subclasses implement it in different ways. But this approach isn't always flexible enough. Inheritance binds an implementation to the abstraction permanently, which makes it difficult to modify, extend, and reuse abstractions and implementations independently.

Consider the implementation of a portable Window abstraction in a user interface toolkit. This abstraction should enable us to write applications that work on both the X Window System and IBM's Presentation Manager (PM), for example. Using inheritance, we could define an abstract class Window and subclasses XWindow and PMWindow that implement the Window interface for the different platforms. But this approach has two drawbacks:

1. It's inconvenient to extend the Window abstraction to cover different kinds of windows or new platforms. Imagine an IconWindow subclass of Window that specializes the Window abstraction for icons. To support IconWindows for both platforms, we have to implement *two* new classes, XIconWindow and PMIconWindow. Worse, we'll have to define two classes for *every* kind of window. Supporting a third platform requires yet another new Window subclass for every kind of window.

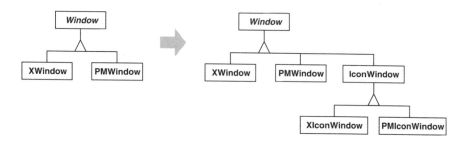

2. It makes client code platform-dependent. Whenever a client creates a window, it instantiates a concrete class that has a specific implementation. For example, creating an XWindow object binds the Window abstraction to the X Window implementation, which makes the client code dependent on the X Window implementation. This, in turn, makes it harder to port the client code to other platforms.

   Clients should be able to create a window without committing to a concrete implementation. Only the window implementation should depend on the platform on which the application runs. Therefore client code should instantiate windows without mentioning specific platforms.

The Bridge pattern addresses these problems by putting the Window abstraction and its implementation in separate class hierarchies. There is one class hierarchy for window interfaces (Window, IconWindow, TransientWindow) and a separate hierarchy for platform-specific window implementations, with WindowImp as its root. The XWindowImp subclass, for example, provides an implementation based on the X Window System.

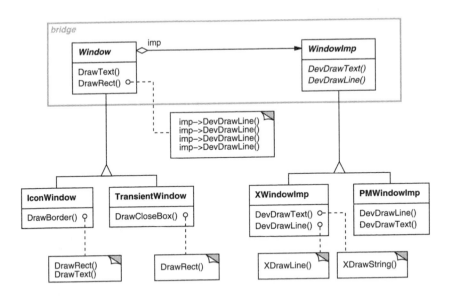

All operations on Window subclasses are implemented in terms of abstract operations from the WindowImp interface. This decouples the window abstractions from the various platform-specific implementations. We refer to the relationship between Window and WindowImp as a **bridge**, because it bridges the abstraction and its implementation, letting them vary independently.

Applicability

Use the Bridge pattern when

- you want to avoid a permanent binding between an abstraction and its implementation. This might be the case, for example, when the implementation must be selected or switched at run-time.

- both the abstractions and their implementations should be extensible by subclassing. In this case, the Bridge pattern lets you combine the different abstractions and implementations and extend them independently.

- changes in the implementation of an abstraction should have no impact on clients; that is, their code should not have to be recompiled.

- (C++) you want to hide the implementation of an abstraction completely from clients. In C++ the representation of a class is visible in the class interface.

- you have a proliferation of classes as shown earlier in the first Motivation diagram. Such a class hierarchy indicates the need for splitting an object into two parts. Rumbaugh uses the term "nested generalizations" [RBP+91] to refer to such class hierarchies.

- you want to share an implementation among multiple objects (perhaps using reference counting), and this fact should be hidden from the client. A simple example is Coplien's String class [Cop92], in which multiple objects can share the same string representation (StringRep).

Structure

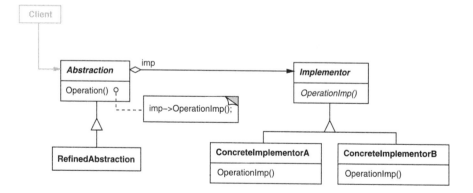

Participants

- **Abstraction** (Window)
  - defines the abstraction's interface.
  - maintains a reference to an object of type Implementor.
- **RefinedAbstraction** (IconWindow)
  - Extends the interface defined by Abstraction.
- **Implementor** (WindowImp)
  - defines the interface for implementation classes. This interface doesn't have to correspond exactly to Abstraction's interface; in fact the two interfaces can be quite different. Typically the Implementor interface provides only primitive operations, and Abstraction defines higher-level operations based on these primitives.
- **ConcreteImplementor** (XWindowImp, PMWindowImp)
  - implements the Implementor interface and defines its concrete implementation.

Collaborations

- Abstraction forwards client requests to its Implementor object.

Consequences

The Bridge pattern has the following consequences:

1. *Decoupling interface and implementation.* An implementation is not bound permanently to an interface. The implementation of an abstraction can be configured at run-time. It's even possible for an object to change its implementation at run-time.

   Decoupling Abstraction and Implementor also eliminates compile-time dependencies on the implementation. Changing an implementation class doesn't require recompiling the Abstraction class and its clients. This property is essential when you must ensure binary compatibility between different versions of a class library.

   Furthermore, this decoupling encourages layering that can lead to a better-structured system. The high-level part of a system only has to know about Abstraction and Implementor.

2. *Improved extensibility.* You can extend the Abstraction and Implementor hierarchies independently.

3. *Hiding implementation details from clients.* You can shield clients from implementation details, like the sharing of implementor objects and the accompanying reference count mechanism (if any).

Implementation

Consider the following implementation issues when applying the Bridge pattern:

1. *Only one Implementor.* In situations where there's only one implementation, creating an abstract Implementor class isn't necessary. This is a degenerate case of the Bridge pattern; there's a one-to-one relationship between Abstraction and Implementor. Nevertheless, this separation is still useful when a change in the implementation of a class must not affect its existing clients—that is, they shouldn't have to be recompiled, just relinked.

   Carolan [Car89] uses the term "Cheshire Cat" to describe this separation. In C++, the class interface of the Implementor class can be defined in a private header file that isn't provided to clients. This lets you hide an implementation of a class completely from its clients.

2. *Creating the right Implementor object.* How, when, and where do you decide which Implementor class to instantiate when there's more than one?

   If Abstraction knows about all ConcreteImplementor classes, then it can instantiate one of them in its constructor; it can decide between them based on parameters passed to its constructor. If, for example, a collection class supports multiple implementations, the decision can be based on the size of the collection. A linked list implementation can be used for small collections and a hash table for larger ones.

   Another approach is to choose a default implementation initially and change it later according to usage. For example, if the collection grows bigger than a certain threshold, then it switches its implementation to one that's more appropriate for a large number of items.

   It's also possible to delegate the decision to another object altogether. In the Window/WindowImp example, we can introduce a factory object (see Abstract Factory (87)) whose sole duty is to encapsulate platform-specifics. The factory knows what kind of WindowImp object to create for the platform in use; a Window simply asks it for a WindowImp, and it returns the right kind. A benefit of this approach is that Abstraction is not coupled directly to any of the Implementor classes.

3. *Sharing implementors.* Coplien illustrates how the Handle/Body idiom in C++ can be used to share implementations among several objects [Cop92]. The Body stores a reference count that the Handle class increments and decrements. The code for assigning handles with shared bodies has the following general form:

```
Handle& Handle::operator= (const Handle& other)  {
    other._body->Ref();
    _body->Unref();

    if (_body->RefCount() == 0) {
        delete _body;
    }
    _body = other._body;

    return *this;
}
```

4. *Using multiple inheritance.* You can use multiple inheritance in C++ to combine an interface with its implementation [Mar91]. For example, a class can inherit publicly from Abstraction and privately from a ConcreteImplementor. But because this approach relies on static inheritance, it binds an implementation permanently to its interface. Therefore you can't implement a true Bridge with multiple inheritance—at least not in C++.

Sample Code

The following C++ code implements the Window/WindowImp example from the Motivation section. The `Window` class defines the window abstraction for client applications:

```
class Window {
public:
    Window(View* contents);

    // requests handled by window
    virtual void DrawContents();

    virtual void Open();
    virtual void Close();
    virtual void Iconify();
    virtual void Deiconify();

    // requests forwarded to implementation
    virtual void SetOrigin(const Point& at);
    virtual void SetExtent(const Point& extent);
    virtual void Raise();
    virtual void Lower();

    virtual void DrawLine(const Point&, const Point&);
    virtual void DrawRect(const Point&, const Point&);
    virtual void DrawPolygon(const Point[], int n);
    virtual void DrawText(const char*, const Point&);

protected:
    WindowImp* GetWindowImp();
    View* GetView();
```

```
    private:
        WindowImp* _imp;
        View* _contents; // the window's contents
    };
```

`Window` maintains a reference to a `WindowImp`, the abstract class that declares an interface to the underlying windowing system.

```
    class WindowImp {
    public:
        virtual void ImpTop() = 0;
        virtual void ImpBottom() = 0;
        virtual void ImpSetExtent(const Point&) = 0;
        virtual void ImpSetOrigin(const Point&) = 0;

        virtual void DeviceRect(Coord, Coord, Coord, Coord) = 0;
        virtual void DeviceText(const char*, Coord, Coord) = 0;
        virtual void DeviceBitmap(const char*, Coord, Coord) = 0;
        // lots more functions for drawing on windows...
    protected:
        WindowImp();
    };
```

Subclasses of `Window` define the different kinds of windows the application might use, such as application windows, icons, transient windows for dialogs, floating palettes of tools, and so on.

For example, `ApplicationWindow` will implement `DrawContents` to draw the `View` instance it stores:

```
    class ApplicationWindow : public Window {
    public:
        // ...
        virtual void DrawContents();
    };

    void ApplicationWindow::DrawContents () {
        GetView()->DrawOn(this);
    }
```

`IconWindow` stores the name of a bitmap for the icon it displays...

```
    class IconWindow : public Window {
    public:
        // ...
        virtual void DrawContents();
    private:
        const char* _bitmapName;
    };
```

...and it implements `DrawContents` to draw the bitmap on the window:

```
void IconWindow::DrawContents() {
    WindowImp* imp = GetWindowImp();
    if (imp != 0) {
        imp->DeviceBitmap(_bitmapName, 0.0, 0.0);
    }
}
```

Many other variations of `Window` are possible. A `TransientWindow` may need to communicate with the window that created it during the dialog; hence it keeps a reference to that window. A `PaletteWindow` always floats above other windows. An `IconDockWindow` holds `IconWindows` and arranges them neatly.

`Window` operations are defined in terms of the `WindowImp` interface. For example, `DrawRect` extracts four coordinates from its two `Point` parameters before calling the `WindowImp` operation that draws the rectangle in the window:

```
void Window::DrawRect (const Point& p1, const Point& p2) {
    WindowImp* imp = GetWindowImp();
    imp->DeviceRect(p1.X(), p1.Y(), p2.X(), p2.Y());
}
```

Concrete subclasses of `WindowImp` support different window systems. The `XWindowImp` subclass supports the X Window System:

```
class XWindowImp : public WindowImp {
public:
    XWindowImp();

    virtual void DeviceRect(Coord, Coord, Coord, Coord);
    // remainder of public interface...
private:
    // lots of X window system-specific state, including:
    Display* _dpy;
    Drawable _winid;  // window id
    GC _gc;           // window graphic context
};
```

For Presentation Manager (PM), we define a `PMWindowImp` class:

```
class PMWindowImp : public WindowImp {
public:
    PMWindowImp();
    virtual void DeviceRect(Coord, Coord, Coord, Coord);

    // remainder of public interface...
private:
    // lots of PM window system-specific state, including:
    HPS _hps;
};
```

These subclasses implement `WindowImp` operations in terms of window system primitives. For example, `DeviceRect` is implemented for X as follows:

```
void XWindowImp::DeviceRect (
    Coord x0, Coord y0, Coord x1, Coord y1
) {
    int x = round(min(x0, x1));
    int y = round(min(y0, y1));
    int w = round(abs(x0 - x1));
    int h = round(abs(y0 - y1));
    XDrawRectangle(_dpy, _winid, _gc, x, y, w, h);
}
```

The PM implementation might look like this:

```
void PMWindowImp::DeviceRect (
    Coord x0, Coord y0, Coord x1, Coord y1
) {
    Coord left = min(x0, x1);
    Coord right = max(x0, x1);
    Coord bottom = min(y0, y1);
    Coord top = max(y0, y1);

    PPOINTL point[4];

    point[0].x = left;      point[0].y = top;
    point[1].x = right;     point[1].y = top;
    point[2].x = right;     point[2].y = bottom;
    point[3].x = left;      point[3].y = bottom;

    if (
        (GpiBeginPath(_hps, 1L) == false) ||
        (GpiSetCurrentPosition(_hps, &point[3]) == false) ||
        (GpiPolyLine(_hps, 4L, point) == GPI_ERROR)  ||
        (GpiEndPath(_hps) == false)
    ) {
        // report error

    } else {
        GpiStrokePath(_hps, 1L, 0L);
    }
}
```

How does a window obtain an instance of the right `WindowImp` subclass? We'll
assume `Window` has that responsibility in this example. Its `GetWindowImp` operation gets the right instance from an abstract factory (see Abstract Factory (87))
that effectively encapsulates all window system specifics.

```
WindowImp* Window::GetWindowImp () {
    if (_imp == 0) {
        _imp = WindowSystemFactory::Instance()->MakeWindowImp();
    }
    return _imp;
}
```

`WindowSystemFactory::Instance()` returns an abstract factory that manufactures all window system-specific objects. For simplicity, we've made it a Singleton (127) and have let the `Window` class access the factory directly.

Known Uses

The Window example above comes from ET++ [WGM88]. In ET++, WindowImp is called "WindowPort" and has subclasses such as XWindowPort and SunWindowPort. The Window object creates its corresponding Implementor object by requesting it from an abstract factory called "WindowSystem." WindowSystem provides an interface for creating platform-specific objects such as fonts, cursors, bitmaps, and so forth.

The ET++ Window/WindowPort design extends the Bridge pattern in that the WindowPort also keeps a reference back to the Window. The WindowPort implementor class uses this reference to notify Window about WindowPort-specific events: the arrival of input events, window resizes, etc.

Both Coplien [Cop92] and Stroustrup [Str91] mention Handle classes and give some examples. Their examples emphasize memory management issues like sharing string representations and support for variable-sized objects. Our focus is more on supporting independent extension of both an abstraction and its implementation.

libg++ [Lea88] defines classes that implement common data structures, such as Set, LinkedSet, HashSet, LinkedList, and HashTable. Set is an abstract class that defines a set abstraction, while LinkedList and HashTable are concrete implementors for a linked list and a hash table, respectively. LinkedSet and HashSet are Set implementors that bridge between Set and their concrete counterparts LinkedList and HashTable. This is an example of a degenerate bridge, because there's no abstract Implementor class.

NeXT's AppKit [Add94] uses the Bridge pattern in the implementation and display of graphical images. An image can be represented in several different ways. The optimal display of an image depends on the properties of a display device, specifically its color capabilities and its resolution. Without help from AppKit, developers would have to determine which implementation to use under various circumstances in every application.

To relieve developers of this responsibility, AppKit provides an NXImage/NXImageRep bridge. NXImage defines the interface for handling images. The implementation of images is defined in a separate NXImageRep class hierarchy having subclasses such as NXEPSImageRep, NXCachedImageRep, and NXBitMapImageRep. NXImage maintains a reference to one or more NXImageRep objects. If there is more than one image implementation, then NXImage selects the most appropriate one for the current display device. NXImage is even capable of converting one implementation to another if necessary. The interesting aspect of this Bridge variant is that NXImage can store more than one NXImageRep implementation at a time.

Related Patterns

An Abstract Factory (87) can create and configure a particular Bridge.

The Adapter (139) pattern is geared toward making unrelated classes work together. It is usually applied to systems after they're designed. Bridge, on the other hand, is used up-front in a design to let abstractions and implementations vary independently.

COMPOSITE   Object Structural

Intent

Compose objects into tree structures to represent part-whole hierarchies. Composite lets clients treat individual objects and compositions of objects uniformly.

Motivation

Graphics applications like drawing editors and schematic capture systems let users build complex diagrams out of simple components. The user can group components to form larger components, which in turn can be grouped to form still larger components. A simple implementation could define classes for graphical primitives such as Text and Lines plus other classes that act as containers for these primitives.

But there's a problem with this approach: Code that uses these classes must treat primitive and container objects differently, even if most of the time the user treats them identically. Having to distinguish these objects makes the application more complex. The Composite pattern describes how to use recursive composition so that clients don't have to make this distinction.

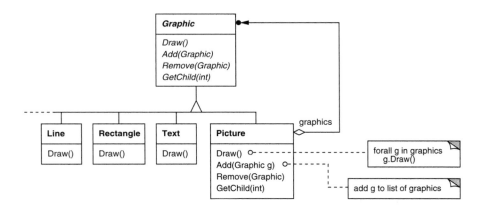

The key to the Composite pattern is an abstract class that represents *both* primitives and their containers. For the graphics system, this class is Graphic. Graphic declares operations like Draw that are specific to graphical objects. It also declares operations that all composite objects share, such as operations for accessing and managing its children.

The subclasses Line, Rectangle, and Text (see preceding class diagram) define primitive graphical objects. These classes implement Draw to draw lines, rectangles, and text, respectively. Since primitive graphics have no child graphics, none of these subclasses implements child-related operations.

The Picture class defines an aggregate of Graphic objects. Picture implements Draw to call Draw on its children, and it implements child-related operations accordingly. Because the Picture interface conforms to the Graphic interface, Picture objects can compose other Pictures recursively.

The following diagram shows a typical composite object structure of recursively composed Graphic objects:

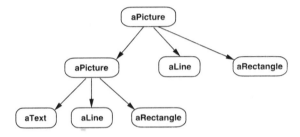

Applicability

Use the Composite pattern when

- you want to represent part-whole hierarchies of objects.
- you want clients to be able to ignore the difference between compositions of objects and individual objects. Clients will treat all objects in the composite structure uniformly.

Structure

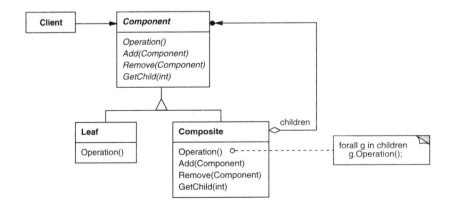

A typical Composite object structure might look like this:

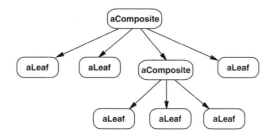

Participants

- **Component** (Graphic)
  - declares the interface for objects in the composition.
  - implements default behavior for the interface common to all classes, as appropriate.
  - declares an interface for accessing and managing its child components.
  - (optional) defines an interface for accessing a component's parent in the recursive structure, and implements it if that's appropriate.
- **Leaf** (Rectangle, Line, Text, etc.)
  - represents leaf objects in the composition. A leaf has no children.
  - defines behavior for primitive objects in the composition.
- **Composite** (Picture)
  - defines behavior for components having children.
  - stores child components.
  - implements child-related operations in the Component interface.
- **Client**
  - manipulates objects in the composition through the Component interface.

Collaborations

- Clients use the Component class interface to interact with objects in the composite structure. If the recipient is a Leaf, then the request is handled directly. If the recipient is a Composite, then it usually forwards requests to its child components, possibly performing additional operations before and/or after forwarding.

Consequences

The Composite pattern

- defines class hierarchies consisting of primitive objects and composite objects. Primitive objects can be composed into more complex objects, which in turn can be composed, and so on recursively. Wherever client code expects a primitive object, it can also take a composite object.

- makes the client simple. Clients can treat composite structures and individual objects uniformly. Clients normally don't know (and shouldn't care) whether they're dealing with a leaf or a composite component. This simplifies client code, because it avoids having to write tag-and-case-statement-style functions over the classes that define the composition.

- makes it easier to add new kinds of components. Newly defined Composite or Leaf subclasses work automatically with existing structures and client code. Clients don't have to be changed for new Component classes.

- can make your design overly general. The disadvantage of making it easy to add new components is that it makes it harder to restrict the components of a composite. Sometimes you want a composite to have only certain components. With Composite, you can't rely on the type system to enforce those constraints for you. You'll have to use run-time checks instead.

Implementation

There are many issues to consider when implementing the Composite pattern:

1. *Explicit parent references.* Maintaining references from child components to their parent can simplify the traversal and management of a composite structure. The parent reference simplifies moving up the structure and deleting a component. Parent references also help support the Chain of Responsibility (223) pattern.

   The usual place to define the parent reference is in the Component class. Leaf and Composite classes can inherit the reference and the operations that manage it.

   With parent references, it's essential to maintain the invariant that all children of a composite have as their parent the composite that in turn has them as children. The easiest way to ensure this is to change a component's parent *only* when it's being added or removed from a composite. If this can be implemented once in the Add and Remove operations of the Composite class, then it can be inherited by all the subclasses, and the invariant will be maintained automatically.

2. *Sharing components.* It's often useful to share components, for example, to reduce storage requirements. But when a component can have no more than one parent, sharing components becomes difficult.

A possible solution is for children to store multiple parents. But that can lead to ambiguities as a request propagates up the structure. The Flyweight (195) pattern shows how to rework a design to avoid storing parents altogether. It works in cases where children can avoid sending parent requests by externalizing some or all of their state.

3. *Maximizing the Component interface.* One of the goals of the Composite pattern is to make clients unaware of the specific Leaf or Composite classes they're using. To attain this goal, the Component class should define as many common operations for Composite and Leaf classes as possible. The Component class usually provides default implementations for these operations, and Leaf and Composite subclasses will override them.

However, this goal will sometimes conflict with the principle of class hierarchy design that says a class should only define operations that are meaningful to its subclasses. There are many operations that Component supports that don't seem to make sense for Leaf classes. How can Component provide a default implementation for them?

Sometimes a little creativity shows how an operation that would appear to make sense only for Composites can be implemented for all Components by moving it to the Component class. For example, the interface for accessing children is a fundamental part of a Composite class but not necessarily Leaf classes. But if we view a Leaf as a Component that *never* has children, then we can define a default operation for child access in the Component class that never *returns* any children. Leaf classes can use the default implementation, but Composite classes will reimplement it to return their children.

The child management operations are more troublesome and are discussed in the next item.

4. *Declaring the child management operations.* Although the Composite class *implements* the Add and Remove operations for managing children, an important issue in the Composite pattern is which classes *declare* these operations in the Composite class hierarchy. Should we declare these operations in the Component and make them meaningful for Leaf classes, or should we declare and define them only in Composite and its subclasses?

The decision involves a trade-off between safety and transparency:

- Defining the child management interface at the root of the class hierarchy gives you transparency, because you can treat all components uniformly. It costs you safety, however, because clients may try to do meaningless things like add and remove objects from leaves.

- Defining child management in the Composite class gives you safety, because any attempt to add or remove objects from leaves will be caught at compile-time in a statically typed language like C++. But you lose transparency, because leaves and composites have different interfaces.

We have emphasized transparency over safety in this pattern. If you opt for
safety, then at times you may lose type information and have to convert a
component into a composite. How can you do this without resorting to a
type-unsafe cast?

One approach is to declare an operation `Composite* GetComposite()` in
the Component class. Component provides a default operation that returns
a null pointer. The Composite class redefines this operation to return itself
through the `this` pointer:

```cpp
class Composite;

class Component {
public:
    //...
    virtual Composite* GetComposite() { return 0; }
};

class Composite : public Component {
public:
    void Add(Component*);
    // ...
    virtual Composite* GetComposite() { return this; }
};

class Leaf : public Component {
    // ...
};
```

`GetComposite` lets you query a component to see if it's a composite. You
can perform `Add` and `Remove` safely on the composite it returns.

```cpp
Composite* aComposite = new Composite;
Leaf* aLeaf = new Leaf;

Component* aComponent;
Composite* test;

aComponent = aComposite;
if (test = aComponent->GetComposite()) {
    test->Add(new Leaf);
}

aComponent = aLeaf;

if (test = aComponent->GetComposite()) {
    test->Add(new Leaf); // will not add leaf
}
```

Similar tests for a Composite can be done using the C++ `dynamic_cast`
construct.

Of course, the problem here is that we don't treat all components uniformly.
We have to revert to testing for different types before taking the appropriate
action.

The only way to provide transparency is to define default Add and Remove operations in Component. That creates a new problem: There's no way to implement Component::Add without introducing the possibility of it failing. You could make it do nothing, but that ignores an important consideration; that is, an attempt to add something to a leaf probably indicates a bug. In that case, the Add operation produces garbage. You could make it delete its argument, but that might not be what clients expect.

Usually it's better to make Add and Remove fail by default (perhaps by raising an exception) if the component isn't allowed to have children or if the argument of Remove isn't a child of the component, respectively.

Another alternative is to change the meaning of "remove" slightly. If the component maintains a parent reference, then we could redefine Component::Remove to remove itself from its parent. However, there still isn't a meaningful interpretation for a corresponding Add.

5. *Should Component implement a list of Components?* You might be tempted to define the set of children as an instance variable in the Component class where the child access and management operations are declared. But putting the child pointer in the base class incurs a space penalty for every leaf, even though a leaf never has children. This is worthwhile only if there are relatively few children in the structure.

6. *Child ordering.* Many designs specify an ordering on the children of Composite. In the earlier Graphics example, ordering may reflect front-to-back ordering. If Composites represent parse trees, then compound statements can be instances of a Composite whose children must be ordered to reflect the program.

   When child ordering is an issue, you must design child access and management interfaces carefully to manage the sequence of children. The Iterator (257) pattern can guide you in this.

7. *Caching to improve performance.* If you need to traverse or search compositions frequently, the Composite class can cache traversal or search information about its children. The Composite can cache actual results or just information that lets it short-circuit the traversal or search. For example, the Picture class from the Motivation example could cache the bounding box of its children. During drawing or selection, this cached bounding box lets the Picture avoid drawing or searching when its children aren't visible in the current window.

   Changes to a component will require invalidating the caches of its parents. This works best when components know their parents. So if you're using caching, you need to define an interface for telling composites that their caches are invalid.

8. *Who should delete components?* In languages without garbage collection, it's usually best to make a Composite responsible for deleting its children when it's destroyed. An exception to this rule is when Leaf objects are immutable and thus can be shared.

9. *What's the best data structure for storing components?* Composites may use a variety of data structures to store their children, including linked lists, trees, arrays, and hash tables. The choice of data structure depends (as always) on efficiency. In fact, it isn't even necessary to use a general-purpose data structure at all. Sometimes composites have a variable for each child, although this requires each subclass of Composite to implement its own management interface. See Interpreter (243) for an example.

Sample Code

Equipment such as computers and stereo components are often organized into part-whole or containment hierarchies. For example, a chassis can contain drives and planar boards, a bus can contain cards, and a cabinet can contain chassis, buses, and so forth. Such structures can be modeled naturally with the Composite pattern.

Equipment class defines an interface for all equipment in the part-whole hierarchy.

```
class Equipment {
public:
    virtual ~Equipment();

    const char* Name() { return _name; }

    virtual Watt Power();
    virtual Currency NetPrice();
    virtual Currency DiscountPrice();

    virtual void Add(Equipment*);
    virtual void Remove(Equipment*);
    virtual Iterator<Equipment*>* CreateIterator();
protected:
    Equipment(const char*);
private:
    const char* _name;
};
```

Equipment declares operations that return the attributes of a piece of equipment, like its power consumption and cost. Subclasses implement these operations for specific kinds of equipment. Equipment also declares a CreateIterator operation that returns an Iterator (see Appendix C) for accessing its parts. The default implementation for this operation returns a NullIterator, which iterates over the empty set.

Subclasses of Equipment might include Leaf classes that represent disk drives, integrated circuits, and switches:

```
class FloppyDisk : public Equipment {
public:
    FloppyDisk(const char*);
    virtual ~FloppyDisk();

    virtual Watt Power();
    virtual Currency NetPrice();
    virtual Currency DiscountPrice();
};
```

CompositeEquipment is the base class for equipment that contains other equipment. It's also a subclass of Equipment.

```
class CompositeEquipment : public Equipment {
public:
    virtual ~CompositeEquipment();

    virtual Watt Power();
    virtual Currency NetPrice();
    virtual Currency DiscountPrice();

    virtual void Add(Equipment*);
    virtual void Remove(Equipment*);
    virtual Iterator<Equipment*>* CreateIterator();

protected:
    CompositeEquipment(const char*);
private:
    List<Equipment*> _equipment;
};
```

CompositeEquipment defines the operations for accessing and managing subequipment. The operations Add and Remove insert and delete equipment from the list of equipment stored in the _equipment member. The operation CreateIterator returns an iterator (specifically, an instance of ListIterator) that will traverse this list.

A default implementation of NetPrice might use CreateIterator to sum the net prices of the subequipment[2]:

```
Currency CompositeEquipment::NetPrice () {
    Iterator<Equipment*>* i = CreateIterator();
    Currency total = 0;

    for (i->First(); !i->IsDone(); i->Next()) {
        total += i->CurrentItem()->NetPrice();
    }
    delete i;
    return total;
}
```

---

[2] It's easy to forget to delete the iterator once you're done with it. The Iterator pattern shows how to guard against such bugs on page 266.

Now we can represent a computer chassis as a subclass of CompositeEquipment called Chassis. Chassis inherits the child-related operations from CompositeEquipment.

```
class Chassis : public CompositeEquipment {
public:
    Chassis(const char*);
    virtual ~Chassis();

    virtual Watt Power();
    virtual Currency NetPrice();
    virtual Currency DiscountPrice();
};
```

We can define other equipment containers such as Cabinet and Bus in a similar way. That gives us everything we need to assemble equipment into a (pretty simple) personal computer:

```
Cabinet* cabinet = new Cabinet("PC Cabinet");
Chassis* chassis = new Chassis("PC Chassis");

cabinet->Add(chassis);

Bus* bus = new Bus("MCA Bus");
bus->Add(new Card("16Mbs Token Ring"));

chassis->Add(bus);
chassis->Add(new FloppyDisk("3.5in Floppy"));

cout << "The net price is " << chassis->NetPrice() << endl;
```

Known Uses

Examples of the Composite pattern can be found in almost all object-oriented systems. The original View class of Smalltalk Model/View/Controller [KP88] was a Composite, and nearly every user interface toolkit or framework has followed in its steps, including ET++ (with its VObjects [WGM88]) and InterViews (Styles [LCI+92], Graphics [VL88], and Glyphs [CL90]). It's interesting to note that the original View of Model/View/Controller had a set of subviews; in other words, View was both the Component class and the Composite class. Release 4.0 of Smalltalk-80 revised Model/View/Controller with a VisualComponent class that has subclasses View and CompositeView.

The RTL Smalltalk compiler framework [JML92] uses the Composite pattern extensively. RTLExpression is a Component class for parse trees. It has subclasses, such as BinaryExpression, that contain child RTLExpression objects. These classes define a composite structure for parse trees. RegisterTransfer is the Component class for a program's intermediate Single Static Assignment (SSA) form. Leaf subclasses of RegisterTransfer define different static assignments such as

- primitive assignments that perform an operation on two registers and assign the result to a third;

- an assignment with a source register but no destination register, which indicates that the register is used after a routine returns; and

- an assignment with a destination register but no source, which indicates that the register is assigned before the routine starts.

Another subclass, RegisterTransferSet, is a Composite class for representing assignments that change several registers at once.

Another example of this pattern occurs in the financial domain, where a portfolio aggregates individual assets. You can support complex aggregations of assets by implementing a portfolio as a Composite that conforms to the interface of an individual asset [BE93].

The Command (233) pattern describes how Command objects can be composed and sequenced with a MacroCommand Composite class.

Related Patterns

Often the component-parent link is used for a Chain of Responsibility (223).

Decorator (175) is often used with Composite. When decorators and composites are used together, they will usually have a common parent class. So decorators will have to support the Component interface with operations like Add, Remove, and GetChild.

Flyweight (195) lets you share components, but they can no longer refer to their parents.

Iterator (257) can be used to traverse composites.

Visitor (331) localizes operations and behavior that would otherwise be distributed across Composite and Leaf classes.

DECORATOR   Object Structural

Intent

Attach additional responsibilities to an object dynamically. Decorators provide a flexible alternative to subclassing for extending functionality.

Also Known As

Wrapper

Motivation

Sometimes we want to add responsibilities to individual objects, not to an entire class. A graphical user interface toolkit, for example, should let you add properties like borders or behaviors like scrolling to any user interface component.

One way to add responsibilities is with inheritance. Inheriting a border from another class puts a border around every subclass instance. This is inflexible, however, because the choice of border is made statically. A client can't control how and when to decorate the component with a border.

A more flexible approach is to enclose the component in another object that adds the border. The enclosing object is called a **decorator**. The decorator conforms to the interface of the component it decorates so that its presence is transparent to the component's clients. The decorator forwards requests to the component and may perform additional actions (such as drawing a border) before or after forwarding. Transparency lets you nest decorators recursively, thereby allowing an unlimited number of added responsibilities.

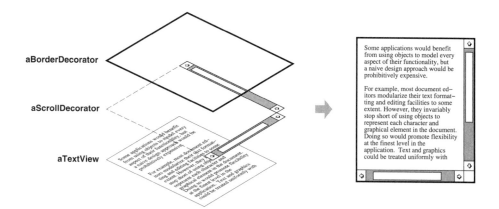

For example, suppose we have a TextView object that displays text in a window. TextView has no scroll bars by default, because we might not always need them. When we do, we can use a ScrollDecorator to add them. Suppose we also want to add a thick black border around the TextView. We can use a BorderDecorator to add this as well. We simply compose the decorators with the TextView to produce the desired result.

The following object diagram shows how to compose a TextView object with BorderDecorator and ScrollDecorator objects to produce a bordered, scrollable text view:

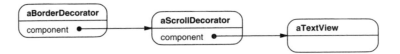

The ScrollDecorator and BorderDecorator classes are subclasses of Decorator, an abstract class for visual components that decorate other visual components.

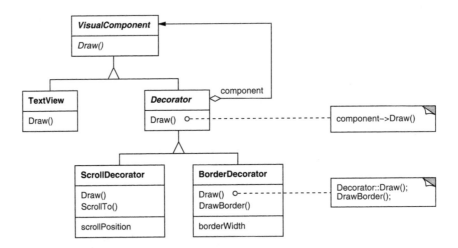

VisualComponent is the abstract class for visual objects. It defines their drawing and event handling interface. Note how the Decorator class simply forwards draw requests to its component, and how Decorator subclasses can extend this operation.

Decorator subclasses are free to add operations for specific functionality. For example, ScrollDecorator's ScrollTo operation lets other objects scroll the interface *if* they know there happens to be a ScrollDecorator object in the interface. The important aspect of this pattern is that it lets decorators appear anywhere a VisualComponent can. That way clients generally can't tell the difference between a decorated component and an undecorated one, and so they don't depend at all on the decoration.

Applicability

Use Decorator

- to add responsibilities to individual objects dynamically and transparently, that is, without affecting other objects.

- for responsibilities that can be withdrawn.

- when extension by subclassing is impractical. Sometimes a large number of independent extensions are possible and would produce an explosion of subclasses to support every combination. Or a class definition may be hidden or otherwise unavailable for subclassing.

Structure

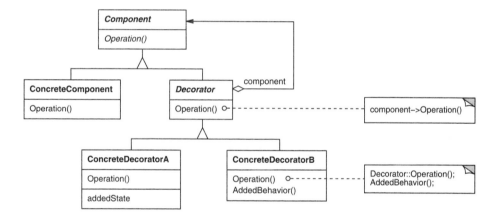

Participants

- **Component** (VisualComponent)
  - defines the interface for objects that can have responsibilities added to them dynamically.

- **ConcreteComponent** (TextView)
  - defines an object to which additional responsibilities can be attached.

- **Decorator**
  - maintains a reference to a Component object and defines an interface that conforms to Component's interface.

- **ConcreteDecorator** (BorderDecorator, ScrollDecorator)

  - adds responsibilities to the component.

Collaborations

- Decorator forwards requests to its Component object. It may optionally perform additional operations before and after forwarding the request.

Consequences

The Decorator pattern has at least two key benefits and two liabilities:

1. *More flexibility than static inheritance.* The Decorator pattern provides a more flexible way to add responsibilities to objects than can be had with static (multiple) inheritance. With decorators, responsibilities can be added and removed at run-time simply by attaching and detaching them. In contrast, inheritance requires creating a new class for each additional responsibility (e.g., BorderedScrollableTextView, BorderedTextView). This gives rise to many classes and increases the complexity of a system. Furthermore, providing different Decorator classes for a specific Component class lets you mix and match responsibilities.

   Decorators also make it easy to add a property twice. For example, to give a TextView a double border, simply attach two BorderDecorators. Inheriting from a Border class twice is error-prone at best.

2. *Avoids feature-laden classes high up in the hierarchy.* Decorator offers a pay-as-you-go approach to adding responsibilities. Instead of trying to support all foreseeable features in a complex, customizable class, you can define a simple class and add functionality incrementally with Decorator objects. Functionality can be composed from simple pieces. As a result, an application needn't pay for features it doesn't use. It's also easy to define new kinds of Decorators independently from the classes of objects they extend, even for unforeseen extensions. Extending a complex class tends to expose details unrelated to the responsibilities you're adding.

3. *A decorator and its component aren't identical.* A decorator acts as a transparent enclosure. But from an object identity point of view, a decorated component is not identical to the component itself. Hence you shouldn't rely on object identity when you use decorators.

4. *Lots of little objects.* A design that uses Decorator often results in systems composed of lots of little objects that all look alike. The objects differ only in the way they are interconnected, not in their class or in the value of their variables. Although these systems are easy to customize by those who understand them, they can be hard to learn and debug.

Implementation

Several issues should be considered when applying the Decorator pattern:

1. *Interface conformance.* A decorator object's interface must conform to the interface of the component it decorates. ConcreteDecorator classes must therefore inherit from a common class (at least in C++).

2. *Omitting the abstract Decorator class.* There's no need to define an abstract Decorator class when you only need to add one responsibility. That's often the case when you're dealing with an existing class hierarchy rather than designing a new one. In that case, you can merge Decorator's responsibility for forwarding requests to the component into the ConcreteDecorator.

3. *Keeping Component classes lightweight.* To ensure a conforming interface, components and decorators must descend from a common Component class. It's important to keep this common class lightweight; that is, it should focus on defining an interface, not on storing data. The definition of the data representation should be deferred to subclasses; otherwise the complexity of the Component class might make the decorators too heavyweight to use in quantity. Putting a lot of functionality into Component also increases the probability that concrete subclasses will pay for features they don't need.

4. *Changing the skin of an object versus changing its guts.* We can think of a decorator as a skin over an object that changes its behavior. An alternative is to change the object's guts. The Strategy (315) pattern is a good example of a pattern for changing the guts.

   Strategies are a better choice in situations where the Component class is intrinsically heavyweight, thereby making the Decorator pattern too costly to apply. In the Strategy pattern, the component forwards some of its behavior to a separate strategy object. The Strategy pattern lets us alter or extend the component's functionality by replacing the strategy object.

   For example, we can support different border styles by having the component defer border-drawing to a separate Border object. The Border object is a Strategy object that encapsulates a border-drawing strategy. By extending the number of strategies from just one to an open-ended list, we achieve the same effect as nesting decorators recursively.

   In MacApp 3.0 [App89] and Bedrock [Sym93a], for example, graphical components (called "views") maintain a list of "adorner" objects that can attach additional adornments like borders to a view component. If a view has any adorners attached, then it gives them a chance to draw additional embellishments. MacApp and Bedrock must use this approach because the View class is heavyweight. It would be too expensive to use a full-fledged View just to add a border.

   Since the Decorator pattern only changes a component from the outside, the component doesn't have to know anything about its decorators; that is, the decorators are transparent to the component:

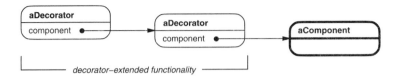

With strategies, the component itself knows about possible extensions. So it has to reference and maintain the corresponding strategies:

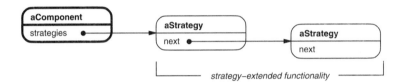

The Strategy-based approach might require modifying the component to accommodate new extensions. On the other hand, a strategy can have its own specialized interface, whereas a decorator's interface must conform to the component's. A strategy for rendering a border, for example, need only define the interface for rendering a border (DrawBorder, GetWidth, etc.), which means that the strategy can be lightweight even if the Component class is heavyweight.

MacApp and Bedrock use this approach for more than just adorning views. They also use it to augment the event-handling behavior of objects. In both systems, a view maintains a list of "behavior" objects that can modify and intercept events. The view gives each of the registered behavior objects a chance to handle the event before nonregistered behaviors, effectively overriding them. You can decorate a view with special keyboard-handling support, for example, by registering a behavior object that intercepts and handles key events.

Sample Code

The following code shows how to implement user interface decorators in C++. We'll assume there's a Component class called `VisualComponent`.

```
class VisualComponent {
public:
    VisualComponent();

    virtual void Draw();
    virtual void Resize();
    // ...
};
```

We define a subclass of VisualComponent called Decorator, which we'll subclass to obtain different decorations.

```
class Decorator : public VisualComponent {
public:
    Decorator(VisualComponent*);

    virtual void Draw();
    virtual void Resize();
    // ...
private:
    VisualComponent* _component;
};
```

Decorator decorates the VisualComponent referenced by the _component instance variable, which is initialized in the constructor. For each operation in VisualComponent's interface, Decorator defines a default implementation that passes the request on to _component:

```
void Decorator::Draw () {
    _component->Draw();
}

void Decorator::Resize () {
    _component->Resize();
}
```

Subclasses of Decorator define specific decorations. For example, the class BorderDecorator adds a border to its enclosing component. Border-Decorator is a subclass of Decorator that overrides the Draw operation to draw the border. BorderDecorator also defines a private DrawBorder helper operation that does the drawing. The subclass inherits all other operation implementations from Decorator.

```
class BorderDecorator : public Decorator {
public:
    BorderDecorator(VisualComponent*, int borderWidth);

    virtual void Draw();
private:
    void DrawBorder(int);
private:
    int _width;
};

void BorderDecorator::Draw () {
    Decorator::Draw();
    DrawBorder(_width);
}
```

A similar implementation would follow for `ScrollDecorator` and `Drop-ShadowDecorator`, which would add scrolling and drop shadow capabilities to a visual component.

Now we can compose instances of these classes to provide different decorations. The following code illustrates how we can use decorators to create a bordered scrollable `TextView`.

First, we need a way to put a visual component into a window object. We'll assume our `Window` class provides a `SetContents` operation for this purpose:

```
void Window::SetContents (VisualComponent* contents) {
    // ...
}
```

Now we can create the text view and a window to put it in:

```
Window* window = new Window;
TextView* textView = new TextView;
```

`TextView` is a `VisualComponent`, which lets us put it into the window:

```
window->SetContents(textView);
```

But we want a bordered and scrollable `TextView`. So we decorate it accordingly before putting it in the window.

```
window->SetContents(
    new BorderDecorator(
        new ScrollDecorator(textView), 1
    )
);
```

Because `Window` accesses its contents through the `VisualComponent` interface, it's unaware of the decorator's presence. You, as the client, can still keep track of the text view if you have to interact with it directly, for example, when you need to invoke operations that aren't part of the `VisualComponent` interface. Clients that rely on the component's identity should refer to it directly as well.

Known Uses

Many object-oriented user interface toolkits use decorators to add graphical embellishments to widgets. Examples include InterViews [LVC89, LCI+92], ET++ [WGM88], and the ObjectWorks\Smalltalk class library [Par90]. More exotic applications of Decorator are the DebuggingGlyph from InterViews and the PassivityWrapper from ParcPlace Smalltalk. A DebuggingGlyph prints out debugging information before and after it forwards a layout request to its component. This trace information can be used to analyze and debug the layout behavior of objects in a complex composition. The PassivityWrapper can enable or disable user interactions with the component.

But the Decorator pattern is by no means limited to graphical user interfaces, as the following example (based on the ET++ streaming classes [WGM88]) illustrates.

Streams are a fundamental abstraction in most I/O facilities. A stream can provide an interface for converting objects into a sequence of bytes or characters. That lets us transcribe an object to a file or to a string in memory for retrieval later. A straightforward way to do this is to define an abstract Stream class with subclasses MemoryStream and FileStream. But suppose we also want to be able to do the following:

- Compress the stream data using different compression algorithms (run-length encoding, Lempel-Ziv, etc.).

- Reduce the stream data to 7-bit ASCII characters so that it can be transmitted over an ASCII communication channel.

The Decorator pattern gives us an elegant way to add these responsibilities to streams. The diagram below shows one solution to the problem:

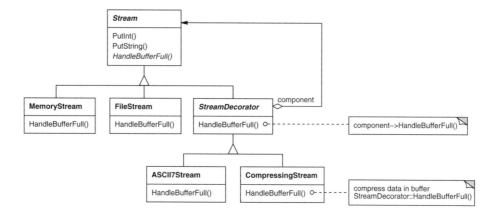

The Stream abstract class maintains an internal buffer and provides operations for storing data onto the stream (PutInt, PutString). Whenever the buffer is full, Stream calls the abstract operation HandleBufferFull, which does the actual data transfer. The FileStream version of this operation overrides this operation to transfer the buffer to a file.

The key class here is StreamDecorator, which maintains a reference to a component stream and forwards requests to it. StreamDecorator subclasses override HandleBufferFull and perform additional actions before calling StreamDecorator's HandleBufferFull operation.

For example, the CompressingStream subclass compresses the data, and the ASCII7Stream converts the data into 7-bit ASCII. Now, to create a FileStream that compresses its data *and* converts the compressed binary data to 7-bit ASCII, we decorate a FileStream with a CompressingStream and an ASCII7Stream:

```
Stream* aStream = new CompressingStream(
    new ASCII7Stream(
        new FileStream("aFileName")
    )
);
aStream->PutInt(12);
aStream->PutString("aString");
```

Related Patterns

Adapter (139): A decorator is different from an adapter in that a decorator only changes an object's responsibilities, not its interface; an adapter will give an object a completely new interface.

Composite (163): A decorator can be viewed as a degenerate composite with only one component. However, a decorator adds additional responsibilities—it isn't intended for object aggregation.

Strategy (315): A decorator lets you change the skin of an object; a strategy lets you change the guts. These are two alternative ways of changing an object.

FACADE   Object Structural

Intent

Provide a unified interface to a set of interfaces in a subsystem. Facade defines a higher-level interface that makes the subsystem easier to use.

Motivation

Structuring a system into subsystems helps reduce complexity. A common design goal is to minimize the communication and dependencies between subsystems. One way to achieve this goal is to introduce a **facade** object that provides a single, simplified interface to the more general facilities of a subsystem.

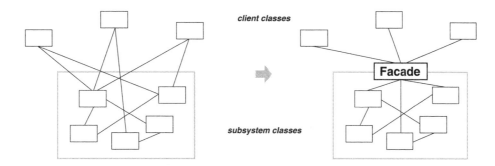

Consider for example a programming environment that gives applications access to its compiler subsystem. This subsystem contains classes such as Scanner, Parser, ProgramNode, BytecodeStream, and ProgramNodeBuilder that implement the compiler. Some specialized applications might need to access these classes directly. But most clients of a compiler generally don't care about details like parsing and code generation; they merely want to compile some code. For them, the powerful but low-level interfaces in the compiler subsystem only complicate their task.

To provide a higher-level interface that can shield clients from these classes, the compiler subsystem also includes a Compiler class. This class defines a unified interface to the compiler's functionality. The Compiler class acts as a facade: It offers clients a single, simple interface to the compiler subsystem. It glues together the classes that implement compiler functionality without hiding them completely. The compiler facade makes life easier for most programmers without hiding the lower-level functionality from the few that need it.

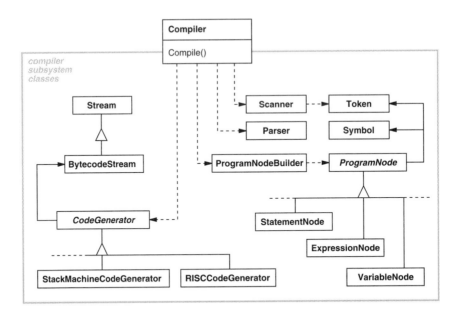

Applicability

Use the Facade pattern when

- you want to provide a simple interface to a complex subsystem. Subsystems often get more complex as they evolve. Most patterns, when applied, result in more and smaller classes. This makes the subsystem more reusable and easier to customize, but it also becomes harder to use for clients that don't need to customize it. A facade can provide a simple default view of the subsystem that is good enough for most clients. Only clients needing more customizability will need to look beyond the facade.

- there are many dependencies between clients and the implementation classes of an abstraction. Introduce a facade to decouple the subsystem from clients and other subsystems, thereby promoting subsystem independence and portability.

- you want to layer your subsystems. Use a facade to define an entry point to each subsystem level. If subsystems are dependent, then you can simplify the dependencies between them by making them communicate with each other solely through their facades.

Structure

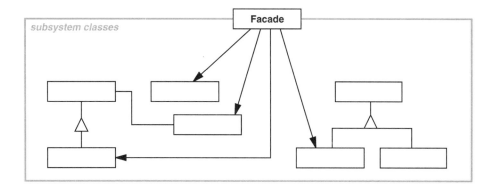

Participants

- **Facade** (Compiler)
    - knows which subsystem classes are responsible for a request.
    - delegates client requests to appropriate subsystem objects.
- **subsystem classes** (Scanner, Parser, ProgramNode, etc.)
    - implement subsystem functionality.
    - handle work assigned by the Facade object.
    - have no knowledge of the facade; that is, they keep no references to it.

Collaborations

- Clients communicate with the subsystem by sending requests to Facade, which forwards them to the appropriate subsystem object(s). Although the subsystem objects perform the actual work, the facade may have to do work of its own to translate its interface to subsystem interfaces.
- Clients that use the facade don't have to access its subsystem objects directly.

Consequences

The Facade pattern offers the following benefits:

1. It shields clients from subsystem components, thereby reducing the number of objects that clients deal with and making the subsystem easier to use.
2. It promotes weak coupling between the subsystem and its clients. Often the components in a subsystem are strongly coupled. Weak coupling lets you vary the components of the subsystem without affecting its clients. Facades

help layer a system and the dependencies between objects. They can eliminate complex or circular dependencies. This can be an important consequence when the client and the subsystem are implemented independently.

Reducing compilation dependencies is vital in large software systems. You want to save time by minimizing recompilation when subsystem classes change. Reducing compilation dependencies with facades can limit the recompilation needed for a small change in an important subsystem. A facade can also simplify porting systems to other platforms, because it's less likely that building one subsystem requires building all others.

3. It doesn't prevent applications from using subsystem classes if they need to. Thus you can choose between ease of use and generality.

Implementation

Consider the following issues when implementing a facade:

1. *Reducing client-subsystem coupling.* The coupling between clients and the subsystem can be reduced even further by making Facade an abstract class with concrete subclasses for different implementations of a subsystem. Then clients can communicate with the subsystem through the interface of the abstract Facade class. This abstract coupling keeps clients from knowing which implementation of a subsystem is used.

An alternative to subclassing is to configure a Facade object with different subsystem objects. To customize the facade, simply replace one or more of its subsystem objects.

2. *Public versus private subsystem classes.* A subsystem is analogous to a class in that both have interfaces, and both encapsulate something—a class encapsulates state and operations, while a subsystem encapsulates classes. And just as it's useful to think of the public and private interface of a class, we can think of the public and private interface of a subsystem.

The public interface to a subsystem consists of classes that all clients can access; the private interface is just for subsystem extenders. The Facade class is part of the public interface, of course, but it's not the only part. Other subsystem classes are usually public as well. For example, the classes Parser and Scanner in the compiler subsystem are part of the public interface.

Making subsystem classes private would be useful, but few object-oriented languages support it. Both C++ and Smalltalk traditionally have had a global name space for classes. Recently, however, the C++ standardization committee added name spaces to the language [Str94], which will let you expose just the public subsystem classes.

Sample Code

Let's take a closer look at how to put a facade on a compiler subsystem.

The compiler subsystem defines a BytecodeStream class that implements a stream of `Bytecode` objects. A `Bytecode` object encapsulates a bytecode, which can specify machine instructions. The subsystem also defines a `Token` class for objects that encapsulate tokens in the programming language.

The `Scanner` class takes a stream of characters and produces a stream of tokens, one token at a time.

```
class Scanner {
public:
    Scanner(istream&);
    virtual ~Scanner();

    virtual Token& Scan();
private:
    istream& _inputStream;
};
```

The class `Parser` uses a `ProgramNodeBuilder` to construct a parse tree from a `Scanner`'s tokens.

```
class Parser {
public:
    Parser();
    virtual ~Parser();

    virtual void Parse(Scanner&, ProgramNodeBuilder&);
};
```

`Parser` calls back on `ProgramNodeBuilder` to build the parse tree incrementally. These classes interact according to the Builder (97) pattern.

```
class ProgramNodeBuilder {
public:
    ProgramNodeBuilder();

    virtual ProgramNode* NewVariable(
        const char* variableName
    ) const;

    virtual ProgramNode* NewAssignment(
        ProgramNode* variable, ProgramNode* expression
    ) const;

    virtual ProgramNode* NewReturnStatement(
        ProgramNode* value
    ) const;

    virtual ProgramNode* NewCondition(
        ProgramNode* condition,
        ProgramNode* truePart, ProgramNode* falsePart
    ) const;
    // ...
```

```
    ProgramNode* GetRootNode();
private:
    ProgramNode* _node;
};
```

The parse tree is made up of instances of `ProgramNode` subclasses such as `StatementNode`, `ExpressionNode`, and so forth. The `ProgramNode` hierarchy is an example of the Composite (163) pattern. `ProgramNode` defines an interface for manipulating the program node and its children, if any.

```
class ProgramNode {
public:
    // program node manipulation
    virtual void GetSourcePosition(int& line, int& index);
    // ...

    // child manipulation
    virtual void Add(ProgramNode*);
    virtual void Remove(ProgramNode*);
    // ...

    virtual void Traverse(CodeGenerator&);
protected:
    ProgramNode();
};
```

The `Traverse` operation takes a `CodeGenerator` object. `ProgramNode` subclasses use this object to generate machine code in the form of `Bytecode` objects on a `BytecodeStream`. The class `CodeGenerator` is a visitor (see Visitor (331)).

```
class CodeGenerator {
public:
    virtual void Visit(StatementNode*);
    virtual void Visit(ExpressionNode*);
    // ...
protected:
    CodeGenerator(BytecodeStream&);
protected:
    BytecodeStream& _output;
};
```

`CodeGenerator` has subclasses, for example, `StackMachineCodeGenerator` and `RISCCodeGenerator`, that generate machine code for different hardware architectures.

Each subclass of `ProgramNode` implements `Traverse` to call `Traverse` on its child `ProgramNode` objects. In turn, each child does the same for its children, and so on recursively. For example, `ExpressionNode` defines `Traverse` as follows:

```
void ExpressionNode::Traverse (CodeGenerator& cg) {
    cg.Visit(this);

    ListIterator<ProgramNode*> i(_children);

    for (i.First(); !i.IsDone(); i.Next()) {
        i.CurrentItem()->Traverse(cg);
    }
}
```

The classes we've discussed so far make up the compiler subsystem. Now we'll introduce a `Compiler` class, a facade that puts all these pieces together. `Compiler` provides a simple interface for compiling source and generating code for a particular machine.

```
class Compiler {
public:
    Compiler();

    virtual void Compile(istream&, BytecodeStream&);
};


void Compiler::Compile (
    istream& input, BytecodeStream& output
) {
    Scanner scanner(input);
    ProgramNodeBuilder builder;
    Parser parser;

    parser.Parse(scanner, builder);

    RISCCodeGenerator generator(output);
    ProgramNode* parseTree = builder.GetRootNode();
    parseTree->Traverse(generator);
}
```

This implementation hard-codes the type of code generator to use so that programmers aren't required to specify the target architecture. That might be reasonable if there's only ever one target architecture. If that's not the case, then we might want to change the `Compiler` constructor to take a `CodeGenerator` parameter. Then programmers can specify the generator to use when they instantiate `Compiler`. The compiler facade can parameterize other participants such as `Scanner` and `ProgramNodeBuilder` as well, which adds flexibility, but it also detracts from the Facade pattern's mission, which is to simplify the interface for the common case.

Known Uses

The compiler example in the Sample Code section was inspired by the Object-Works\Smalltalk compiler system [Par90].

In the ET++ application framework [WGM88], an application can have built-in browsing tools for inspecting its objects at run-time. These browsing tools are implemented in a separate subsystem that includes a Facade class called "ProgrammingEnvironment." This facade defines operations such as InspectObject and InspectClass for accessing the browsers.

An ET++ application can also forgo built-in browsing support. In that case, ProgrammingEnvironment implements these requests as null operations; that is, they do nothing. Only the ETProgrammingEnvironment subclass implements these requests with operations that display the corresponding browsers. The application has no knowledge of whether a browsing environment is available or not; there's abstract coupling between the application and the browsing subsystem.

The Choices operating system [CIRM93] uses facades to compose many frameworks into one. The key abstractions in Choices are processes, storage, and address spaces. For each of these abstractions there is a corresponding subsystem, implemented as a framework, that supports porting Choices to a variety of different hardware platforms. Two of these subsystems have a "representative" (i.e., facade). These representatives are FileSystemInterface (storage) and Domain (address spaces).

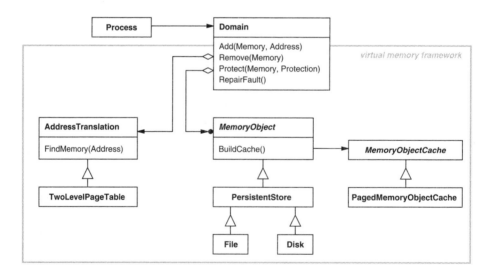

For example, the virtual memory framework has Domain as its facade. A Domain represents an address space. It provides a mapping between virtual addresses and offsets into memory objects, files, or backing store. The main operations on Domain support adding a memory object at a particular address, removing a memory object, and handling a page fault.

As the preceding diagram shows, the virtual memory subsystem uses the following components internally:

- MemoryObject represents a data store.

- MemoryObjectCache caches the data of MemoryObjects in physical memory. MemoryObjectCache is actually a Strategy (315) that localizes the caching policy.

- AddressTranslation encapsulates the address translation hardware.

The RepairFault operation is called whenever a page fault interrupt occurs. The Domain finds the memory object at the address causing the fault and delegates the RepairFault operation to the cache associated with that memory object. Domains can be customized by changing their components.

Related Patterns

Abstract Factory (87) can be used with Facade to provide an interface for creating subsystem objects in a subsystem-independent way. Abstract Factory can also be used as an alternative to Facade to hide platform-specific classes.

Mediator (273) is similar to Facade in that it abstracts functionality of existing classes. However, Mediator's purpose is to abstract arbitrary communication between colleague objects, often centralizing functionality that doesn't belong in any one of them. A mediator's colleagues are aware of and communicate with the mediator instead of communicating with each other directly. In contrast, a facade merely abstracts the interface to subsystem objects to make them easier to use; it doesn't define new functionality, and subsystem classes don't know about it.

Usually only one Facade object is required. Thus Facade objects are often Singletons (127).

FLYWEIGHT   Object Structural

Intent

Use sharing to support large numbers of fine-grained objects efficiently.

Motivation

Some applications could benefit from using objects throughout their design, but a naive implementation would be prohibitively expensive.

For example, most document editor implementations have text formatting and editing facilities that are modularized to some extent. Object-oriented document editors typically use objects to represent embedded elements like tables and figures. However, they usually stop short of using an object for each character in the document, even though doing so would promote flexibility at the finest levels in the application. Characters and embedded elements could then be treated uniformly with respect to how they are drawn and formatted. The application could be extended to support new character sets without disturbing other functionality. The application's object structure could mimic the document's physical structure. The following diagram shows how a document editor can use objects to represent characters.

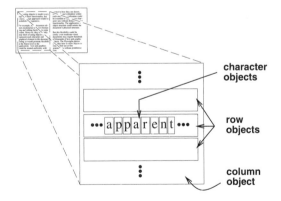

The drawback of such a design is its cost. Even moderate-sized documents may require hundreds of thousands of character objects, which will consume lots of memory and may incur unacceptable run-time overhead. The Flyweight pattern describes how to share objects to allow their use at fine granularities without prohibitive cost.

A **flyweight** is a shared object that can be used in multiple contexts simultaneously. The flyweight acts as an independent object in each context—it's indistinguishable from an instance of the object that's not shared. Flyweights cannot make assumptions about the context in which they operate. The key concept here is the distinction between **intrinsic** and **extrinsic** state. Intrinsic state is stored in the flyweight; it consists of information that's independent of the flyweight's context, thereby making it sharable. Extrinsic state depends on and varies with the flyweight's context and therefore can't be shared. Client objects are responsible for passing extrinsic state to the flyweight when it needs it.

Flyweights model concepts or entities that are normally too plentiful to represent with objects. For example, a document editor can create a flyweight for each letter of the alphabet. Each flyweight stores a character code, but its coordinate position in the document and its typographic style can be determined from the text layout algorithms and formatting commands in effect wherever the character appears. The character code is intrinsic state, while the other information is extrinsic.

Logically there is an object for every occurrence of a given character in the document:

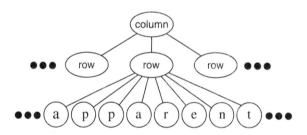

Physically, however, there is one shared flyweight object per character, and it appears in different contexts in the document structure. Each occurrence of a particular character object refers to the same instance in the shared pool of flyweight objects:

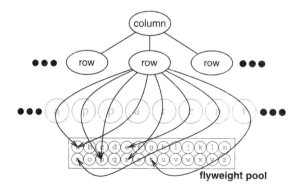

flyweight pool

The class structure for these objects is shown next. Glyph is the abstract class for graphical objects, some of which may be flyweights. Operations that may depend on extrinsic state have it passed to them as a parameter. For example, Draw and Intersects must know which context the glyph is in before they can do their job.

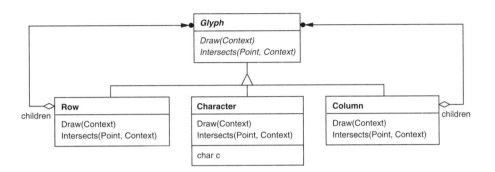

A flyweight representing the letter "a" only stores the corresponding character code; it doesn't need to store its location or font. Clients supply the context-dependent information that the flyweight needs to draw itself. For example, a Row glyph knows where its children should draw themselves so that they are tiled horizontally. Thus it can pass each child its location in the draw request.

Because the number of different character objects is far less than the number of characters in the document, the total number of objects is substantially less than what a naive implementation would use. A document in which all characters appear in the same font and color will allocate on the order of 100 character objects (roughly the size of the ASCII character set) regardless of the document's length. And since most documents use no more than 10 different font-color combinations, this number won't grow appreciably in practice. An object abstraction thus becomes practical for individual characters.

Applicability

The Flyweight pattern's effectiveness depends heavily on how and where it's used. Apply the Flyweight pattern when *all* of the following are true:

- An application uses a large number of objects.
- Storage costs are high because of the sheer quantity of objects.
- Most object state can be made extrinsic.
- Many groups of objects may be replaced by relatively few shared objects once extrinsic state is removed.
- The application doesn't depend on object identity. Since flyweight objects may be shared, identity tests will return true for conceptually distinct objects.

Structure

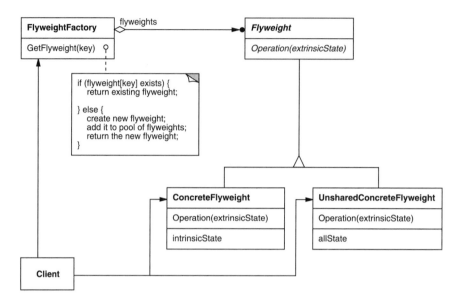

The following object diagram shows how flyweights are shared:

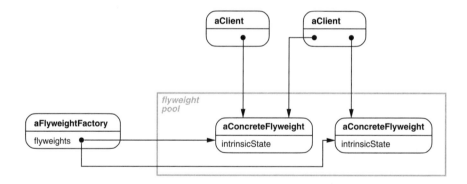

Participants

- **Flyweight** (Glyph)
    - declares an interface through which flyweights can receive and act on extrinsic state.

- **ConcreteFlyweight** (Character)

    – implements the Flyweight interface and adds storage for intrinsic state, if any. A ConcreteFlyweight object must be sharable. Any state it stores must be intrinsic; that is, it must be independent of the ConcreteFlyweight object's context.

- **UnsharedConcreteFlyweight** (Row, Column)

    – not all Flyweight subclasses need to be shared. The Flyweight interface *enables* sharing; it doesn't enforce it. It's common for UnsharedConcrete-Flyweight objects to have ConcreteFlyweight objects as children at some level in the flyweight object structure (as the Row and Column classes have).

- **FlyweightFactory**

    – creates and manages flyweight objects.

    – ensures that flyweights are shared properly. When a client requests a flyweight, the FlyweightFactory object supplies an existing instance or creates one, if none exists.

- **Client**

    – maintains a reference to flyweight(s).

    – computes or stores the extrinsic state of flyweight(s).

Collaborations

- State that a flyweight needs to function must be characterized as either intrinsic or extrinsic. Intrinsic state is stored in the ConcreteFlyweight object; extrinsic state is stored or computed by Client objects. Clients pass this state to the flyweight when they invoke its operations.

- Clients should not instantiate ConcreteFlyweights directly. Clients must obtain ConcreteFlyweight objects exclusively from the FlyweightFactory object to ensure they are shared properly.

Consequences

Flyweights may introduce run-time costs associated with transferring, finding, and/or computing extrinsic state, especially if it was formerly stored as intrinsic state. However, such costs are offset by space savings, which increase as more flyweights are shared.

Storage savings are a function of several factors:

- the reduction in the total number of instances that comes from sharing

- the amount of intrinsic state per object

- whether extrinsic state is computed or stored.

The more flyweights are shared, the greater the storage savings. The savings increase with the amount of shared state. The greatest savings occur when the objects use substantial quantities of both intrinsic and extrinsic state, and the extrinsic state can be computed rather than stored. Then you save on storage in two ways: Sharing reduces the cost of intrinsic state, and you trade extrinsic state for computation time.

The Flyweight pattern is often combined with the Composite (163) pattern to represent a hierarchical structure as a graph with shared leaf nodes. A consequence of sharing is that flyweight leaf nodes cannot store a pointer to their parent. Rather, the parent pointer is passed to the flyweight as part of its extrinsic state. This has a major impact on how the objects in the hierarchy communicate with each other.

Implementation

Consider the following issues when implementing the Flyweight pattern:

1. *Removing extrinsic state.* The pattern's applicability is determined largely by how easy it is to identify extrinsic state and remove it from shared objects. Removing extrinsic state won't help reduce storage costs if there are as many different kinds of extrinsic state as there are objects before sharing. Ideally, extrinsic state can be computed from a separate object structure, one with far smaller storage requirements.

   In our document editor, for example, we can store a map of typographic information in a separate structure rather than store the font and type style with each character object. The map keeps track of runs of characters with the same typographic attributes. When a character draws itself, it receives its typographic attributes as a side-effect of the draw traversal. Because documents normally use just a few different fonts and styles, storing this information externally to each character object is far more efficient than storing it internally.

2. *Managing shared objects.* Because objects are shared, clients shouldn't instantiate them directly. FlyweightFactory lets clients locate a particular flyweight. FlyweightFactory objects often use an associative store to let clients look up flyweights of interest. For example, the flyweight factory in the document editor example can keep a table of flyweights indexed by character codes. The manager returns the proper flyweight given its code, creating the flyweight if it does not already exist.

   Sharability also implies some form of reference counting or garbage collection to reclaim a flyweight's storage when it's no longer needed. However, neither is necessary if the number of flyweights is fixed and small (e.g., flyweights for the ASCII character set). In that case, the flyweights are worth keeping around permanently.

Sample Code

Returning to our document formatter example, we can define a Glyph base class for flyweight graphical objects. Logically, glyphs are Composites (see Composite (163)) that have graphical attributes and can draw themselves. Here we focus on just the font attribute, but the same approach can be used for any other graphical attributes a glyph might have.

```
class Glyph {
public:
    virtual ~Glyph();

    virtual void Draw(Window*, GlyphContext&);

    virtual void SetFont(Font*, GlyphContext&);
    virtual Font* GetFont(GlyphContext&);

    virtual void First(GlyphContext&);
    virtual void Next(GlyphContext&);
    virtual bool IsDone(GlyphContext&);
    virtual Glyph* Current(GlyphContext&);

    virtual void Insert(Glyph*, GlyphContext&);
    virtual void Remove(GlyphContext&);
protected:
    Glyph();
};
```

The Character subclass just stores a character code:

```
class Character : public Glyph {
public:
    Character(char);

    virtual void Draw(Window*, GlyphContext&);
private:
    char _charcode;
};
```

To keep from allocating space for a font attribute in every glyph, we'll store the attribute extrinsically in a GlyphContext object. GlyphContext acts as a repository of extrinsic state. It maintains a compact mapping between a glyph and its font (and any other graphical attributes it might have) in different contexts. Any operation that needs to know the glyph's font in a given context will have a GlyphContext instance passed to it as a parameter. The operation can then query the GlyphContext for the font in that context. The context depends on the glyph's location in the glyph structure. Therefore Glyph's child iteration and manipulation operations must update the GlyphContext whenever they're used.

```
class GlyphContext {
public:
    GlyphContext();
    virtual ~GlyphContext();

    virtual void Next(int step = 1);
    virtual void Insert(int quantity = 1);

    virtual Font* GetFont();
    virtual void SetFont(Font*, int span = 1);
private:
    int _index;
    BTree* _fonts;
};
```

GlyphContext must be kept informed of the current position in the glyph structure during traversal. GlyphContext::Next increments _index as the traversal proceeds. Glyph subclasses that have children (e.g., Row and Column) must implement Next so that it calls GlyphContext::Next at each point in the traversal.

GlyphContext::GetFont uses the index as a key into a BTree structure that stores the glyph-to-font mapping. Each node in the tree is labeled with the length of the string for which it gives font information. Leaves in the tree point to a font, while interior nodes break the string into substrings, one for each child.

Consider the following excerpt from a glyph composition:

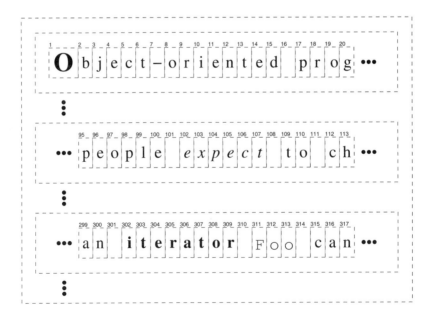

The BTree structure for font information might look like

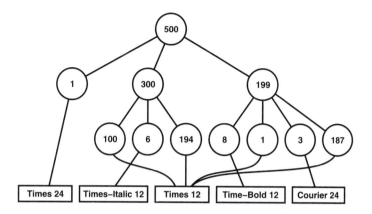

Interior nodes define ranges of glyph indices. BTree is updated in response to font changes and whenever glyphs are added to or removed from the glyph structure. For example, assuming we're at index 102 in the traversal, the following code sets the font of each character in the word "expect" to that of the surrounding text (that is, times12, an instance of Font for 12-point Times Roman):

```
GlyphContext gc;
Font* times12 = new Font("Times-Roman-12");
Font* timesItalic12 = new Font("Times-Italic-12");
// ...

gc.SetFont(times12, 6);
```

The new BTree structure (with changes shown in black) looks like

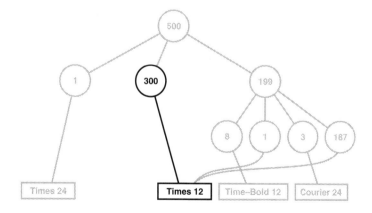

Suppose we add the word "don't " (including a trailing space) in 12-point Times Italic before "expect." The following code informs the gc of this event, assuming it is still at index 102:

```
gc.Insert(6);
gc.SetFont(timesItalic12, 6);
```

The BTree structure becomes

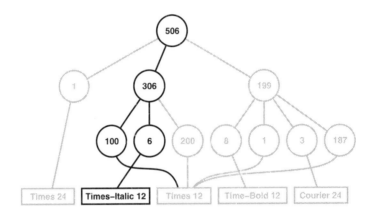

When the GlyphContext is queried for the font of the current glyph, it descends the BTree, adding up indices as it goes until it finds the font for the current index. Because the frequency of font changes is relatively low, the tree stays small relative to the size of the glyph structure. This keeps storage costs down without an inordinate increase in look-up time.[3]

The last object we need is a FlyweightFactory that creates glyphs and ensures they're shared properly. Class GlyphFactory instantiates Character and other kinds of glyphs. We only share Character objects; composite glyphs are far less plentiful, and their important state (i.e., their children) is intrinsic anyway.

```
const int NCHARCODES = 128;

class GlyphFactory {
public:
    GlyphFactory();
    virtual ~GlyphFactory();
```

---

[3] Look-up time in this scheme is proportional to the font change frequency. Worst-case performance occurs when a font change occurs on every character, but that's unusual in practice.

```
        virtual Character* CreateCharacter(char);
        virtual Row* CreateRow();
        virtual Column* CreateColumn();
        // ...
    private:
        Character* _character[NCHARCODES];
    };
```

The _character array contains pointers to Character glyphs indexed by character code. The array is initialized to zero in the constructor.

```
        GlyphFactory::GlyphFactory () {
            for (int i = 0; i < NCHARCODES; ++i) {
                _character[i] = 0;
            }
        }
```

CreateCharacter looks up a character in the character glyph in the array, and it returns the corresponding glyph if it exists. If it doesn't, then CreateCharacter creates the glyph, puts it in the array, and returns it:

```
        Character* GlyphFactory::CreateCharacter (char c) {
            if (!_character[c]) {
                _character[c] = new Character(c);
            }

            return _character[c];
        }
```

The other operations simply instantiate a new object each time they're called, since noncharacter glyphs won't be shared:

```
        Row* GlyphFactory::CreateRow () {
            return new Row;
        }


        Column* GlyphFactory::CreateColumn () {
            return new Column;
        }
```

We could omit these operations and let clients instantiate unshared glyphs directly. However, if we decide to make these glyphs sharable later, we'll have to change client code that creates them.

Known Uses

The concept of flyweight objects was first described and explored as a design technique in InterViews 3.0 [CL90]. Its developers built a powerful document editor called Doc as a proof of concept [CL92]. Doc uses glyph objects to represent each character in the document. The editor builds one Glyph instance for each character in a particular style (which defines its graphical attributes); hence a character's intrinsic state consists of the character code and its style information (an index into a style table).[4] That means only position is extrinsic, making Doc fast. Documents are represented by a class Document, which also acts as the FlyweightFactory. Measurements on Doc have shown that sharing flyweight characters is quite effective. In a typical case, a document containing 180,000 characters required allocation of only 480 character objects.

ET++ [WGM88] uses flyweights to support look-and-feel independence.[5] The look-and-feel standard affects the layout of user interface elements (e.g., scroll bars, buttons, menus—known collectively as "widgets") and their decorations (e.g., shadows, beveling). A widget delegates all its layout and drawing behavior to a separate Layout object. Changing the Layout object changes the look and feel, even at run-time.

For each widget class there is a corresponding Layout class (e.g., ScrollbarLayout, MenubarLayout, etc.). An obvious problem with this approach is that using separate layout objects doubles the number of user interface objects: For each user interface object there is an additional Layout object. To avoid this overhead, Layout objects are implemented as flyweights. They make good flyweights because they deal mostly with defining behavior, and it's easy to pass them what little extrinsic state they need to lay out or draw an object.

The Layout objects are created and managed by Look objects. The Look class is an Abstract Factory (87) that retrieves a specific Layout object with operations like GetButtonLayout, GetMenuBarLayout, and so forth. For each look-and-feel standard there is a corresponding Look subclass (e.g., MotifLook, OpenLook) that supplies the appropriate Layout objects.

By the way, Layout objects are essentially strategies (see Strategy (315)). They are an example of a strategy object implemented as a flyweight.

Related Patterns

The Flyweight pattern is often combined with the Composite (163) pattern to implement a logically hierarchical structure in terms of a directed-acyclic graph with shared leaf nodes.

It's often best to implement State (305) and Strategy (315) objects as flyweights.

---

[4] In the Sample Code given earlier, style information is made extrinsic, leaving the character code as the only intrinsic state.

[5] See Abstract Factory (87) for another approach to look-and-feel independence.

PROXY

Object Structural

Intent

Provide a surrogate or placeholder for another object to control access to it.

Also Known As

Surrogate

Motivation

One reason for controlling access to an object is to defer the full cost of its creation and initialization until we actually need to use it. Consider a document editor that can embed graphical objects in a document. Some graphical objects, like large raster images, can be expensive to create. But opening a document should be fast, so we should avoid creating all the expensive objects at once when the document is opened. This isn't necessary anyway, because not all of these objects will be visible in the document at the same time.

These constraints would suggest creating each expensive object *on demand,* which in this case occurs when an image becomes visible. But what do we put in the document in place of the image? And how can we hide the fact that the image is created on demand so that we don't complicate the editor's implementation? This optimization shouldn't impact the rendering and formatting code, for example.

The solution is to use another object, an image **proxy**, that acts as a stand-in for the real image. The proxy acts just like the image and takes care of instantiating it when it's required.

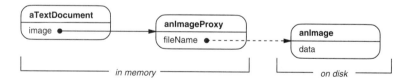

The image proxy creates the real image only when the document editor asks it to display itself by invoking its Draw operation. The proxy forwards subsequent requests directly to the image. It must therefore keep a reference to the image after creating it.

Let's assume that images are stored in separate files. In this case we can use the file name as the reference to the real object. The proxy also stores its **extent**, that is, its width and height. The extent lets the proxy respond to requests for its size from the formatter without actually instantiating the image.

The following class diagram illustrates this example in more detail.

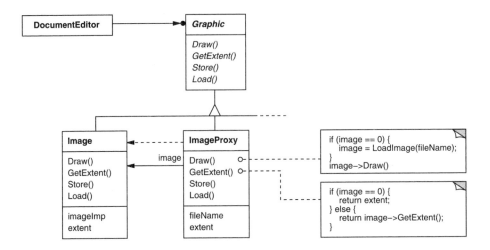

The document editor accesses embedded images through the interface defined by the abstract Graphic class. ImageProxy is a class for images that are created on demand. ImageProxy maintains the file name as a reference to the image on disk. The file name is passed as an argument to the ImageProxy constructor.

ImageProxy also stores the bounding box of the image and a reference to the real Image instance. This reference won't be valid until the proxy instantiates the real image. The Draw operation makes sure the image is instantiated before forwarding it the request. GetExtent forwards the request to the image only if it's instantiated; otherwise ImageProxy returns the extent it stores.

Applicability

Proxy is applicable whenever there is a need for a more versatile or sophisticated reference to an object than a simple pointer. Here are several common situations in which the Proxy pattern is applicable:

1. A **remote proxy** provides a local representative for an object in a different address space. NEXTSTEP [Add94] uses the class NXProxy for this purpose. Coplien [Cop92] calls this kind of proxy an "Ambassador."

2. A **virtual proxy** creates expensive objects on demand. The ImageProxy described in the Motivation is an example of such a proxy.

3. A **protection proxy** controls access to the original object. Protection proxies are useful when objects should have different access rights. For example,

KernelProxies in the Choices operating system [CIRM93] provide protected access to operating system objects.

4. A **smart reference** is a replacement for a bare pointer that performs additional actions when an object is accessed. Typical uses include

- counting the number of references to the real object so that it can be freed automatically when there are no more references (also called **smart pointers** [Ede92]).

- loading a persistent object into memory when it's first referenced.

- checking that the real object is locked before it's accessed to ensure that no other object can change it.

Structure

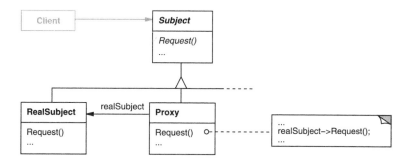

Here's a possible object diagram of a proxy structure at run-time:

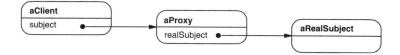

Participants

- **Proxy** (ImageProxy)

  - maintains a reference that lets the proxy access the real subject. Proxy may refer to a Subject if the RealSubject and Subject interfaces are the same.

  - provides an interface identical to Subject's so that a proxy can by substituted for the real subject.

  - controls access to the real subject and may be responsible for creating and deleting it.

      – other responsibilities depend on the kind of proxy:

- *remote proxies* are responsible for encoding a request and its arguments and for sending the encoded request to the real subject in a different address space.

- *virtual proxies* may cache additional information about the real subject so that they can postpone accessing it. For example, the ImageProxy from the Motivation caches the real image's extent.

- *protection proxies* check that the caller has the access permissions required to perform a request.

- **Subject** (Graphic)
  - defines the common interface for RealSubject and Proxy so that a Proxy can be used anywhere a RealSubject is expected.

- **RealSubject** (Image)
  - defines the real object that the proxy represents.

Collaborations

- Proxy forwards requests to RealSubject when appropriate, depending on the kind of proxy.

Consequences

The Proxy pattern introduces a level of indirection when accessing an object. The additional indirection has many uses, depending on the kind of proxy:

1. A remote proxy can hide the fact that an object resides in a different address space.

2. A virtual proxy can perform optimizations such as creating an object on demand.

3. Both protection proxies and smart references allow additional housekeeping tasks when an object is accessed.

There's another optimization that the Proxy pattern can hide from the client. It's called **copy-on-write**, and it's related to creation on demand. Copying a large and complicated object can be an expensive operation. If the copy is never modified, then there's no need to incur this cost. By using a proxy to postpone the copying process, we ensure that we pay the price of copying the object only if it's modified.

To make copy-on-write work, the subject must be reference counted. Copying the proxy will do nothing more than increment this reference count. Only when the client requests an operation that modifies the subject does the proxy actually copy it. In that case the proxy must also decrement the subject's reference count. When the reference count goes to zero, the subject gets deleted.

Copy-on-write can reduce the cost of copying heavyweight subjects significantly.

Implementation

The Proxy pattern can exploit the following language features:

1. *Overloading the member access operator in C++.* C++ supports overloading `operator->`, the member access operator. Overloading this operator lets you perform additional work whenever an object is dereferenced. This can be helpful for implementing some kinds of proxy; the proxy behaves just like a pointer.

   The following example illustrates how to use this technique to implement a virtual proxy called `ImagePtr`.

```
class Image;
extern Image* LoadAnImageFile(const char*);
    // external function

class ImagePtr {
public:
    ImagePtr(const char* imageFile);
    virtual ~ImagePtr();

    virtual Image* operator->();
    virtual Image& operator*();
private:
    Image* LoadImage();
private:
    Image* _image;
    const char* _imageFile;
};

ImagePtr::ImagePtr (const char* theImageFile) {
    _imageFile = theImageFile;
    _image = 0;
}

Image* ImagePtr::LoadImage () {
    if (_image == 0) {
        _image = LoadAnImageFile(_imageFile);
    }
    return _image;
}
```

   The overloaded `->` and `*` operators use `LoadImage` to return `_image` to callers (loading it if necessary).

```
Image* ImagePtr::operator-> () {
    return LoadImage();
}

Image& ImagePtr::operator* () {
    return *LoadImage();
}
```

This approach lets you call Image operations through ImagePtr objects without going to the trouble of making the operations part of the ImagePtr interface:

```
ImagePtr image = ImagePtr("anImageFileName");
image->Draw(Point(50, 100));
    // (image.operator->())->Draw(Point(50, 100))
```

Notice how the image proxy acts like a pointer, but it's not declared to be a pointer to an Image. That means you can't use it exactly like a real pointer to an Image. Hence clients must treat Image and ImagePtr objects differently in this approach.

Overloading the member access operator isn't a good solution for every kind of proxy. Some proxies need to know precisely *which* operation is called, and overloading the member access operator doesn't work in those cases.

Consider the virtual proxy example in the Motivation. The image should be loaded at a specific time—namely when the Draw operation is called— and not whenever the image is referenced. Overloading the access operator doesn't allow this distinction. In that case we must manually implement each proxy operation that forwards the request to the subject.

These operations are usually very similar to each other, as the Sample Code demonstrates. Typically all operations verify that the request is legal, that the original object exists, etc., before forwarding the request to the subject. It's tedious to write this code again and again. So it's common to use a preprocessor to generate it automatically.

2. *Using* doesNotUnderstand *in Smalltalk.* Smalltalk provides a hook that you can use to support automatic forwarding of requests. Smalltalk calls doesNotUnderstand: aMessage when a client sends a message to a receiver that has no corresponding method. The Proxy class can redefine doesNotUnderstand so that the message is forwarded to its subject.

To ensure that a request is forwarded to the subject and not just absorbed by the proxy silently, you can define a Proxy class that doesn't understand *any* messages. Smalltalk lets you do this by defining Proxy as a class with no superclass.[6]

The main disadvantage of doesNotUnderstand: is that most Smalltalk systems have a few special messages that are handled directly by the virtual machine, and these do not cause the usual method look-up. The only one that's usually implemented in Object (and so can affect proxies) is the identity operation ==.

If you're going to use doesNotUnderstand: to implement Proxy, then you must design around this problem. You can't expect identity on proxies to mean identity on their real subjects. An added disadvantage is that

---

[6] The implementation of distributed objects in NEXTSTEP [Add94] (specifically, the class NXProxy) uses this technique. The implementation redefines forward, the equivalent hook in NEXTSTEP.

`doesNotUnderstand:` was developed for error handling, not for building proxies, and so it's generally not very fast.

3. *Proxy doesn't always have to know the type of real subject.* If a Proxy class can deal with its subject solely through an abstract interface, then there's no need to make a Proxy class for each RealSubject class; the proxy can deal with all RealSubject classes uniformly. But if Proxies are going to instantiate RealSubjects (such as in a virtual proxy), then they have to know the concrete class.

Another implementation issue involves how to refer to the subject before it's instantiated. Some proxies have to refer to their subject whether it's on disk or in memory. That means they must use some form of address space-independent object identifiers. We used a file name for this purpose in the Motivation.

Sample Code

The following code implements two kinds of proxy: the virtual proxy described in the Motivation section, and a proxy implemented with `doesNotUnderstand:`.[7]

1. *A virtual proxy.* The `Graphic` class defines the interface for graphical objects:

```
class Graphic {
public:
    virtual ~Graphic();

    virtual void Draw(const Point& at) = 0;
    virtual void HandleMouse(Event& event) = 0;

    virtual const Point& GetExtent() = 0;

    virtual void Load(istream& from) = 0;
    virtual void Save(ostream& to) = 0;
protected:
    Graphic();
};
```

The `Image` class implements the `Graphic` interface to display image files. `Image` overrides `HandleMouse` to let users resize the image interactively.

```
class Image : public Graphic {
public:
    Image(const char* file);  // loads image from a file
    virtual ~Image();

    virtual void Draw(const Point& at);
    virtual void HandleMouse(Event& event);

    virtual const Point& GetExtent();
```

---

[7] Iterator (257) describes another kind of proxy on page 266.

```
    virtual void Load(istream& from);
    virtual void Save(ostream& to);
private:
    // ...
};
```

`ImageProxy` has the same interface as `Image`:

```
class ImageProxy : public Graphic {
public:
    ImageProxy(const char* imageFile);
    virtual ~ImageProxy();

    virtual void Draw(const Point& at);
    virtual void HandleMouse(Event& event);

    virtual const Point& GetExtent();

    virtual void Load(istream& from);
    virtual void Save(ostream& to);
protected:
    Image* GetImage();
private:
    Image* _image;
    Point _extent;
    char* _fileName;
};
```

The constructor saves a local copy of the name of the file that stores the image, and it initializes _extent and _image:

```
ImageProxy::ImageProxy (const char* fileName)  {
    _fileName = strdup(fileName);
    _extent = Point::Zero;  // don't know extent yet
    _image = 0;
}

Image* ImageProxy::GetImage() {
    if (_image == 0) {
        _image = new Image(_fileName);
    }
    return _image;
}
```

The implementation of `GetExtent` returns the cached extent if possible; otherwise the image is loaded from the file. `Draw` loads the image, and `HandleMouse` forwards the event to the real image.

```
const Point& ImageProxy::GetExtent () {
    if (_extent == Point::Zero) {
        _extent = GetImage()->GetExtent();
    }
    return _extent;
}
```

```
void ImageProxy::Draw (const Point& at) {
    GetImage()->Draw(at);
}

void ImageProxy::HandleMouse (Event& event) {
    GetImage()->HandleMouse(event);
}
```

The Save operation saves the cached image extent and the image file name to a stream. Load retrieves this information and initializes the corresponding members.

```
void ImageProxy::Save (ostream& to) {
    to << _extent << _fileName;
}

void ImageProxy::Load (istream& from) {
    from >> _extent >> _fileName;
}
```

Finally, suppose we have a class TextDocument that can contain Graphic objects:

```
class TextDocument {
public:
    TextDocument();

    void Insert(Graphic*);
    // ...
};
```

We can insert an ImageProxy into a text document like this:

```
TextDocument* text = new TextDocument;
// ...
text->Insert(new ImageProxy("anImageFileName"));
```

2. *Proxies that use* doesNotUnderstand. You can make generic proxies in Smalltalk by defining classes whose superclass is nil[8] and defining the doesNotUnderstand: method to handle messages.

The following method assumes the proxy has a realSubject method that returns its real subject. In the case of ImageProxy, this method would check to see if the the Image had been created, create it if necessary, and finally return it. It uses perform:withArguments: to perform the message being trapped on the real subject.

```
doesNotUnderstand: aMessage
    ^ self realSubject
        perform: aMessage selector
        withArguments: aMessage arguments
```

---

[8] Almost all classes ultimately have Object as their superclass. Hence this is the same as saying "defining a class that doesn't have Object as its superclass."

The argument to `doesNotUnderstand:` is an instance of `Message` that represents the message not understood by the proxy. So the proxy responds to all messages by making sure that the real subject exists before forwarding the message to it.

One of the advantages of `doesNotUnderstand:` is it can perform arbitrary processing. For example, we could produce a protection proxy by specifying a set `legalMessages` of messages to accept and then giving the proxy the following method:

```
doesNotUnderstand: aMessage
    ^ (legalMessages includes: aMessage selector)
        ifTrue: [self realSubject
            perform: aMessage selector
            withArguments: aMessage arguments]
        ifFalse: [self error: 'Illegal operator']
```

This method checks to see that a message is legal before forwarding it to the real subject. If it isn't legal, then it will send `error:` to the proxy, which will result in an infinite loop of errors unless the proxy defines `error:`. Consequently, the definition of `error:` should be copied from class Object along with any methods it uses.

Known Uses

The virtual proxy example in the Motivation section is from the ET++ text building block classes.

NEXTSTEP [Add94] uses proxies (instances of class NXProxy) as local representatives for objects that may be distributed. A server creates proxies for remote objects when clients request them. On receiving a message, the proxy encodes it along with its arguments and then forwards the encoded message to the remote subject. Similarly, the subject encodes any return results and sends them back to the NXProxy object.

McCullough [McC87] discusses using proxies in Smalltalk to access remote objects. Pascoe [Pas86] describes how to provide side-effects on method calls and access control with "Encapsulators."

Related Patterns

Adapter (139): An adapter provides a different interface to the object it adapts. In contrast, a proxy provides the same interface as its subject. However, a proxy used for access protection might refuse to perform an operation that the subject will perform, so its interface may be effectively a subset of the subject's.

Decorator (175): Although decorators can have similar implementations as proxies, decorators have a different purpose. A decorator adds one or more responsibilities to an object, whereas a proxy controls access to an object.

Proxies vary in the degree to which they are implemented like a decorator. A protection proxy might be implemented exactly like a decorator. On the other hand, a remote proxy will not contain a direct reference to its real subject but only an indirect reference, such as "host ID and local address on host." A virtual proxy will start off with an indirect reference such as a file name but will eventually obtain and use a direct reference.

Discussion of Structural Patterns

You may have noticed similarities between the structural patterns, especially in their participants and collaborations. This is so probably because structural patterns rely on the same small set of language mechanisms for structuring code and objects: single and multiple inheritance for class-based patterns, and object composition for object patterns. But the similarities belie the different intents among these patterns. In this section we compare and contrast groups of structural patterns to give you a feel for their relative merits.

Adapter versus Bridge

The Adapter (139) and Bridge (151) patterns have some common attributes. Both promote flexibility by providing a level of indirection to another object. Both involve forwarding requests to this object from an interface other than its own.

The key difference between these patterns lies in their intents. Adapter focuses on resolving incompatibilities between two existing interfaces. It doesn't focus on how those interfaces are implemented, nor does it consider how they might evolve independently. It's a way of making two independently designed classes work together without reimplementing one or the other. Bridge, on the other hand, bridges an abstraction and its (potentially numerous) implementations. It provides a stable interface to clients even as it lets you vary the classes that implement it. It also accommodates new implementations as the system evolves.

As a result of these differences, Adapter and Bridge are often used at different points in the software lifecycle. An adapter often becomes necessary when you discover that two incompatible classes should work together, generally to avoid replicating code. The coupling is unforeseen. In contrast, the user of a bridge understands up-front that an abstraction must have several implementations, and both may evolve independently. The Adapter pattern makes things work *after* they're designed; Bridge makes them work *before* they are. That doesn't mean Adapter is somehow inferior to Bridge; each pattern merely addresses a different problem.

You might think of a facade (see Facade (185)) as an adapter to a set of other objects. But that interpretation overlooks the fact that a facade defines a *new* interface, whereas an adapter reuses an old interface. Remember that an adapter makes two *existing* interfaces work together as opposed to defining an entirely new one.

Composite versus Decorator versus Proxy

Composite (163) and Decorator (175) have similar structure diagrams, reflecting the fact that both rely on recursive composition to organize an open-ended number of objects. This commonality might tempt you to think of a decorator object as a degenerate composite, but that misses the point of the Decorator pattern. The similarity ends at recursive composition, again because of differing intents.

Decorator is designed to let you add responsibilities to objects without subclassing. It avoids the explosion of subclasses that can arise from trying to cover every combination of responsibilities statically. Composite has a different intent. It focuses on structuring classes so that many related objects can be treated uniformly, and multiple objects can be treated as one. Its focus is not on embellishment but on representation.

These intents are distinct but complementary. Consequently, the Composite and Decorator patterns are often used in concert. Both lead to the kind of design in which you can build applications just by plugging objects together without defining any new classes. There will be an abstract class with some subclasses that are composites, some that are decorators, and some that implement the fundamental building blocks of the system. In this case, both composites and decorators will have a common interface. From the point of view of the Decorator pattern, a composite is a ConcreteComponent. From the point of view of the Composite pattern, a decorator is a Leaf. Of course, they don't *have* to be used together and, as we have seen, their intents are quite different.

Another pattern with a structure similar to Decorator's is Proxy (207). Both patterns describe how to provide a level of indirection to an object, and the implementations of both the proxy and decorator object keep a reference to another object to which they forward requests. Once again, however, they are intended for different purposes.

Like Decorator, the Proxy pattern composes an object and provides an identical interface to clients. Unlike Decorator, the Proxy pattern is not concerned with attaching or detaching properties dynamically, and it's not designed for recursive composition. Its intent is to provide a stand-in for a subject when it's inconvenient or undesirable to access the subject directly because, for example, it lives on a remote machine, has restricted access, or is persistent.

In the Proxy pattern, the subject defines the key functionality, and the proxy provides (or refuses) access to it. In Decorator, the component provides only part of the functionality, and one or more decorators furnish the rest. Decorator addresses the situation where an object's total functionality can't be determined at compile time, at least not conveniently. That open-endedness makes recursive composition an essential part of Decorator. That isn't the case in Proxy, because Proxy focuses on one relationship—between the proxy and its subject—and that relationship can be expressed statically.

These differences are significant because they capture solutions to specific recurring problems in object-oriented design. But that doesn't mean these patterns can't be combined. You might envision a proxy-decorator that adds functionality to a proxy, or a decorator-proxy that embellishes a remote object. Although such hybrids *might* be useful (we don't have real examples handy), they are divisible into patterns that *are* useful.

Chapter 5

Behavioral Patterns

Behavioral patterns are concerned with algorithms and the assignment of responsibilities between objects. Behavioral patterns describe not just patterns of objects or classes but also the patterns of communication between them. These patterns characterize complex control flow that's difficult to follow at run-time. They shift your focus away from flow of control to let you concentrate just on the way objects are interconnected.

Behavioral class patterns use inheritance to distribute behavior between classes. This chapter includes two such patterns. Template Method (325) is the simpler and more common of the two. A template method is an abstract definition of an algorithm. It defines the algorithm step by step. Each step invokes either an abstract operation or a primitive operation. A subclass fleshes out the algorithm by defining the abstract operations. The other behavioral class pattern is Interpreter (243), which represents a grammar as a class hierarchy and implements an interpreter as an operation on instances of these classes.

Behavioral object patterns use object composition rather than inheritance. Some describe how a group of peer objects cooperate to perform a task that no single object can carry out by itself. An important issue here is how peer objects know about each other. Peers could maintain explicit references to each other, but that would increase their coupling. In the extreme, every object would know about every other. The Mediator (273) pattern avoids this by introducing a mediator object between peers. The mediator provides the indirection needed for loose coupling.

Chain of Responsibility (223) provides even looser coupling. It lets you send requests to an object implicitly through a chain of candidate objects. Any candidate may fulfill the request depending on run-time conditions. The number of candidates is open-ended, and you can select which candidates participate in the chain at run-time.

The Observer (293) pattern defines and maintains a dependency between objects. The classic example of Observer is in Smalltalk Model/View/Controller, where all views of the model are notified whenever the model's state changes.

Other behavioral object patterns are concerned with encapsulating behavior in an object and delegating requests to it. The Strategy (315) pattern encapsulates an algorithm in an object. Strategy makes it easy to specify and change the algorithm an object uses. The Command (233) pattern encapsulates a request in an object so that it can be passed as a parameter, stored on a history list, or manipulated in other ways. The State (305) pattern encapsulates the states of an object so that the object can change its behavior when its state object changes. Visitor (331) encapsulates behavior that would otherwise be distributed across classes, and Iterator (257) abstracts the way you access and traverse objects in an aggregate.

CHAIN OF RESPONSIBILITY   Object Behavioral

Intent

Avoid coupling the sender of a request to its receiver by giving more than one object a chance to handle the request. Chain the receiving objects and pass the request along the chain until an object handles it.

Motivation

Consider a context-sensitive help facility for a graphical user interface. The user can obtain help information on any part of the interface just by clicking on it. The help that's provided depends on the part of the interface that's selected and its context; for example, a button widget in a dialog box might have different help information than a similar button in the main window. If no specific help information exists for that part of the interface, then the help system should display a more general help message about the immediate context—the dialog box as a whole, for example.

Hence it's natural to organize help information according to its generality—from the most specific to the most general. Furthermore, it's clear that a help request is handled by one of several user interface objects; which one depends on the context and how specific the available help is.

The problem here is that the object that ultimately *provides* the help isn't known explicitly to the object (e.g., the button) that *initiates* the help request. What we need is a way to decouple the button that initiates the help request from the objects that might provide help information. The Chain of Responsibility pattern defines how that happens.

The idea of this pattern is to decouple senders and receivers by giving multiple objects a chance to handle a request. The request gets passed along a chain of objects until one of them handles it.

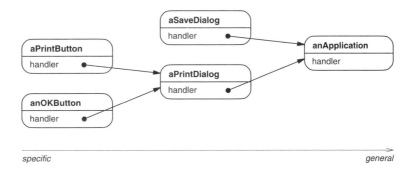

The first object in the chain receives the request and either handles it or forwards it to the next candidate on the chain, which does likewise. The object that made the request has no explicit knowledge of who will handle it—we say the request has an **implicit receiver**.

Let's assume the user clicks for help on a button widget marked "Print." The button is contained in an instance of PrintDialog, which knows the application object it belongs to (see preceding object diagram). The following interaction diagram illustrates how the help request gets forwarded along the chain:

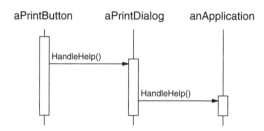

In this case, neither aPrintButton nor aPrintDialog handles the request; it stops at anApplication, which can handle it or ignore it. The client that issued the request has no direct reference to the object that ultimately fulfills it.

To forward the request along the chain, and to ensure receivers remain implicit, each object on the chain shares a common interface for handling requests and for accessing its **successor** on the chain. For example, the help system might define a HelpHandler class with a corresponding HandleHelp operation. HelpHandler can be the parent class for candidate object classes, or it can be defined as a mixin class. Then classes that want to handle help requests can make HelpHandler a parent:

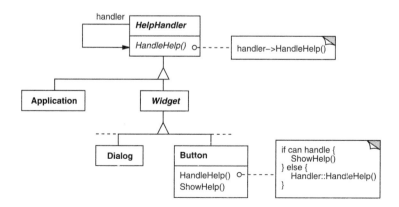

The Button, Dialog, and Application classes use HelpHandler operations to handle help requests. HelpHandler's HandleHelp operation forwards the request to the successor by default. Subclasses can override this operation to provide help under the right circumstances; otherwise they can use the default implementation to forward the request.

Applicability

Use Chain of Responsibility when

- more than one object may handle a request, and the handler isn't known *a priori*. The handler should be ascertained automatically.

- you want to issue a request to one of several objects without specifying the receiver explicitly.

- the set of objects that can handle a request should be specified dynamically.

Structure

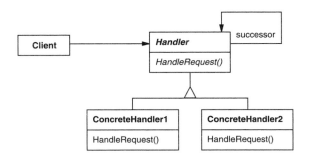

A typical object structure might look like this:

Participants

- **Handler** (HelpHandler)
  - defines an interface for handling requests.
  - (optional) implements the successor link.

- **ConcreteHandler** (PrintButton, PrintDialog)

  - handles requests it is responsible for.

  - can access its successor.

  - if the ConcreteHandler can handle the request, it does so; otherwise it forwards the request to its successor.

- **Client**

  - initiates the request to a ConcreteHandler object on the chain.

Collaborations

- When a client issues a request, the request propagates along the chain until a ConcreteHandler object takes responsibility for handling it.

Consequences

Chain of Responsibility has the following benefits and liabilities:

1. *Reduced coupling.* The pattern frees an object from knowing which other object handles a request. An object only has to know that a request will be handled "appropriately." Both the receiver and the sender have no explicit knowledge of each other, and an object in the chain doesn't have to know about the chain's structure.

   As a result, Chain of Responsibility can simplify object interconnections. Instead of objects maintaining references to all candidate receivers, they keep a single reference to their successor.

2. *Added flexibility in assigning responsibilities to objects.* Chain of Responsibility gives you added flexibility in distributing responsibilities among objects. You can add or change responsibilities for handling a request by adding to or otherwise changing the chain at run-time. You can combine this with subclassing to specialize handlers statically.

3. *Receipt isn't guaranteed.* Since a request has no explicit receiver, there's no *guarantee* it'll be handled—the request can fall off the end of the chain without ever being handled. A request can also go unhandled when the chain is not configured properly.

Implementation

Here are implementation issues to consider in Chain of Responsibility:

1. *Implementing the successor chain.* There are two possible ways to implement the successor chain:

   (a) Define new links (usually in the Handler, but ConcreteHandlers could define them instead).

(b) Use existing links.

Our examples so far define new links, but often you can use existing object references to form the successor chain. For example, parent references in a part-whole hierarchy can define a part's successor. A widget structure might already have such links. Composite (163) discusses parent references in more detail.

Using existing links works well when the links support the chain you need. It saves you from defining links explicitly, and it saves space. But if the structure doesn't reflect the chain of responsibility your application requires, then you'll have to define redundant links.

2. *Connecting successors.* If there are no preexisting references for defining a chain, then you'll have to introduce them yourself. In that case, the Handler not only defines the interface for the requests but usually maintains the successor as well. That lets the handler provide a default implementation of HandleRequest that forwards the request to the successor (if any). If a ConcreteHandler subclass isn't interested in the request, it doesn't have to override the forwarding operation, since its default implementation forwards unconditionally.

Here's a HelpHandler base class that maintains a successor link:

```
class HelpHandler {
public:
    HelpHandler(HelpHandler* s) : _successor(s) { }
    virtual void HandleHelp();
private:
    HelpHandler* _successor;
};

void HelpHandler::HandleHelp () {
    if (_successor) {
        _successor->HandleHelp();
    }
}
```

3. *Representing requests.* Different options are available for representing requests. In the simplest form, the request is a hard-coded operation invocation, as in the case of HandleHelp. This is convenient and safe, but you can forward only the fixed set of requests that the Handler class defines.

An alternative is to use a single handler function that takes a request code (e.g., an integer constant or a string) as parameter. This supports an open-ended set of requests. The only requirement is that the sender and receiver agree on how the request should be encoded.

This approach is more flexible, but it requires conditional statements for dispatching the request based on its code. Moreover, there's no type-safe way to pass parameters, so they must be packed and unpacked manually. Obviously this is less safe than invoking an operation directly.

To address the parameter-passing problem, we can use separate request *objects* that bundle request parameters. A `Request` class can represent requests explicitly, and new kinds of requests can be defined by subclassing. Subclasses can define different parameters. Handlers must know the kind of request (that is, which `Request` subclass they're using) to access these parameters.

To identify the request, `Request` can define an accessor function that returns an identifier for the class. Alternatively, the receiver can use run-time type information if the implementation languages supports it.

Here is a sketch of a dispatch function that uses request objects to identify requests. A `GetKind` operation defined in the base `Request` class identifies the kind of request:

```
void Handler::HandleRequest (Request* theRequest) {
    switch (theRequest->GetKind()) {
    case Help:
        // cast argument to appropriate type
        HandleHelp((HelpRequest*) theRequest);
        break;

    case Print:
        HandlePrint((PrintRequest*) theRequest);
        // ...
        break;

    default:
        // ...
        break;
    }
}
```

Subclasses can extend the dispatch by overriding `HandleRequest`. The subclass handles only the requests in which it's interested; other requests are forwarded to the parent class. In this way, subclasses effectively extend (rather than override) the `HandleRequest` operation. For example, here's how an `ExtendedHandler` subclass extends `Handler`'s version of `HandleRequest`:

```
class ExtendedHandler : public Handler {
public:
    virtual void HandleRequest(Request* theRequest);
    // ...
};

void ExtendedHandler::HandleRequest (Request* theRequest) {
    switch (theRequest->GetKind()) {
    case Preview:
        // handle the Preview request
        break;
```

```
        default:
            // let Handler handle other requests
            Handler::HandleRequest(theRequest);
        }
    }
```

4. *Automatic forwarding in Smalltalk.* You can use the doesNotUnderstand mechanism in Smalltalk to forward requests. Messages that have no corresponding methods are trapped in the implementation of doesNotUnderstand, which can be overridden to forward the message to an object's successor. Thus it isn't necessary to implement forwarding manually; the class handles only the request in which it's interested, and it relies on doesNotUnderstand to forward all others.

Sample Code

The following example illustrates how a chain of responsibility can handle requests for an on-line help system like the one described earlier. The help request is an explicit operation. We'll use existing parent references in the widget hierarchy to propagate requests between widgets in the chain, and we'll define a reference in the Handler class to propagate help requests between nonwidgets in the chain.

The HelpHandler class defines the interface for handling help requests. It maintains a help topic (which is empty by default) and keeps a reference to its successor on the chain of help handlers. The key operation is HandleHelp, which subclasses override. HasHelp is a convenience operation for checking whether there is an associated help topic.

```
typedef int Topic;
const Topic NO_HELP_TOPIC = -1;

class HelpHandler {
public:
    HelpHandler(HelpHandler* = 0, Topic = NO_HELP_TOPIC);
    virtual bool HasHelp();
    virtual void SetHandler(HelpHandler*, Topic);
    virtual void HandleHelp();
private:
    HelpHandler* _successor;
    Topic _topic;
};

HelpHandler::HelpHandler (
    HelpHandler* h, Topic t
) : _successor(h), _topic(t) { }

bool HelpHandler::HasHelp () {
    return _topic != NO_HELP_TOPIC;
}
```

```
void HelpHandler::HandleHelp () {
    if (_successor != 0) {
        _successor->HandleHelp();
    }
}
```

All widgets are subclasses of the `Widget` abstract class. `Widget` is a subclass of `HelpHandler`, since all user interface elements can have help associated with them. (We could have used a mixin-based implementation just as well.)

```
class Widget : public HelpHandler {
protected:
    Widget(Widget* parent, Topic t = NO_HELP_TOPIC);
private:
    Widget* _parent;
};


Widget::Widget (Widget* w, Topic t) : HelpHandler(w, t) {
    _parent = w;
}
```

In our example, a button is the first handler on the chain. The `Button` class is a subclass of `Widget`. The `Button` constructor takes two parameters: a reference to its enclosing widget and the help topic.

```
class Button : public Widget {
public:
    Button(Widget* d, Topic t = NO_HELP_TOPIC);

    virtual void HandleHelp();
    // Widget operations that Button overrides...
};
```

`Button`'s version of `HandleHelp` first tests to see if there is a help topic for buttons. If the developer hasn't defined one, then the request gets forwarded to the successor using the `HandleHelp` operation in `HelpHandler`. If there *is* a help topic, then the button displays it, and the search ends.

```
Button::Button (Widget* h, Topic t) : Widget(h, t) { }

void Button::HandleHelp () {
    if (HasHelp()) {
        // offer help on the button
    } else {
        HelpHandler::HandleHelp();
    }
}
```

`Dialog` implements a similar scheme, except that its successor is not a widget but *any* help handler. In our application this successor will be an instance of `Application`.

```
class Dialog : public Widget {
public:
    Dialog(HelpHandler* h, Topic t = NO_HELP_TOPIC);
    virtual void HandleHelp();

    // Widget operations that Dialog overrides...
    // ...
};

Dialog::Dialog (HelpHandler* h,  Topic t) : Widget(0) {
    SetHandler(h, t);
}

void Dialog::HandleHelp () {
    if (HasHelp()) {
        // offer help on the dialog
    } else {
        HelpHandler::HandleHelp();
    }
}
```

At the end of the chain is an instance of Application. The application is not
a widget, so Application is subclassed directly from HelpHandler. When a
help request propagates to this level, the application can supply information on
the application in general, or it can offer a list of different help topics:

```
class Application : public HelpHandler {
public:
    Application(Topic t) : HelpHandler(0, t) { }

    virtual void HandleHelp();
    // application-specific operations...
};

void Application::HandleHelp () {
    // show a list of help topics
}
```

The following code creates and connects these objects. Here the dialog concerns
printing, and so the objects have printing-related topics assigned.

```
const Topic PRINT_TOPIC = 1;
const Topic PAPER_ORIENTATION_TOPIC = 2;
const Topic APPLICATION_TOPIC = 3;

Application* application = new Application(APPLICATION_TOPIC);
Dialog* dialog = new Dialog(application, PRINT_TOPIC);
Button* button = new Button(dialog, PAPER_ORIENTATION_TOPIC);
```

We can invoke the help request by calling HandleHelp on any object on the chain.
To start the search at the button object, just call HandleHelp on it:

```
button->HandleHelp();
```

In this case, the button will handle the request immediately. Note that any `HelpHandler` class could be made the successor of `Dialog`. Moreover, its successor could be changed dynamically. So no matter where a dialog is used, you'll get the proper context-dependent help information for it.

Known Uses

Several class libraries use the Chain of Responsibility pattern to handle user events. They use different names for the Handler class, but the idea is the same: When the user clicks the mouse or presses a key, an event gets generated and passed along the chain. MacApp [App89] and ET++ [WGM88] call it "Event-Handler," Symantec's TCL library [Sym93b] calls it "Bureaucrat," and NeXT's AppKit [Add94] uses the name "Responder."

The Unidraw framework for graphical editors defines Command objects that encapsulate requests to Component and ComponentView objects [VL90]. Commands are requests in the sense that a component or component view may interpret a command to perform an operation. This corresponds to the "requests as objects" approach described in Implementation. Components and component views may be structured hierarchically. A component or a component view may forward command interpretation to its parent, which may in turn forward it to its parent, and so on, thereby forming a chain of responsibility.

ET++ uses Chain of Responsibility to handle graphical update. A graphical object calls the InvalidateRect operation whenever it must update a part of its appearance. A graphical object can't handle InvalidateRect by itself, because it doesn't know enough about its context. For example, a graphical object can be enclosed in objects like Scrollers or Zoomers that transform its coordinate system. That means the object might be scrolled or zoomed so that it's partially out of view. Therefore the default implementation of InvalidateRect forwards the request to the enclosing container object. The last object in the forwarding chain is a Window instance. By the time Window receives the request, the invalidation rectangle is guaranteed to be transformed properly. The Window handles InvalidateRect by notifying the window system interface and requesting an update.

Related Patterns

Chain of Responsibility is often applied in conjunction with Composite (163). There, a component's parent can act as its successor.

COMMAND   Object Behavioral

Intent

Encapsulate a request as an object, thereby letting you parameterize clients with different requests, queue or log requests, and support undoable operations.

Also Known As

Action, Transaction

Motivation

Sometimes it's necessary to issue requests to objects without knowing anything about the operation being requested or the receiver of the request. For example, user interface toolkits include objects like buttons and menus that carry out a request in response to user input. But the toolkit can't implement the request explicitly in the button or menu, because only applications that use the toolkit know what should be done on which object. As toolkit designers we have no way of knowing the receiver of the request or the operations that will carry it out.

The Command pattern lets toolkit objects make requests of unspecified application objects by turning the request itself into an object. This object can be stored and passed around like other objects. The key to this pattern is an abstract Command class, which declares an interface for executing operations. In the simplest form this interface includes an abstract Execute operation. Concrete Command subclasses specify a receiver-action pair by storing the receiver as an instance variable and by implementing Execute to invoke the request. The receiver has the knowledge required to carry out the request.

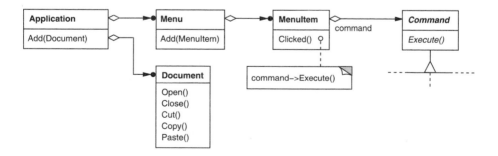

Menus can be implemented easily with Command objects. Each choice in a Menu is an instance of a MenuItem class. An Application class creates these menus and their menu items along with the rest of the user interface. The Application class also keeps track of Document objects that a user has opened.

The application configures each MenuItem with an instance of a concrete Command subclass. When the user selects a MenuItem, the MenuItem calls Execute on its command, and Execute carries out the operation. MenuItems don't know which subclass of Command they use. Command subclasses store the receiver of the request and invoke one or more operations on the receiver.

For example, PasteCommand supports pasting text from the clipboard into a Document. PasteCommand's receiver is the Document object it is supplied upon instantiation. The Execute operation invokes Paste on the receiving Document.

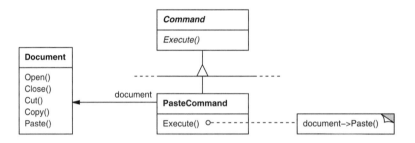

OpenCommand's Execute operation is different: it prompts the user for a document name, creates a corresponding Document object, adds the document to the receiving application, and opens the document.

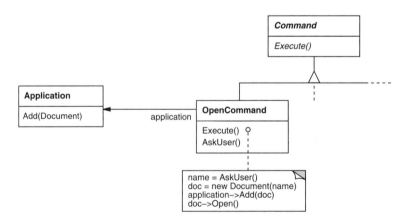

Sometimes a MenuItem needs to execute a *sequence* of commands. For example, a MenuItem for centering a page at normal size could be constructed from a CenterDocumentCommand object and a NormalSizeCommand object. Because it's common to string commands together in this way, we can define a MacroCommand class to allow a MenuItem to execute an open-ended number of commands.

MacroCommand is a concrete Command subclass that simply executes a sequence of Commands. MacroCommand has no explicit receiver, because the commands it sequences define their own receiver.

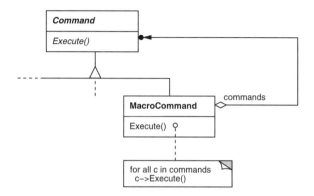

In each of these examples, notice how the Command pattern decouples the object that invokes the operation from the one having the knowledge to perform it. This gives us a lot of flexibility in designing our user interface. An application can provide both a menu and a push button interface to a feature just by making the menu and the push button share an instance of the same concrete Command subclass. We can replace commands dynamically, which would be useful for implementing context-sensitive menus. We can also support command scripting by composing commands into larger ones. All of this is possible because the object that issues a request only needs to know how to issue it; it doesn't need to know how the request will be carried out.

Applicability

Use the Command pattern when you want to

- parameterize objects by an action to perform, as MenuItem objects did above. You can express such parameterization in a procedural language with a **callback** function, that is, a function that's registered somewhere to be called at a later point. Commands are an object-oriented replacement for callbacks.

- specify, queue, and execute requests at different times. A Command object can have a lifetime independent of the original request. If the receiver of a request can be represented in an address space-independent way, then you can transfer a command object for the request to a different process and fulfill the request there.

- support undo. The Command's Execute operation can store state for reversing its effects in the command itself. The Command interface must have an added Unexecute operation that reverses the effects of a previous call to Execute. Executed commands are stored in a history list. Unlimited-level undo and redo is achieved by traversing this list backwards and forwards calling Unexecute and Execute, respectively.

- support logging changes so that they can be reapplied in case of a system crash. By augmenting the Command interface with load and store operations, you can keep a persistent log of changes. Recovering from a crash involves reloading logged commands from disk and reexecuting them with the Execute operation.

- structure a system around high-level operations built on primitives operations. Such a structure is common in information systems that support **transactions**. A transaction encapsulates a set of changes to data. The Command pattern offers a way to model transactions. Commands have a common interface, letting you invoke all transactions the same way. The pattern also makes it easy to extend the system with new transactions.

Structure

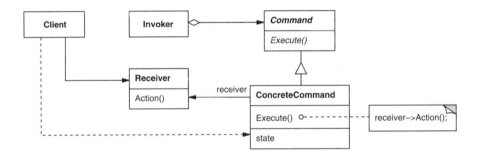

Participants

- **Command**
  - declares an interface for executing an operation.
- **ConcreteCommand** (PasteCommand, OpenCommand)
  - defines a binding between a Receiver object and an action.
  - implements Execute by invoking the corresponding operation(s) on Receiver.
- **Client** (Application)
  - creates a ConcreteCommand object and sets its receiver.
- **Invoker** (MenuItem)
  - asks the command to carry out the request.

- **Receiver** (Document, Application)
    - knows how to perform the operations associated with carrying out a request. Any class may serve as a Receiver.

Collaborations

- The client creates a ConcreteCommand object and specifies its receiver.
- An Invoker object stores the ConcreteCommand object.
- The invoker issues a request by calling Execute on the command. When commands are undoable, ConcreteCommand stores state for undoing the command prior to invoking Execute.
- The ConcreteCommand object invokes operations on its receiver to carry out the request.

The following diagram shows the interactions between these objects. It illustrates how Command decouples the invoker from the receiver (and the request it carries out).

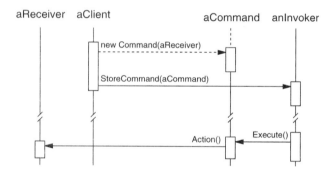

Consequences

The Command pattern has the following consequences:

1. Command decouples the object that invokes the operation from the one that knows how to perform it.

2. Commands are first-class objects. They can be manipulated and extended like any other object.

3. You can assemble commands into a composite command. An example is the MacroCommand class described earlier. In general, composite commands are an instance of the Composite (163) pattern.

4. It's easy to add new Commands, because you don't have to change existing classes.

Implementation

Consider the following issues when implementing the Command pattern:

1. *How intelligent should a command be?* A command can have a wide range of abilities. At one extreme it merely defines a binding between a receiver and the actions that carry out the request. At the other extreme it implements everything itself without delegating to a receiver at all. The latter extreme is useful when you want to define commands that are independent of existing classes, when no suitable receiver exists, or when a command knows its receiver implicitly. For example, a command that creates another application window may be just as capable of creating the window as any other object. Somewhere in between these extremes are commands that have enough knowledge to find their receiver dynamically.

2. *Supporting undo and redo.* Commands can support undo and redo capabilities if they provide a way to reverse their execution (e.g., an Unexecute or Undo operation). A ConcreteCommand class might need to store additional state to do so. This state can include

   - the Receiver object, which actually carries out operations in response to the request,

   - the arguments to the operation performed on the receiver, and

   - any original values in the receiver that can change as a result of handling the request. The receiver must provide operations that let the command return the receiver to its prior state.

   To support one level of undo, an application needs to store only the command that was executed last. For multiple-level undo and redo, the application needs a **history list** of commands that have been executed, where the maximum length of the list determines the number of undo/redo levels. The history list stores sequences of commands that have been executed. Traversing backward through the list and reverse-executing commands cancels their effect; traversing forward and executing commands reexecutes them.

   An undoable command might have to be copied before it can be placed on the history list. That's because the command object that carried out the original request, say, from a MenuItem, will perform other requests at later times. Copying is required to distinguish different invocations of the same command if its state can vary across invocations.

   For example, a DeleteCommand that deletes selected objects must store different sets of objects each time it's executed. Therefore the DeleteCommand object must be copied following execution, and the copy is placed on the history list. If the command's state never changes on execution, then copying is not required—only a reference to the command need be placed on the history list. Commands that must be copied before being placed on the history list act as prototypes (see Prototype (117)).

3. *Avoiding error accumulation in the undo process.* Hysteresis can be a problem in ensuring a reliable, semantics-preserving undo/redo mechanism. Errors can accumulate as commands are executed, unexecuted, and reexecuted repeatedly so that an application's state eventually diverges from original values. It may be necessary therefore to store more information in the command to ensure that objects are restored to their original state. The Memento (283) pattern can be applied to give the command access to this information without exposing the internals of other objects.

4. *Using C++ templates.* For commands that (1) aren't undoable and (2) don't require arguments, we can use C++ templates to avoid creating a Command subclass for every kind of action and receiver. We show how to do this in the Sample Code section.

Sample Code

The C++ code shown here sketches the implementation of the Command classes in the Motivation section. We'll define `OpenCommand`, `PasteCommand`, and `MacroCommand`. First the abstract `Command` class:

```
class Command {
public:
    virtual ~Command();

    virtual void Execute() = 0;
protected:
    Command();
};
```

`OpenCommand` opens a document whose name is supplied by the user. An `OpenCommand` must be passed an `Application` object in its constructor. `AskUser` is an implementation routine that prompts the user for the name of the document to open.

```
class OpenCommand : public Command {
public:
    OpenCommand(Application*);

    virtual void Execute();
protected:
    virtual const char* AskUser();
private:
    Application* _application;
    char* _response;
};


OpenCommand::OpenCommand (Application* a) {
    _application = a;
}
```

```
void OpenCommand::Execute () {
    const char* name = AskUser();

    if (name != 0) {
        Document* document = new Document(name);
        _application->Add(document);
        document->Open();
    }
}
```

A `PasteCommand` must be passed a `Document` object as its receiver. The receiver is given as a parameter to `PasteCommand`'s constructor.

```
class PasteCommand : public Command {
public:
    PasteCommand(Document*);

    virtual void Execute();
private:
    Document* _document;
};

PasteCommand::PasteCommand (Document* doc) {
    _document = doc;
}

void PasteCommand::Execute () {
    _document->Paste();
}
```

For simple commands that aren't undoable and don't require arguments, we can use a class template to parameterize the command's receiver. We'll define a template subclass `SimpleCommand` for such commands. `SimpleCommand` is parameterized by the `Receiver` type and maintains a binding between a receiver object and an action stored as a pointer to a member function.

```
template <class Receiver>
class SimpleCommand : public Command {
public:
    typedef void (Receiver::* Action)();

    SimpleCommand(Receiver* r, Action a) :
        _receiver(r), _action(a) { }

    virtual void Execute();
private:
    Action _action;
    Receiver* _receiver;
};
```

The constructor stores the receiver and the action in the corresponding instance variables. `Execute` simply applies the action to the receiver.

```
template <class Receiver>
void SimpleCommand<Receiver>::Execute () {
    (_receiver->*_action) ();
}
```

To create a command that calls `Action` on an instance of class `MyClass`, a client simply writes

```
MyClass* receiver = new MyClass;
// ...
Command* aCommand =
    new SimpleCommand<MyClass>(receiver, &MyClass::Action);
// ...
aCommand->Execute();
```

Keep in mind that this solution only works for simple commands. More complex commands that keep track of not only their receivers but also arguments and/or undo state require a `Command` subclass.

A `MacroCommand` manages a sequence of subcommands and provides operations for adding and removing subcommands. No explicit receiver is required, because the subcommands already define their receiver.

```
class MacroCommand : public Command {
public:
    MacroCommand();
    virtual ~MacroCommand();

    virtual void Add(Command*);
    virtual void Remove(Command*);

    virtual void Execute();
private:
    List<Command*>* _cmds;
};
```

The key to the `MacroCommand` is its `Execute` member function. This traverses all the subcommands and performs `Execute` on each of them.

```
void MacroCommand::Execute () {
    ListIterator<Command*> i(_cmds);

    for (i.First(); !i.IsDone(); i.Next()) {
        Command* c = i.CurrentItem();
        c->Execute();
    }
}
```

Note that should the `MacroCommand` implement an `Unexecute` operation, then its subcommands must be unexecuted in *reverse* order relative to `Execute`'s implementation.

Finally, `MacroCommand` must provide operations to manage its subcommands. The `MacroCommand` is also responsible for deleting its subcommands.

```
void MacroCommand::Add (Command* c) {
    _cmds->Append(c);
}

void MacroCommand::Remove (Command* c) {
    _cmds->Remove(c);
}
```

Known Uses

Perhaps the first example of the Command pattern appears in a paper by Lieberman [Lie85]. MacApp [App89] popularized the notion of commands for implementing undoable operations. ET++ [WGM88], InterViews [LCI+92], and Unidraw [VL90] also define classes that follow the Command pattern. InterViews defines an Action abstract class that provides command functionality. It also defines an ActionCallback template, parameterized by action method, that can instantiate command subclasses automatically.

The THINK class library [Sym93b] also uses commands to support undoable actions. Commands in THINK are called "Tasks." Task objects are passed along a Chain of Responsibility (223) for consumption.

Unidraw's command objects are unique in that they can behave like messages. A Unidraw command may be sent to another object for interpretation, and the result of the interpration varies with the receiving object. Moreover, the receiver may delegate the interpretation to another object, typically the receiver's parent in a larger structure as in a Chain of Responsibility. The receiver of a Unidraw command is thus computed rather than stored. Unidraw's interpretation mechanism depends on run-time type information.

Coplien describes how to implement **functors**, objects that are functions, in C++ [Cop92]. He achieves a degree of transparency in their use by overloading the function call operator (`operator()`). The Command pattern is different; its focus is on maintaining a *binding between* a receiver and a function (i.e., action), not just maintaining a function.

Related Patterns

A Composite (163) can be used to implement MacroCommands.

A Memento (283) can keep state the command requires to undo its effect.

A command that must be copied before being placed on the history list acts as a Prototype (117).

INTERPRETER   Class Behavioral

Intent

Given a language, define a represention for its grammar along with an interpreter that uses the representation to interpret sentences in the language.

Motivation

If a particular kind of problem occurs often enough, then it might be worthwhile to express instances of the problem as sentences in a simple language. Then you can build an interpreter that solves the problem by interpreting these sentences.

For example, searching for strings that match a pattern is a common problem. Regular expressions are a standard language for specifying patterns of strings. Rather than building custom algorithms to match each pattern against strings, search algorithms could interpret a regular expression that specifies a set of strings to match.

The Interpreter pattern describes how to define a grammar for simple languages, represent sentences in the language, and interpret these sentences. In this example, the pattern describes how to define a grammar for regular expressions, represent a particular regular expression, and how to interpret that regular expression.

Suppose the following grammar defines the regular expressions:

```
expression ::= literal | alternation | sequence | repetition |
               '(' expression ')'
alternation ::= expression '|' expression
sequence ::= expression '&' expression
repetition ::= expression '*'
literal ::= 'a' | 'b' | 'c' | ... { 'a' | 'b' | 'c' | ... }*
```

The symbol expression is the start symbol, and literal is a terminal symbol defining simple words.

The Interpreter pattern uses a class to represent each grammar rule. Symbols on the right-hand side of the rule are instance variables of these classes. The grammar above is represented by five classes: an abstract class RegularExpression and its four subclasses LiteralExpression, AlternationExpression, SequenceExpression, and RepetitionExpression. The last three classes define variables that hold subexpressions.

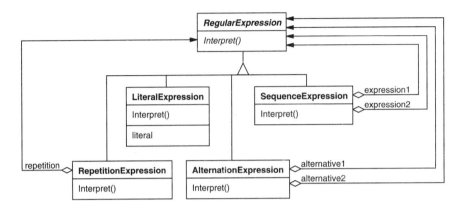

Every regular expression defined by this grammar is represented by an abstract syntax tree made up of instances of these classes. For example, the abstract syntax tree

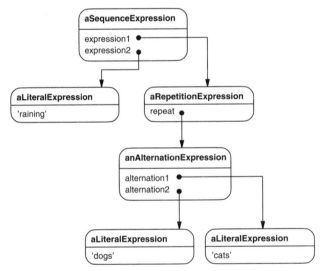

represents the regular expression

```
raining & (dogs | cats) *
```

We can create an interpreter for these regular expressions by defining the Interpret operation on each subclass of RegularExpression. Interpret takes as an argument the context in which to interpret the expression. The context contains the input string and information on how much of it has been matched so far. Each subclass of RegularExpression implements Interpret to match the next part of the input string based on the current context. For example,

- LiteralExpression will check if the input matches the literal it defines,

- AlternationExpression will check if the input matches any of its alternatives,

- RepetitionExpression will check if the input has multiple copies of expression it repeats,

and so on.

Applicability

Use the Interpreter pattern when there is a language to interpret, and you can represent statements in the language as abstract syntax trees. The Interpreter pattern works best when

- the grammar is simple. For complex grammars, the class hierarchy for the grammar becomes large and unmanageable. Tools such as parser generators are a better alternative in such cases. They can interpret expressions without building abstract syntax trees, which can save space and possibly time.

- efficiency is not a critical concern. The most efficient interpreters are usually *not* implemented by interpreting parse trees directly but by first translating them into another form. For example, regular expressions are often transformed into state machines. But even then, the *translator* can be implemented by the Interpreter pattern, so the pattern is still applicable.

Structure

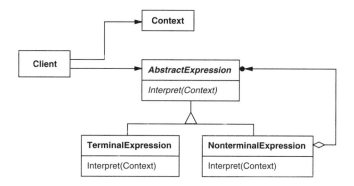

Participants

- **AbstractExpression** (RegularExpression)
  - declares an abstract Interpret operation that is common to all nodes in the abstract syntax tree.

- **TerminalExpression** (LiteralExpression)

  - implements an Interpret operation associated with terminal symbols in the grammar.

  - an instance is required for every terminal symbol in a sentence.

- **NonterminalExpression** (AlternationExpression, RepetitionExpression, SequenceExpressions)

  - one such class is required for every rule $R ::= R_1 R_2 \ldots R_n$ in the grammar.

  - maintains instance variables of type AbstractExpression for each of the symbols R_1 through R_n.

  - implements an Interpret operation for nonterminal symbols in the grammar. Interpret typically calls itself recursively on the variables representing R_1 through R_n.

- **Context**

  - contains information that's global to the interpreter.

- **Client**

  - builds (or is given) an abstract syntax tree representing a particular sentence in the language that the grammar defines. The abstract syntax tree is assembled from instances of the NonterminalExpression and TerminalExpression classes.

  - invokes the Interpret operation.

Collaborations

- The client builds (or is given) the sentence as an abstract syntax tree of NonterminalExpression and TerminalExpression instances. Then the client initializes the context and invokes the Interpret operation.

- Each NonterminalExpression node defines Interpret in terms of Interpret on each subexpression. The Interpret operation of each TerminalExpression defines the base case in the recursion.

- The Interpret operations at each node use the context to store and access the state of the interpreter.

Consequences

The Interpreter pattern has the following benefits and liabilities:

1. *It's easy to change and extend the grammar.* Because the pattern uses classes to represent grammar rules, you can use inheritance to change or extend the grammar. Existing expressions can be modified incrementally, and new expressions can be defined as variations on old ones.

2. *Implementing the grammar is easy, too.* Classes defining nodes in the abstract syntax tree have similar implementations. These classes are easy to write, and often their generation can be automated with a compiler or parser generator.

3. *Complex grammars are hard to maintain.* The Interpreter pattern defines at least one class for every rule in the grammar (grammar rules defined using BNF may require multiple classes). Hence grammars containing many rules can be hard to manage and maintain. Other design patterns can be applied to mitigate the problem (see Implementation). But when the grammar is very complex, other techniques such as parser or compiler generators are more appropriate.

4. *Adding new ways to interpret expressions.* The Interpreter pattern makes it easier to evaluate an expression in a new way. For example, you can support pretty printing or type-checking an expression by defining a new operation on the expression classes. If you keep creating new ways of interpreting an expression, then consider using the Visitor (331) pattern to avoid changing the grammar classes.

Implementation

The Interpreter and Composite (163) patterns share many implementation issues. The following issues are specific to Interpreter:

1. *Creating the abstract syntax tree.* The Interpreter pattern doesn't explain how to *create* an abstract syntax tree. In other words, it doesn't address parsing. The abstract syntax tree can be created by a table-driven parser, by a hand-crafted (usually recursive descent) parser, or directly by the client.

2. *Defining the Interpret operation.* You don't have to define the Interpret operation in the expression classes. If it's common to create a new interpreter, then it's better to use the Visitor (331) pattern to put Interpret in a separate "visitor" object. For example, a grammar for a programming language will have many operations on abstract syntax trees, such as as type-checking, optimization, code generation, and so on. It will be more likely to use a visitor to avoid defining these operations on every grammar class.

3. *Sharing terminal symbols with the Flyweight pattern.* Grammars whose sentences contain many occurrences of a terminal symbol might benefit from sharing a single copy of that symbol. Grammars for computer programs are good examples—each program variable will appear in many places throughout the code. In the Motivation example, a sentence can have the terminal symbol dog (modeled by the LiteralExpression class) appearing many times.

Terminal nodes generally don't store information about their position in the abstract syntax tree. Parent nodes pass them whatever context they need during interpretation. Hence there is a distinction between shared (intrinsic) state and passed-in (extrinsic) state, and the Flyweight (195) pattern applies.

For example, each instance of LiteralExpression for dog receives a context containing the substring matched so far. And every such LiteralExpression does the same thing in its Interpret operation—it checks whether the next part of the input contains a dog—no matter where the instance appears in the tree.

Sample Code

Here are two examples. The first is a complete example in Smalltalk for checking whether a sequence matches a regular expression. The second is a C++ program for evaluating Boolean expressions.

The regular expression matcher tests whether a string is in the language defined by the regular expression. The regular expression is defined by the following grammar:

```
expression ::= literal | alternation | sequence | repetition |
               '(' expression ')'
alternation ::= expression '|' expression
sequence ::= expression '&' expression
repetition ::= expression 'repeat'
literal ::= 'a' | 'b' | 'c' | ... { 'a' | 'b' | 'c' | ... }*
```

This grammar is a slight modification of the Motivation example. We changed the concrete syntax of regular expressions a little, because symbol "*" can't be a postfix operation in Smalltalk. So we use repeat instead. For example, the regular expression

```
(('dog ' | 'cat ') repeat & 'weather')
```

matches the input string "dog dog cat weather".

To implement the matcher, we define the five classes described on page 243. The class SequenceExpression has instance variables expression1 and expression2 for its children in the abstract syntax tree. AlternationExpression stores its alternatives in the instance variables alternative1 and alternative2, while RepetitionExpression holds the expression it repeats in its repetition instance variable. LiteralExpression has a components instance variable that holds a list of objects (probably characters). These represent the literal string that must match the input sequence.

The match: operation implements an interpreter for the regular expression. Each of the classes defining the abstract syntax tree implements this operation. It takes inputState as an argument representing the current state of the matching process, having read part of the input string.

This current state is characterized by a set of input streams representing the set of inputs that the regular expression could have accepted so far. (This is roughly equivalent to recording all states that the equivalent finite state automata would be in, having recognized the input stream to this point).

The current state is most important to the `repeat` operation. For example, if the regular expression were

```
'a' repeat
```

then the interpreter could match "a", "aa", "aaa", and so on. If it were

```
'a' repeat & 'bc'
```

then it could match "abc", "aabc", "aaabc", and so on. But if the regular expression were

```
'a' repeat & 'abc'
```

then matching the input "aabc" against the subexpression "`'a' repeat`" would yield two input streams, one having matched one character of the input, and the other having matched two characters. Only the stream that has accepted one character will match the remaining "abc".

Now we consider the definitions of `match:` for each class defining the regular expression. The definition for `SequenceExpression` matches each of its subexpressions in sequence. Usually it will eliminate input streams from its `inputState`.

```
match: inputState
    ^ expression2 match: (expression1 match: inputState).
```

An `AlternationExpression` will return a state that consists of the union of states from either alternative. The definition of `match:` for `AlternationExpression` is

```
match: inputState
    | finalState |
    finalState := alternative1 match: inputState.
    finalState addAll: (alternative2 match: inputState).
    ^ finalState
```

The `match:` operation for `RepetitionExpression` tries to find as many states that could match as possible:

```
match: inputState
    | aState finalState |
    aState := inputState.
    finalState := inputState copy.
    [aState isEmpty]
        whileFalse:
            [aState := repetition match: aState.
             finalState addAll: aState].
        ^ finalState
```

Its output state usually contains more states than its input state, because a `RepetitionExpression` can match one, two, or many occurrences of `repetition` on the input state. The output states represent all these possibilities, allowing subsequent elements of the regular expression to decide which state is the correct one.

Finally, the definition of `match:` for `LiteralExpression` tries to match its components against each possible input stream. It keeps only those input streams that have a match:

```
match: inputState
    | finalState tStream |
    finalState := Set new.
    inputState
        do:
            [:stream | tStream := stream copy.
                (tStream nextAvailable:
                    components size
                ) = components
                    ifTrue: [finalState add: tStream]
            ].
        ^ finalState
```

The `nextAvailable:` message advances the input stream. This is the only `match:` operation that advances the stream. Notice how the state that's returned contains a copy of the input stream, thereby ensuring that matching a literal never changes the input stream. This is important because each alternative of an `AlternationExpression` should see identical copies of the input stream.

Now that we've defined the classes that make up an abstract syntax tree, we can describe how to build it. Rather than write a parser for regular expressions, we'll define some operations on the `RegularExpression` classes so that evaluating a Smalltalk expression will produce an abstract syntax tree for the corresponding regular expression. That lets us use the built-in Smalltalk compiler as if it were a parser for regular expressions.

To build the abstract syntax tree, we'll need to define "|", "repeat", and "&" as operations on `RegularExpression`. These operations are defined in class `RegularExpression` like this:

```
& aNode
    ^ SequenceExpression new
        expression1: self expression2: aNode asRExp


repeat
    ^ RepetitionExpression new repetition: self
```

```
| aNode
    ^ AlternationExpression new
    alternative1: self alternative2: aNode asRExp

asRExp
    ^ self
```

The `asRExp` operation will convert literals into `RegularExpressions`. These operations are defined in class `String`:

```
& aNode
    ^ SequenceExpression new
        expression1: self asRExp expression2: aNode asRExp

repeat
    ^ RepetitionExpression new repetition: self

| aNode
    ^ AlternationExpression new
        alternative1: self asRExp alternative2: aNode asRExp

asRExp
    ^ LiteralExpression new components: self
```

If we defined these operations higher up in the class hierarchy (`Sequenceable-Collection` in Smalltalk-80, `IndexedCollection` in Smalltalk/V), then they would also be defined for classes such as `Array` and `OrderedCollection`. This would let regular expressions match sequences of any kind of object.

The second example is a system for manipulating and evaluating Boolean expressions implemented in C++. The terminal symbols in this language are Boolean variables, that is, the constants `true` and `false`. Nonterminal symbols represent expressions containing the operators `and`, `or`, and `not`. The grammar is defined as follows[1]:

```
BooleanExp ::= VariableExp | Constant | OrExp | AndExp | NotExp |
                '(' BooleanExp ')'
AndExp ::= BooleanExp 'and' BooleanExp
OrExp ::= BooleanExp 'or' BooleanExp
NotExp ::= 'not' BooleanExp
Constant ::= 'true' | 'false'
VariableExp ::= 'A' | 'B' | ... | 'X' | 'Y' | 'Z'
```

We define two operations on Boolean expressions. The first, `Evaluate`, evaluates a Boolean expression in a context that assigns a true or false value to each variable. The second operation, `Replace`, produces a new Boolean expression by replacing a variable with an expression. `Replace` shows how the Interpreter pattern can be used for more than just evaluating expressions. In this case, it manipulates the expression itself.

---

[1] For simplicity, we ignore operator precedence and assume it's the responsibility of whichever object constructs the syntax tree.

We give details of just the `BooleanExp`, `VariableExp`, and `AndExp` classes here. Classes `OrExp` and `NotExp` are similar to `AndExp`. The `Constant` class represents the Boolean constants.

`BooleanExp` defines the interface for all classes that define a Boolean expression:

```
class BooleanExp {
public:
    BooleanExp();
    virtual ~BooleanExp();

    virtual bool Evaluate(Context&) = 0;
    virtual BooleanExp* Replace(const char*, BooleanExp&) = 0;
    virtual BooleanExp* Copy() const = 0;
};
```

The class `Context` defines a mapping from variables to Boolean values, which we represent with the C++ constants `true` and `false`. `Context` has the following interface:

```
class Context {
public:
    bool Lookup(const char*) const;
    void Assign(VariableExp*, bool);
};
```

A `VariableExp` represents a named variable:

```
class VariableExp : public BooleanExp {
public:
    VariableExp(const char*);
    virtual ~VariableExp();

    virtual bool Evaluate(Context&);
    virtual BooleanExp* Replace(const char*, BooleanExp&);
    virtual BooleanExp* Copy() const;
private:
    char* _name;
};
```

The constructor takes the variable's name as an argument:

```
VariableExp::VariableExp (const char* name) {
    _name = strdup(name);
}
```

Evaluating a variable returns its value in the current context.

```
bool VariableExp::Evaluate (Context& aContext) {
    return aContext.Lookup(_name);
}
```

Copying a variable returns a new `VariableExp`:

```
BooleanExp* VariableExp::Copy () const {
    return new VariableExp(_name);
}
```

To replace a variable with an expression, we check to see if the variable has the same name as the one it is passed as an argument:

```
BooleanExp* VariableExp::Replace (
    const char* name, BooleanExp& exp
) {
    if (strcmp(name, _name) == 0) {
        return exp.Copy();
    } else {
        return new VariableExp(_name);
    }
}
```

An `AndExp` represents an expression made by ANDing two Boolean expressions together.

```
class AndExp : public BooleanExp {
public:
    AndExp(BooleanExp*, BooleanExp*);
    virtual ~AndExp();

    virtual bool Evaluate(Context&);
    virtual BooleanExp* Replace(const char*, BooleanExp&);
    virtual BooleanExp* Copy() const;
private:
    BooleanExp* _operand1;
    BooleanExp* _operand2;
};

AndExp::AndExp (BooleanExp* op1, BooleanExp* op2) {
    _operand1 = op1;
    _operand2 = op2;
}
```

Evaluating an `AndExp` evaluates its operands and returns the logical "and" of the results.

```
bool AndExp::Evaluate (Context& aContext) {
    return
        _operand1->Evaluate(aContext) &&
        _operand2->Evaluate(aContext);
}
```

An `AndExp` implements `Copy` and `Replace` by making recursive calls on its operands:

```
BooleanExp* AndExp::Copy () const {
    return
        new AndExp(_operand1->Copy(), _operand2->Copy());
}

BooleanExp* AndExp::Replace (const char* name, BooleanExp& exp) {
    return
        new AndExp(
            _operand1->Replace(name, exp),
            _operand2->Replace(name, exp)
        );
}
```

Now we can define the Boolean expression

```
(true and x) or (y and (not x))
```

and evaluate it for a given assignment of `true` or `false` to the variables `x` and `y`:

```
BooleanExp* expression;
Context context;

VariableExp* x = new VariableExp("X");
VariableExp* y = new VariableExp("Y");

expression = new OrExp(
    new AndExp(new Constant(true), x),
    new AndExp(y, new NotExp(x))
);

context.Assign(x, false);
context.Assign(y, true);

bool result = expression->Evaluate(context);
```

The expression evaluates to `true` for this assignment to `x` and `y`. We can evaluate the expression with a different assignment to the variables simply by changing the context.

Finally, we can replace the variable `y` with a new expression and then reevaluate it:

```
VariableExp* z = new VariableExp("Z");
NotExp not_z(z);

BooleanExp* replacement = expression->Replace("Y", not_z);

context.Assign(z, true);

result = replacement->Evaluate(context);
```

This example illustrates an important point about the Interpreter pattern: many kinds of operations can "interpret" a sentence. Of the three operations defined for `BooleanExp`, `Evaluate` fits our idea of what an interpreter should do most closely—that is, it interprets a program or expression and returns a simple result.

However, `Replace` can be viewed as an interpreter as well. It's an interpreter whose context is the name of the variable being replaced along with the expression that replaces it, and whose result is a new expression. Even `Copy` can be thought of as an interpreter with an empty context. It may seem a little strange to consider `Replace` and `Copy` to be interpreters, because these are just basic operations on trees. The examples in Visitor (331) illustrate how all three operations can be refactored into a separate "interpreter" visitor, thus showing that the similarity is deep.

The Interpreter pattern is more than just an operation distributed over a class hierarchy that uses the Composite (163) pattern. We consider `Evaluate` an interpreter because we think of the `BooleanExp` class hierarchy as representing a language. Given a similar class hierarchy for representing automotive part assemblies, it's unlikely we'd consider operations like `Weight` and `Copy` as interpreters even though they are distributed over a class hierarchy that uses the Composite pattern—we just don't think of automotive parts as a language. It's a matter of perspective; if we started publishing grammars of automotive parts, then we could consider operations on those parts to be ways of interpreting the language.

Known Uses

The Interpreter pattern is widely used in compilers implemented with object-oriented languages, as the Smalltalk compilers are. SPECTalk uses the pattern to interpret descriptions of input file formats [Sza92]. The QOCA constraint-solving toolkit uses it to evaluate constraints [HHMV92].

Considered in its most general form (i.e., an operation distributed over a class hierarchy based on the Composite pattern), nearly every use of the Composite pattern will also contain the Interpreter pattern. But the Interpreter pattern should be reserved for those cases in which you want to think of the class hierarchy as defining a language.

Related Patterns

Composite (163): The abstract syntax tree is an instance of the Composite pattern.

Flyweight (195) shows how to share terminal symbols within the abstract syntax tree.

Iterator (257): The interpreter can use an Iterator to traverse the structure.

Visitor (331) can be used to maintain the behavior in each node in the abstract syntax tree in one class.

ITERATOR   Object Behavioral

Intent

Provide a way to access the elements of an aggregate object sequentially without exposing its underlying representation.

Also Known As

Cursor

Motivation

An aggregate object such as a list should give you a way to access its elements without exposing its internal structure. Moreover, you might want to traverse the list in different ways, depending on what you want to accomplish. But you probably don't want to bloat the List interface with operations for different traversals, even if you could anticipate the ones you will need. You might also need to have more than one traversal pending on the same list.

The Iterator pattern lets you do all this. The key idea in this pattern is to take the responsibility for access and traversal out of the list object and put it into an **iterator** object. The Iterator class defines an interface for accessing the list's elements. An iterator object is responsible for keeping track of the current element; that is, it knows which elements have been traversed already.

For example, a List class would call for a ListIterator with the following relationship between them:

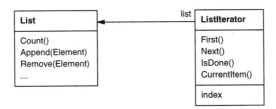

Before you can instantiate ListIterator, you must supply the List to traverse. Once you have the ListIterator instance, you can access the list's elements sequentially. The CurrentItem operation returns the current element in the list, First initializes the current element to the first element, Next advances the current element to the next element, and IsDone tests whether we've advanced beyond the last element—that is, we're finished with the traversal.

Separating the traversal mechanism from the List object lets us define iterators for different traversal policies without enumerating them in the List interface. For example, FilteringListIterator might provide access only to those elements that satisfy specific filtering constraints.

Notice that the iterator and the list are coupled, and the client must know that it is a *list* that's traversed as opposed to some other aggregate structure. Hence the client commits to a particular aggregate structure. It would be better if we could change the aggregate class without changing client code. We can do this by generalizing the iterator concept to support **polymorphic iteration**.

As an example, let's assume that we also have a SkipList implementation of a list. A skiplist [Pug90] is a probabilistic data structure with characteristics similar to balanced trees. We want to be able to write code that works for both List and SkipList objects.

We define an AbstractList class that provides a common interface for manipulating lists. Similarly, we need an abstract Iterator class that defines a common iteration interface. Then we can define concrete Iterator subclasses for the different list implementations. As a result, the iteration mechanism becomes independent of concrete aggregate classes.

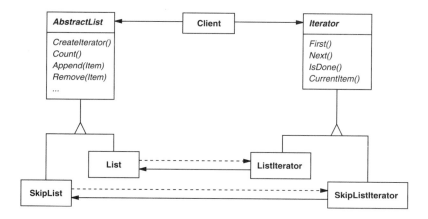

The remaining problem is how to create the iterator. Since we want to write code that's independent of the concrete List subclasses, we cannot simply instantiate a specific class. Instead, we make the list objects responsible for creating their corresponding iterator. This requires an operation like CreateIterator through which clients request an iterator object.

CreateIterator is an example of a factory method (see Factory Method (107)). We use it here to let a client ask a list object for the appropriate iterator. The Factory Method approach give rise to two class hierarchies, one for lists and another for iterators. The CreateIterator factory method "connects" the two hierarchies.

Applicability

Use the Iterator pattern

- to access an aggregate object's contents without exposing its internal representation.
- to support multiple traversals of aggregate objects.
- to provide a uniform interface for traversing different aggregate structures (that is, to support polymorphic iteration).

Structure

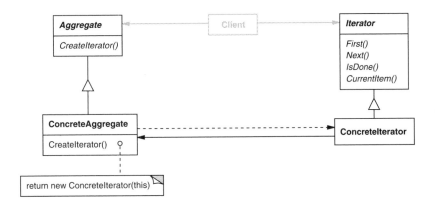

Participants

- **Iterator**
  - defines an interface for accessing and traversing elements.
- **ConcreteIterator**
  - implements the Iterator interface.
  - keeps track of the current position in the traversal of the aggregate.
- **Aggregate**
  - defines an interface for creating an Iterator object.
- **ConcreteAggregate**
  - implements the Iterator creation interface to return an instance of the proper ConcreteIterator.

Collaborations

- A ConcreteIterator keeps track of the current object in the aggregate and can compute the succeeding object in the traversal.

Consequences

The Iterator pattern has three important consequences:

1. *It supports variations in the traversal of an aggregate.* Complex aggregates may be traversed in many ways. For example, code generation and semantic checking involve traversing parse trees. Code generation may traverse the parse tree inorder or preorder. Iterators make it easy to change the traversal algorithm: Just replace the iterator instance with a different one. You can also define Iterator subclasses to support new traversals.

2. *Iterators simplify the Aggregate interface.* Iterator's traversal interface obviates the need for a similar interface in Aggregate, thereby simplifying the aggregate's interface.

3. *More than one traversal can be pending on an aggregate.* An iterator keeps track of its own traversal state. Therefore you can have more than one traversal in progress at once.

Implementation

Iterator has many implementation variants and alternatives. Some important ones follow. The trade-offs often depend on the control structures your language provides. Some languages (CLU [LG86], for example) even support this pattern directly.

1. *Who controls the iteration?* A fundamental issue is deciding which party controls the iteration, the iterator or the client that uses the iterator. When the client controls the iteration, the iterator is called an **external iterator**, and when the iterator controls it, the iterator is an **internal iterator**.[2] Clients that use an external iterator must advance the traversal and request the next element explicitly from the iterator. In contrast, the client hands an internal iterator an operation to perform, and the iterator applies that operation to every element in the aggregate.

   External iterators are more flexible than internal iterators. It's easy to compare two collections for equality with an external iterator, for example, but it's practically impossible with internal iterators. Internal iterators are especially weak in a language like C++ that does not provide anonymous functions, closures, or continuations like Smalltalk and CLOS. But on the other hand,

---

[2] Booch refers to external and internal iterators as **active** and **passive** iterators, respectively [Boo94]. The terms "active" and "passive" describe the role of the client, not the level of activity in the iterator.

ITERATOR   261

internal iterators are easier to use, because they define the iteration logic for you.

2. *Who defines the traversal algorithm?* The iterator is not the only place where the traversal algorithm can be defined. The aggregate might define the traversal algorithm and use the iterator to store just the state of the iteration. We call this kind of iterator a **cursor**, since it merely points to the current position in the aggregate. A client will invoke the Next operation on the aggregate with the cursor as an argument, and the Next operation will change the state of the cursor.[3]

   If the iterator is responsible for the traversal algorithm, then it's easy to use different iteration algorithms on the same aggregate, and it can also be easier to reuse the same algorithm on different aggregates. On the other hand, the traversal algorithm might need to access the private variables of the aggregate. If so, putting the traversal algorithm in the iterator violates the encapsulation of the aggregate.

3. *How robust is the iterator?* It can be dangerous to modify an aggregate while you're traversing it. If elements are added or deleted from the aggregate, you might end up accessing an element twice or missing it completely. A simple solution is to copy the aggregate and traverse the copy, but that's too expensive to do in general.

   A **robust iterator** ensures that insertions and removals won't interfere with traversal, and it does it without copying the aggregate. There are many ways to implement robust iterators. Most rely on registering the iterator with the aggregate. On insertion or removal, the aggregate either adjusts the internal state of iterators it has produced, or it maintains information internally to ensure proper traversal.

   Kofler provides a good discussion of how robust iterators are implemented in ET++ [Kof93]. Murray discusses the implementation of robust iterators for the USL StandardComponents' List class [Mur93].

4. *Additional Iterator operations.* The minimal interface to Iterator consists of the operations First, Next, IsDone, and CurrentItem.[4] Some additional operations might prove useful. For example, ordered aggregates can have a Previous operation that positions the iterator to the previous element. A SkipTo operation is useful for sorted or indexed collections. SkipTo positions the iterator to an object matching specific criteria.

5. *Using polymorphic iterators in C++.* Polymorphic iterators have their cost. They require the iterator object to be allocated dynamically by a factory method. Hence they should be used only when there's a need for polymorphism. Otherwise use concrete iterators, which can be allocated on the stack.

---

[3] Cursors are a simple example of the Memento (283) pattern and share many of its implementation issues.
[4] We can make this interface even *smaller* by merging Next, IsDone, and CurrentItem into a single operation that advances to the next object and returns it. If the traversal is finished, then this operation returns a special value (0, for instance) that marks the end of the iteration.

Polymorphic iterators have another drawback: the client is responsible for deleting them. This is error-prone, because it's easy to forget to free a heap-allocated iterator object when you're finished with it. That's especially likely when there are multiple exit points in an operation. And if an exception is triggered, the iterator object will never be freed.

The Proxy (207) pattern provides a remedy. We can use a stack-allocated proxy as a stand-in for the real iterator. The proxy deletes the iterator in its destructor. Thus when the proxy goes out of scope, the real iterator will get deallocated along with it. The proxy ensures proper cleanup, even in the face of exceptions. This is an application of the well-known C++ technique "resource allocation is initialization" [ES90]. The Sample Code gives an example.

6. *Iterators may have privileged access.* An iterator can be viewed as an extension of the aggregate that created it. The iterator and the aggregate are tightly coupled. We can express this close relationship in C++ by making the iterator a `friend` of its aggregate. Then you don't need to define aggregate operations whose sole purpose is to let iterators implement traversal efficiently.

However, such privileged access can make defining new traversals difficult, since it'll require changing the aggregate interface to add another friend. To avoid this problem, the Iterator class can include `protected` operations for accessing important but publicly unavailable members of the aggregate. Iterator subclasses (and *only* Iterator subclasses) may use these protected operations to gain privileged access to the aggregate.

7. *Iterators for composites.* External iterators can be difficult to implement over recursive aggregate structures like those in the Composite (163) pattern, because a position in the structure may span many levels of nested aggregates. Therefore an external iterator has to store a path through the Composite to keep track of the current object. Sometimes it's easier just to use an internal iterator. It can record the current position simply by calling itself recursively, thereby storing the path implicitly in the call stack.

If the nodes in a Composite have an interface for moving from a node to its siblings, parents, and children, then a cursor-based iterator may offer a better alternative. The cursor only needs to keep track of the current node; it can rely on the node interface to traverse the Composite.

Composites often need to be traversed in more than one way. Preorder, postorder, inorder, and breadth-first traversals are common. You can support each kind of traversal with a different class of iterator.

8. *Null iterators.* A **NullIterator** is a degenerate iterator that's helpful for handling boundary conditions. By definition, a NullIterator is *always* done with traversal; that is, its IsDone operation always evaluates to true.

NullIterator can make traversing tree-structured aggregates (like Composites) easier. At each point in the traversal, we ask the current element for an iterator for its children. Aggregate elements return a concrete iterator as usual. But leaf elements return an instance of NullIterator. That lets us implement traversal over the entire structure in a uniform way.

Sample Code

We'll look at the implementation of a simple List class, which is part of our foundation library (Appendix C). We'll show two Iterator implementations, one for traversing the List in front-to-back order, and another for traversing back-to-front (the foundation library supports only the first one). Then we show how to use these iterators and how to avoid committing to a particular implementation. After that, we change the design to make sure iterators get deleted properly. The last example illustrates an internal iterator and compares it to its external counterpart.

1. *List and Iterator interfaces.* First let's look at the part of the List interface that's relevant to implementing iterators. Refer to Appendix C for the full interface.

```
template <class Item>
class List {
public:
    List(long size = DEFAULT_LIST_CAPACITY);

    long Count() const;
    Item& Get(long index) const;
    // ...
};
```

The List class provides a reasonably efficient way to support iteration through its public interface. It's sufficient to implement both traversals. So there's no need to give iterators privileged access to the underlying data structure; that is, the iterator classes are not friends of List. To enable transparent use of the different traversals we define an abstract Iterator class, which defines the iterator interface.

```
template <class Item>
class Iterator {
public:
    virtual void First() = 0;
    virtual void Next() = 0;
    virtual bool IsDone() const = 0;
    virtual Item CurrentItem() const = 0;
protected:
    Iterator();
};
```

2. *Iterator subclass implementations.* ListIterator is a subclass of Iterator.

```
template <class Item>
class ListIterator : public Iterator<Item> {
public:
    ListIterator(const List<Item>* aList);
    virtual void First();
    virtual void Next();
    virtual bool IsDone() const;
    virtual Item CurrentItem() const;

private:
    const List<Item>* _list;
    long _current;
};
```

The implementation of ListIterator is straightforward. It stores the List along with an index _current into the list:

```
template <class Item>
ListIterator<Item>::ListIterator (
    const List<Item>* aList
) : _list(aList), _current(0) {
}
```

First positions the iterator to the first element:

```
template <class Item>
void ListIterator<Item>::First () {
    _current = 0;
}
```

Next advances the current element:

```
template <class Item>
void ListIterator<Item>::Next () {
    _current++;
}
```

IsDone checks whether the index refers to an element within the List:

```
template <class Item>
bool ListIterator<Item>::IsDone () const {
    return _current >= _list->Count();
}
```

Finally, CurrentItem returns the item at the current index. If the iteration has already terminated, then we throw an IteratorOutOfBounds exception:

```
template <class Item>
Item ListIterator<Item>::CurrentItem () const {
    if (IsDone()) {
        throw IteratorOutOfBounds;
    }
    return _list->Get(_current);
}
```

The implementation of ReverseListIterator is identical, except its `First` operation positions `_current` to the end of the list, and `Next` decrements `_current` toward the first item.

3. *Using the iterators.* Let's assume we have a `List` of `Employee` objects, and we would like to print all the contained employees. The `Employee` class supports this with a `Print` operation. To print the list, we define a `PrintEmployees` operation that takes an iterator as an argument. It uses the iterator to traverse and print the list.

```
void PrintEmployees (Iterator<Employee*>& i) {
    for (i.First(); !i.IsDone(); i.Next()) {
        i.CurrentItem()->Print();
    }
}
```

Since we have iterators for both back-to-front and front-to-back traversals, we can reuse this operation to print the employees in both orders.

```
List<Employee*>* employees;
// ...
ListIterator<Employee*> forward(employees);
ReverseListIterator<Employee*> backward(employees);

PrintEmployees(forward);
PrintEmployees(backward);
```

4. *Avoiding commitment to a specific list implementation.* Let's consider how a skiplist variation of `List` would affect our iteration code. A `SkipList` subclass of `List` must provide a `SkipListIterator` that implements the `Iterator` interface. Internally, the `SkipListIterator` has to keep more than just an index to do the iteration efficiently. But since `SkipListIterator` conforms to the `Iterator` interface, the `PrintEmployees` operation can also be used when the employees are stored in a `SkipList` object.

```
SkipList<Employee*>* employees;
// ...

SkipListIterator<Employee*> iterator(employees);
PrintEmployees(iterator);
```

Although this approach works, it would be better if we didn't have to commit to a specific `List` implementation, namely `SkipList`. We can introduce an `AbstractList` class to standardize the list interface for different list implementations. `List` and `SkipList` become subclasses of `AbstractList`.

To enable polymorphic iteration, `AbstractList` defines a factory method `CreateIterator`, which subclasses override to return their corresponding iterator:

```
template <class Item>
class AbstractList {
public:
    virtual Iterator<Item>* CreateIterator() const = 0;
    // ...
};
```

An alternative would be to define a general mixin class `Traversable` that defines the interface for creating an iterator. Aggregate classes can mix in `Traversable` to support polymorphic iteration.

`List` overrides `CreateIterator` to return a `ListIterator` object:

```
template <class Item>
Iterator<Item>* List<Item>::CreateIterator () const {
    return new ListIterator<Item>(this);
}
```

Now we're in a position to write the code for printing the employees independent of a concrete representation.

```
// we know only that we have an AbstractList
AbstractList<Employee*>* employees;
// ...

Iterator<Employee*>* iterator = employees->CreateIterator();
PrintEmployees(*iterator);
delete iterator;
```

5. *Making sure iterators get deleted.* Notice that `CreateIterator` returns a newly allocated iterator object. We're responsible for deleting it. If we forget, then we've created a storage leak. To make life easier for clients, we'll provide an `IteratorPtr` that acts as a proxy for an iterator. It takes care of cleaning up the `Iterator` object when it goes out of scope.

`IteratorPtr` is always allocated on the stack.[5] C++ automatically takes care of calling its destructor, which deletes the real iterator. `IteratorPtr` overloads both `operator->` and `operator*` in such a way that an `IteratorPtr` can be treated just like a pointer to an iterator. The members of `IteratorPtr` are all implemented inline; thus they can incur no overhead.

```
template <class Item>
class IteratorPtr {
public:
    IteratorPtr(Iterator<Item>* i): _i(i) { }
    ~IteratorPtr() { delete _i; }
```

---

[5] You can ensure this at compile-time just by declaring private `new` and `delete` operators. An accompanying implementation isn't needed.

```
            Iterator<Item>* operator->() { return _i; }
            Iterator<Item>& operator*() { return *_i; }
        private:
            // disallow copy and assignment to avoid
            // multiple deletions of _i:

            IteratorPtr(const IteratorPtr&);
            IteratorPtr& operator=(const IteratorPtr&);
        private:
            Iterator<Item>* _i;
        };
```

`IteratorPtr` lets us simplify our printing code:

```
        AbstractList<Employee*>* employees;
        // ...

        IteratorPtr<Employee*> iterator(employees->CreateIterator());
        PrintEmployees(*iterator);
```

6. *An internal ListIterator.* As a final example, let's look at a possible implementation of an internal or passive `ListIterator` class. Here the iterator controls the iteration, and it applies an operation to each element.

   The issue in this case is how to parameterize the iterator with the operation we want to perform on each element. C++ does not support anonymous functions or closures that other languages provide for this task. There are at least two options: (1) Pass in a pointer to a function (global or static), or (2) rely on subclassing. In the first case, the iterator calls the operation passed to it at each point in the iteration. In the second case, the iterator calls an operation that a subclass overrides to enact specific behavior.

   Neither option is perfect. Often you want to accumulate state during the iteration, and functions aren't well-suited to that; we would have to use static variables to remember the state. An `Iterator` subclass provides us with a convenient place to store the accumulated state, like in an instance variable. But creating a subclass for every different traversal is more work.

   Here's a sketch of the second option, which uses subclassing. We call the internal iterator a `ListTraverser`.

```
        template <class Item>
        class ListTraverser {
        public:
            ListTraverser(List<Item>* aList);
            bool Traverse();
        protected:
            virtual bool ProcessItem(const Item&) = 0;
        private:
            ListIterator<Item> _iterator;
        };
```

`ListTraverser` takes a `List` instance as a parameter. Internally it uses an external `ListIterator` to do the traversal. `Traverse` starts the traversal and calls `ProcessItem` for each item. The internal iterator can choose to terminate a traversal by returning `false` from `ProcessItem`. `Traverse` returns whether the traversal terminated prematurely.

```
template <class Item>
ListTraverser<Item>::ListTraverser (
    List<Item>* aList
) : _iterator(aList) { }

template <class Item>
bool ListTraverser<Item>::Traverse () {
    bool result = false;

    for (
        _iterator.First();
        !_iterator.IsDone();
        _iterator.Next()
    ) {
        result = ProcessItem(_iterator.CurrentItem());

        if (result == false) {
            break;
        }
    }
    return result;
}
```

Let's use a `ListTraverser` to print the first 10 employees from our employee list. To do it we have to subclass `ListTraverser` and override `ProcessItem`. We count the number of printed employees in a `_count` instance variable.

```
class PrintNEmployees : public ListTraverser<Employee*> {
public:
    PrintNEmployees(List<Employee*>* aList, int n) :
        ListTraverser<Employee*>(aList),
        _total(n), _count(0) { }

protected:
    bool ProcessItem(Employee* const&);
private:
    int _total;
    int _count;
};

bool PrintNEmployees::ProcessItem (Employee* const& e) {
    _count++;
    e->Print();
    return _count < _total;
}
```

Here's how `PrintNEmployees` prints the first 10 employees on the list:

```
List<Employee*>* employees;
// ...

PrintNEmployees pa(employees, 10);
pa.Traverse();
```

Note how the client doesn't specify the iteration loop. The entire iteration logic can be reused. This is the primary benefit of an internal iterator. It's a bit more work than an external iterator, though, because we have to define a new class. Contrast this with using an external iterator:

```
ListIterator<Employee*> i(employees);
int count = 0;

for (i.First(); !i.IsDone(); i.Next()) {
    count++;
    i.CurrentItem()->Print();

    if (count >= 10) {
        break;
    }
}
```

Internal iterators can encapsulate different kinds of iteration. For example, `FilteringListTraverser` encapsulates an iteration that processes only items that satisfy a test:

```
template <class Item>
class FilteringListTraverser {
public:
    FilteringListTraverser(List<Item>* aList);
    bool Traverse();
protected:
    virtual bool ProcessItem(const Item&) = 0;
    virtual bool TestItem(const Item&) = 0;
private:
    ListIterator<Item> _iterator;
};
```

This interface is the same as `ListTraverser`'s except for an added `TestItem` member function that defines the test. Subclasses override `TestItem` to specify the test.

`Traverse` decides to continue the traversal based on the outcome of the test:

```
template <class Item>
void FilteringListTraverser<Item>::Traverse () {
    bool result = false;

    for (
        _iterator.First();
        !_iterator.IsDone();
        _iterator.Next()
    ) {
        if (TestItem(_iterator.CurrentItem())) {
            result = ProcessItem(_iterator.CurrentItem());
```

```
                    if (result == false) {
                        break;
                    }
                }
            }
            return result;
        }
```

A variant of this class could define `Traverse` to return if at least one item satisfies the test.[6]

Known Uses

Iterators are common in object-oriented systems. Most collection class libraries offer iterators in one form or another.

Here's an example from the Booch components [Boo94], a popular collection class library. It provides both a fixed size (bounded) and dynamically growing (unbounded) implementation of a queue. The queue interface is defined by an abstract Queue class. To support polymorphic iteration over the different queue implementations, the queue iterator is implemented in the terms of the abstract Queue class interface. This variation has the advantage that you don't need a factory method to ask the queue implementations for their appropriate iterator. However, it requires the interface of the abstract Queue class to be powerful enough to implement the iterator efficiently.

Iterators don't have to be defined as explicitly in Smalltalk. The standard collection classes (Bag, Set, Dictionary, OrderedCollection, String, etc.) define an internal iterator method `do:`, which takes a block (i.e., closure) as an argument. Each element in the collection is bound to the local variable in the block; then the block is executed. Smalltalk also includes a set of Stream classes that support an iterator-like interface. ReadStream is essentially an Iterator, and it can act as an external iterator for all the sequential collections. There are no standard external iterators for nonsequential collections such as Set and Dictionary.

Polymorphic iterators and the cleanup Proxy described earlier are provided by the ET++ container classes [WGM88]. The Unidraw graphical editing framework classes use cursor-based iterators [VL90].

ObjectWindows 2.0 [Bor94] provides a class hierarchy of iterators for containers. You can iterate over different container types in the same way. The ObjectWindow iteration syntax relies on overloading the postincrement operator ++ to advance the iteration.

Related Patterns

Composite (163): Iterators are often applied to recursive structures such as Composites.

---

[6] The `Traverse` operation in these examples is a Template Method (325) with primitive operations `TestItem` and `ProcessItem`.

Factory Method (107): Polymorphic iterators rely on factory methods to instantiate the appropriate Iterator subclass.

Memento (283) is often used in conjunction with the Iterator pattern. An iterator can use a memento to capture the state of an iteration. The iterator stores the memento internally.

MEDIATOR

Object Behavioral

Intent

Define an object that encapsulates how a set of objects interact. Mediator promotes loose coupling by keeping objects from referring to each other explicitly, and it lets you vary their interaction independently.

Motivation

Object-oriented design encourages the distribution of behavior among objects. Such distribution can result in an object structure with many connections between objects; in the worst case, every object ends up knowing about every other.

Though partitioning a system into many objects generally enhances reusability, proliferating interconnections tend to reduce it again. Lots of interconnections make it less likely that an object can work without the support of others—the system acts as though it were monolithic. Moreover, it can be difficult to change the system's behavior in any significant way, since behavior is distributed among many objects. As a result, you may be forced to define many subclasses to customize the system's behavior.

As an example, consider the implementation of dialog boxes in a graphical user interface. A dialog box uses a window to present a collection of widgets such as buttons, menus, and entry fields, as shown here:

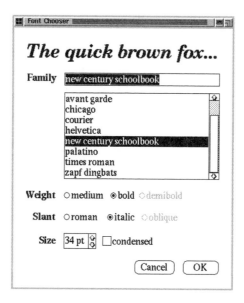

Often there are dependencies between the widgets in the dialog. For example, a button gets disabled when a certain entry field is empty. Selecting an entry in a list of choices called a **list box** might change the contents of an entry field. Conversely, typing text into the entry field might automatically select one or more corresponding entries in the list box. Once text appears in the entry field, other buttons may become enabled that let the user do something with the text, such as changing or deleting the thing to which it refers.

Different dialog boxes will have different dependencies between widgets. So even though dialogs display the same kinds of widgets, they can't simply reuse stock widget classes; they have to be customized to reflect dialog-specific dependencies. Customizing them individually by subclassing will be tedious, since many classes are involved.

You can avoid these problems by encapsulating collective behavior in a separate **mediator** object. A mediator is responsible for controlling and coordinating the interactions of a group of objects. The mediator serves as an intermediary that keeps objects in the group from referring to each other explicitly. The objects only know the mediator, thereby reducing the number of interconnections.

For example, **FontDialogDirector** can be the mediator between the widgets in a dialog box. A FontDialogDirector object knows the widgets in a dialog and coordinates their interaction. It acts as a hub of communication for widgets:

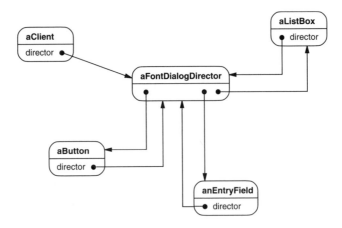

The following interaction diagram illustrates how the objects cooperate to handle a change in a list box's selection:

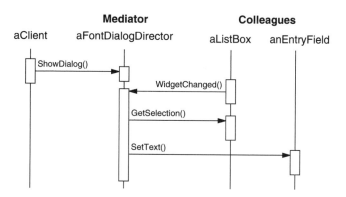

Here's the succession of events by which a list box's selection passes to an entry field:

1. The list box tells its director that it's changed.

2. The director gets the selection from the list box.

3. The director passes the selection to the entry field.

4. Now that the entry field contains some text, the director enables button(s) for initiating an action (e.g., "demibold," "oblique").

Note how the director mediates between the list box and the entry field. Widgets communicate with each other only indirectly, through the director. They don't have to know about each other; all they know is the director. Furthermore, because the behavior is localized in one class, it can be changed or replaced by extending or replacing that class.

Here's how the FontDialogDirector abstraction can be integrated into a class library:

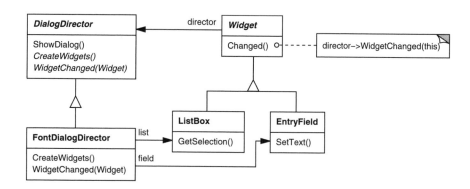

DialogDirector is an abstract class that defines the overall behavior of a dialog. Clients call the ShowDialog operation to display the dialog on the screen. CreateWidgets is an abstract operation for creating the widgets of a dialog. WidgetChanged is another abstract operation; widgets call it to inform their director that they have changed. DialogDirector subclasses override CreateWidgets to create the proper widgets, and they override WidgetChanged to handle the changes.

Applicability

Use the Mediator pattern when

- a set of objects communicate in well-defined but complex ways. The resulting interdependencies are unstructured and difficult to understand.

- reusing an object is difficult because it refers to and communicates with many other objects.

- a behavior that's distributed between several classes should be customizable without a lot of subclassing.

Structure

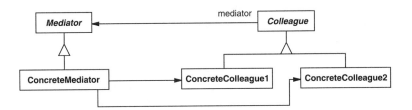

A typical object structure might look like this:

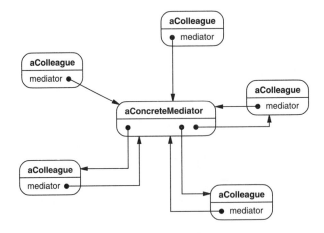

Participants

- **Mediator** (DialogDirector)

    - defines an interface for communicating with Colleague objects.

- **ConcreteMediator** (FontDialogDirector)

    - implements cooperative behavior by coordinating Colleague objects.

    - knows and maintains its colleagues.

- **Colleague classes** (ListBox, EntryField)

    - each Colleague class knows its Mediator object.

    - each colleague communicates with its mediator whenever it would have otherwise communicated with another colleague.

Collaborations

- Colleagues send and receive requests from a Mediator object. The mediator implements the cooperative behavior by routing requests between the appropriate colleague(s).

Consequences

The Mediator pattern has the following benefits and drawbacks:

1. *It limits subclassing.* A mediator localizes behavior that otherwise would be distributed among several objects. Changing this behavior requires subclassing Mediator only; Colleague classes can be reused as is.

2. *It decouples colleagues.* A mediator promotes loose coupling between colleagues. You can vary and reuse Colleague and Mediator classes independently.

3. *It simplifies object protocols.* A mediator replaces many-to-many interactions with one-to-many interactions between the mediator and its colleagues. One-to-many relationships are easier to understand, maintain, and extend.

4. *It abstracts how objects cooperate.* Making mediation an independent concept and encapsulating it in an object lets you focus on how objects interact apart from their individual behavior. That can help clarify how objects interact in a system.

5. *It centralizes control.* The Mediator pattern trades complexity of interaction for complexity in the mediator. Because a mediator encapsulates protocols, it can become more complex than any individual colleague. This can make the mediator itself a monolith that's hard to maintain.

Implementation

The following implementation issues are relevant to the Mediator pattern:

1. *Omitting the abstract Mediator class.* There's no need to define an abstract Mediator class when colleagues work with only one mediator. The abstract coupling that the Mediator class provides lets colleagues work with different Mediator subclasses, and vice versa.

2. *Colleague-Mediator communication.* Colleagues have to communicate with their mediator when an event of interest occurs. One approach is to implement the Mediator as an Observer using the Observer (293) pattern. Colleague classes act as Subjects, sending notifications to the mediator whenever they change state. The mediator responds by propagating the effects of the change to other colleagues.

   Another approach defines a specialized notification interface in Mediator that lets colleagues be more direct in their communication. Smalltalk/V for Windows uses a form of delegation: When communicating with the mediator, a colleague passes itself as an argument, allowing the mediator to identify the sender. The Sample Code uses this approach, and the Smalltalk/V implementation is discussed further in the Known Uses.

Sample Code

We'll use a DialogDirector to implement the font dialog box shown in the Motivation. The abstract class `DialogDirector` defines the interface for directors.

```
class DialogDirector {
public:
    virtual ~DialogDirector();

    virtual void ShowDialog();
    virtual void WidgetChanged(Widget*) = 0;

protected:
    DialogDirector();
    virtual void CreateWidgets() = 0;
};
```

`Widget` is the abstract base class for widgets. A widget knows its director.

```
class Widget {
public:
    Widget(DialogDirector*);
    virtual void Changed();

    virtual void HandleMouse(MouseEvent& event);
    // ...
private:
    DialogDirector* _director;
};
```

Changed calls the director's WidgetChanged operation. Widgets call WidgetChanged on their director to inform it of a significant event.

```
void Widget::Changed () {
    _director->WidgetChanged(this);
}
```

Subclasses of DialogDirector override WidgetChanged to affect the appropriate widgets. The widget passes a reference to itself as an argument to WidgetChanged to let the director identify the widget that changed. DialogDirector subclasses redefine the CreateWidgets pure virtual to construct the widgets in the dialog.

The ListBox, EntryField, and Button are subclasses of Widget for specialized user interface elements. ListBox provides a GetSelection operation to get the current selection, and EntryField's SetText operation puts new text into the field.

```
class ListBox : public Widget {
public:
    ListBox(DialogDirector*);

    virtual const char* GetSelection();
    virtual void SetList(List<char*>* listItems);
    virtual void HandleMouse(MouseEvent& event);
    // ...
};

class EntryField : public Widget {
public:
    EntryField(DialogDirector*);

    virtual void SetText(const char* text);
    virtual const char* GetText();
    virtual void HandleMouse(MouseEvent& event);
    // ...
};
```

Button is a simple widget that calls Changed whenever it's pressed. This gets done in its implementation of HandleMouse:

```
class Button : public Widget {
public:
    Button(DialogDirector*);

    virtual void SetText(const char* text);
    virtual void HandleMouse(MouseEvent& event);
    // ...
};
```

```
void Button::HandleMouse (MouseEvent& event) {
    // ...
    Changed();
}
```

The `FontDialogDirector` class mediates between widgets in the dialog box. `FontDialogDirector` is a subclass of `DialogDirector`:

```
class FontDialogDirector : public DialogDirector {
public:
    FontDialogDirector();
    virtual ~FontDialogDirector();
    virtual void WidgetChanged(Widget*);

protected:
    virtual void CreateWidgets();

private:
    Button* _ok;
    Button* _cancel;
    ListBox* _fontList;
    EntryField* _fontName;
};
```

`FontDialogDirector` keeps track of the widgets it displays. It redefines `CreateWidgets` to create the widgets and initialize its references to them:

```
void FontDialogDirector::CreateWidgets () {
    _ok = new Button(this);
    _cancel = new Button(this);
    _fontList = new ListBox(this);
    _fontName = new EntryField(this);

    // fill the listBox with the available font names

    // assemble the widgets in the dialog
}
```

`WidgetChanged` ensures that the widgets work together properly:

```
void FontDialogDirector::WidgetChanged (
    Widget* theChangedWidget
) {
    if (theChangedWidget == _fontList) {
        _fontName->SetText(_fontList->GetSelection());

    } else if (theChangedWidget == _ok) {
        // apply font change and dismiss dialog
        // ...
```

```
        } else if (theChangedWidget == _cancel) {
            // dismiss dialog
        }
    }
```

The complexity of `WidgetChanged` increases proportionally with the complexity of the dialog. Large dialogs are undesirable for other reasons, of course, but mediator complexity might mitigate the pattern's benefits in other applications.

Known Uses

Both ET++ [WGM88] and the THINK C class library [Sym93b] use director-like objects in dialogs as mediators between widgets.

The application architecture of Smalltalk/V for Windows is based on a mediator structure [LaL94]. In that environment, an application consists of a Window containing a set of panes. The library contains several predefined Pane objects; examples include TextPane, ListBox, Button, and so on. These panes can be used without subclassing. An application developer only subclasses from ViewManager, a class that's responsible for doing inter-pane coordination. ViewManager is the Mediator, and each pane only knows its view manager, which is considered the "owner" of the pane. Panes don't refer to each other directly.

The following object diagram shows a snapshot of an application at run-time:

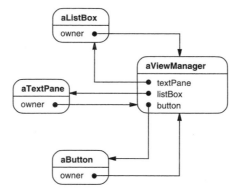

Smalltalk/V uses an event mechanism for Pane-ViewManager communication. A pane generates an event when it wants to get information from the mediator or when it wants to inform the mediator that something significant happened. An event defines a symbol (e.g., `#select`) that identifies the event. To handle the event, the view manager registers a method selector with the pane. This selector is the event's handler; it will be invoked whenever the event occurs.

The following code excerpt shows how a ListPane object gets created inside a ViewManager subclass and how ViewManager registers an event handler for the `#select` event:

```
self addSubpane: (ListPane new
    paneName: 'myListPane';
    owner: self;
    when: #select perform: #listSelect:).
```

Another application of the Mediator pattern is in coordinating complex updates. An example is the ChangeManager class mentioned in Observer (293). Change-Manager mediates between subjects and observers to avoid redundant updates. When an object changes, it notifies the ChangeManager, which in turn coordinates the update by notifying the object's dependents.

A similar application appears in the Unidraw drawing framework [VL90] and uses a class called CSolver to enforce connectivity constraints between "connectors." Objects in graphical editors can appear to stick to one another in different ways. Connectors are useful in applications that maintain connectivity automatically, like diagram editors and circuit design systems. CSolver is a mediator between connectors. It solves the connectivity constraints and updates the connectors' positions to reflect them.

Related Patterns

Facade (185) differs from Mediator in that it abstracts a subsystem of objects to provide a more convenient interface. Its protocol is unidirectional; that is, Facade objects make requests of the subsystem classes but not vice versa. In contrast, Mediator enables cooperative behavior that colleague objects don't or can't provide, and the protocol is multidirectional.

Colleagues can communicate with the mediator using the Observer (293) pattern.

MEMENTO   Object Behavioral

Intent

Without violating encapsulation, capture and externalize an object's internal state so that the object can be restored to this state later.

Also Known As

Token

Motivation

Sometimes it's necessary to record the internal state of an object. This is required when implementing checkpoints and undo mechanisms that let users back out of tentative operations or recover from errors. You must save state information somewhere so that you can restore objects to their previous states. But objects normally encapsulate some or all of their state, making it inaccessible to other objects and impossible to save externally. Exposing this state would violate encapsulation, which can compromise the application's reliability and extensibility.

Consider for example a graphical editor that supports connectivity between objects. A user can connect two rectangles with a line, and the rectangles stay connected when the user moves either of them. The editor ensures that the line stretches to maintain the connection.

A well-known way to maintain connectivity relationships between objects is with a constraint-solving system. We can encapsulate this functionality in a **Constraint-Solver** object. ConstraintSolver records connections as they are made and generates mathematical equations that describe them. It solves these equations whenever the user makes a connection or otherwise modifies the diagram. ConstraintSolver uses the results of its calculations to rearrange the graphics so that they maintain the proper connections.

Supporting undo in this application isn't as easy as it may seem. An obvious way to undo a move operation is to store the original distance moved and move the object back an equivalent distance. However, this does not guarantee all objects will appear where they did before. Suppose there is some slack in the connection. In that case, simply moving the rectangle back to its original location won't necessarily achieve the desired effect.

In general, the ConstraintSolver's public interface might be insufficient to allow precise reversal of its effects on other objects. The undo mechanism must work more closely with ConstraintSolver to reestablish previous state, but we should also avoid exposing the ConstraintSolver's internals to the undo mechanism.

We can solve this problem with the Memento pattern. A **memento** is an object that stores a snapshot of the internal state of another object—the memento's **originator**. The undo mechanism will request a memento from the originator when it needs to checkpoint the originator's state. The originator initializes the memento with information that characterizes its current state. Only the originator can store and retrieve information from the memento—the memento is "opaque" to other objects.

In the graphical editor example just discussed, the ConstraintSolver can act as an originator. The following sequence of events characterizes the undo process:

1. The editor requests a memento from the ConstraintSolver as a side-effect of the move operation.

2. The ConstraintSolver creates and returns a memento, an instance of a class SolverState in this case. A SolverState memento contains data structures that describe the current state of the ConstraintSolver's internal equations and variables.

3. Later when the user undoes the move operation, the editor gives the SolverState back to the ConstraintSolver.

4. Based on the information in the SolverState, the ConstraintSolver changes its internal structures to return its equations and variables to their exact previous state.

This arrangement lets the ConstraintSolver entrust other objects with the information it needs to revert to a previous state without exposing its internal structure and representations.

Applicability

Use the Memento pattern when

- a snapshot of (some portion of) an object's state must be saved so that it can be restored to that state later, *and*

- a direct interface to obtaining the state would expose implementation details and break the object's encapsulation.

Structure

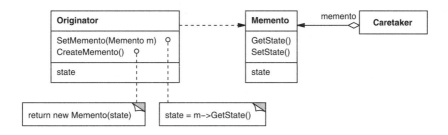

Participants

- **Memento** (SolverState)
  - stores internal state of the Originator object. The memento may store as much or as little of the originator's internal state as necessary at its originator's discretion.
  - protects against access by objects other than the originator. Mementos have effectively two interfaces. Caretaker sees a *narrow* interface to the Memento—it can only pass the memento to other objects. Originator, in contrast, sees a *wide* interface, one that lets it access all the data necessary to restore itself to its previous state. Ideally, only the originator that produced the memento would be permitted to access the memento's internal state.

- **Originator** (ConstraintSolver)
  - creates a memento containing a snapshot of its current internal state.
  - uses the memento to restore its internal state.

- **Caretaker** (undo mechanism)
  - is responsible for the memento's safekeeping.
  - never operates on or examines the contents of a memento.

Collaborations

- A caretaker requests a memento from an originator, holds it for a time, and passes it back to the originator, as the following interaction diagram illustrates:

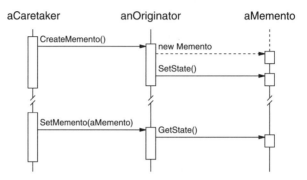

Sometimes the caretaker won't pass the memento back to the originator, because the originator might never need to revert to an earlier state.

- Mementos are passive. Only the originator that created a memento will assign or retrieve its state.

Consequences

The Memento pattern has several consequences:

1. *Preserving encapsulation boundaries.* Memento avoids exposing information that only an originator should manage but that must be stored nevertheless outside the originator. The pattern shields other objects from potentially complex Originator internals, thereby preserving encapsulation boundaries.

2. *It simplifies Originator.* In other encapsulation-preserving designs, Originator keeps the versions of internal state that clients have requested. That puts all the storage management burden on Originator. Having clients manage the state they ask for simplifies Originator and keeps clients from having to notify originators when they're done.

3. *Using mementos might be expensive.* Mementos might incur considerable overhead if Originator must copy large amounts of information to store in the memento or if clients create and return mementos to the originator often enough. Unless encapsulating and restoring Originator state is cheap, the pattern might not be appropriate. See the discussion of incrementality in the Implementation section.

4. *Defining narrow and wide interfaces.* It may be difficult in some languages to ensure that only the originator can access the memento's state.

5. *Hidden costs in caring for mementos.* A caretaker is responsible for deleting the mementos it cares for. However, the caretaker has no idea how much state is

in the memento. Hence an otherwise lightweight caretaker might incur large storage costs when it stores mementos.

Implementation

Here are two issues to consider when implementing the Memento pattern:

1. *Language support.* Mementos have two interfaces: a wide one for originators and a narrow one for other objects. Ideally the implementation language will support two levels of static protection. C++ lets you do this by making the Originator a friend of Memento and making Memento's wide interface private. Only the narrow interface should be declared public. For example:

```cpp
class State;

class Originator {
public:
    Memento* CreateMemento();
    void SetMemento(const Memento*);
    // ...
private:
    State* _state;       // internal data structures
    // ...
};

class Memento {
public:
    // narrow public interface
    virtual ~Memento();
private:
    // private members accessible only to Originator
    friend class Originator;
    Memento();

    void SetState(State*);
    State* GetState();
    // ...
private:
    State* _state;
    // ...
};
```

2. *Storing incremental changes.* When mementos get created and passed back to their originator in a predictable sequence, then Memento can save just the *incremental change* to the originator's internal state.

   For example, undoable commands in a history list can use mementos to ensure that commands are restored to their exact state when they're undone (see Command (233)). The history list defines a specific order in which commands can be undone and redone. That means mementos can store just the incremental change that a command makes rather than the full state of every object they affect. In the Motivation example given earlier, the constraint solver can store only those internal structures that change to keep the line connecting the rectangles, as opposed to storing the absolute positions of these objects.

Sample Code

The C++ code given here illustrates the ConstraintSolver example discussed earlier. We use MoveCommand objects (see Command (233)) to (un)do the translation of a graphical object from one position to another. The graphical editor calls the command's Execute operation to move a graphical object and Unexecute to undo the move. The command stores its target, the distance moved, and an instance of ConstraintSolverMemento, a memento containing state from the constraint solver.

```
class Graphic;
    // base class for graphical objects in the graphical editor

class MoveCommand {
public:
    MoveCommand(Graphic* target, const Point& delta);
    void Execute();
    void Unexecute();
private:
    ConstraintSolverMemento* _state;
    Point _delta;
    Graphic* _target;
};
```

The connection constraints are established by the class ConstraintSolver. Its key member function is Solve, which solves the constraints registered with the AddConstraint operation. To support undo, ConstraintSolver's state can be externalized with CreateMemento into a ConstraintSolverMemento instance. The constraint solver can be returned to a previous state by calling SetMemento. ConstraintSolver is a Singleton (127).

```
class ConstraintSolver {
public:
    static ConstraintSolver* Instance();

    void Solve();
    void AddConstraint(
        Graphic* startConnection, Graphic* endConnection
    );
    void RemoveConstraint(
        Graphic* startConnection, Graphic* endConnection
    );
```

```
    ConstraintSolverMemento* CreateMemento();
    void SetMemento(ConstraintSolverMemento*);
private:
    // nontrivial state and operations for enforcing
    // connectivity semantics
};

class ConstraintSolverMemento {
public:
    virtual ~ConstraintSolverMemento();
private:
    friend class ConstraintSolver;
    ConstraintSolverMemento();

    // private constraint solver state
};
```

Given these interfaces, we can implement MoveCommand members Execute and Unexecute as follows:

```
void MoveCommand::Execute () {
    ConstraintSolver* solver = ConstraintSolver::Instance();
    _state = solver->CreateMemento(); // create a memento
    _target->Move(_delta);
    solver->Solve();
}

void MoveCommand::Unexecute () {
    ConstraintSolver* solver = ConstraintSolver::Instance();
    _target->Move(-_delta);
    solver->SetMemento(_state); // restore solver state
    solver->Solve();
}
```

Execute acquires a ConstraintSolverMemento memento before it moves the graphic. Unexecute moves the graphic back, sets the constraint solver's state to the previous state, and finally tells the constraint solver to solve the constraints.

Known Uses

The preceding sample code is based on Unidraw's support for connectivity through its CSolver class [VL90].

Collections in Dylan [App92] provide an iteration interface that reflects the Memento pattern. Dylan's collections have the notion of a "state" object, which is a memento that represents the state of the iteration. Each collection can represent the current state of the iteration in any way it chooses; the representation is completely hidden from clients. The Dylan iteration approach might be translated to C++ as follows:

```
template <class Item>
class Collection {
public:
    Collection();

    IterationState* CreateInitialState();
    void Next(IterationState*);
    bool IsDone(const IterationState*) const;
    Item CurrentItem(const IterationState*) const;
    IterationState* Copy(const IterationState*) const;

    void Append(const Item&);
    void Remove(const Item&);
    // ...
};
```

CreateInitialState returns an initialized IterationState object for the collection. Next advances the state object to the next position in the iteration; it effectively increments the iteration index. IsDone returns true if Next has advanced beyond the last element in the collection. CurrentItem dereferences the state object and returns the element in the collection to which it refers. Copy returns a copy of the given state object. This is useful for marking a point in an iteration.

Given a class ItemType, we can iterate over a collection of its instances as follows[7]:

```
class ItemType {
public:
    void Process();
    // ...
};

Collection<ItemType*> aCollection;
IterationState* state;

state = aCollection.CreateInitialState();

while (!aCollection.IsDone(state)) {
    aCollection.CurrentItem(state)->Process();
    aCollection.Next(state);
}
delete state;
```

The memento-based iteration interface has two interesting benefits:

1. More than one state can work on the same collection. (The same is true of the Iterator (257) pattern.)

---

[7] Note that our example deletes the state object at the end of the iteration. But delete won't get called if ProcessItem throws an exception, thus creating garbage. This is a problem in C++ but not in Dylan, which has garbage collection. We discuss a solution to this problem on page 266.

2. It doesn't require breaking a collection's encapsulation to support iteration. The memento is only interpreted by the collection itself; no one else has access to it. Other approaches to iteration require breaking encapsulation by making iterator classes friends of their collection classes (see Iterator (257)). The situation is reversed in the memento-based implementation: `Collection` is a friend of the `IteratorState`.

The QOCA constraint-solving toolkit stores incremental information in mementos [HHMV92]. Clients can obtain a memento that characterizes the current solution to a system of constraints. The memento contains only those constraint variables that have changed since the last solution. Usually only a small subset of the solver's variables changes for each new solution. This subset is enough to return the solver to the preceding solution; reverting to earlier solutions requires restoring mementos from the intervening solutions. Hence you can't set mementos in any order; QOCA relies on a history mechanism to revert to earlier solutions.

Related Patterns

Command (233): Commands can use mementos to maintain state for undoable operations.

Iterator (257): Mementos can be used for iteration as described earlier.

Session

profile

order

OBSERVER   Object Behavioral

Intent

Define a one-to-many dependency between objects so that when one object changes state, all its dependents are notified and updated automatically.

Also Known As

Dependents, Publish-Subscribe

Motivation

A common side-effect of partitioning a system into a collection of cooperating classes is the need to maintain consistency between related objects. You don't want to achieve consistency by making the classes tightly coupled, because that reduces their reusability.

For example, many graphical user interface toolkits separate the presentational aspects of the user interface from the underlying application data [KP88, LVC89, P+88, WGM88]. Classes defining application data and presentations can be reused independently. They can work together, too. Both a spreadsheet object and bar chart object can depict information in the same application data object using different presentations. The spreadsheet and the bar chart don't know about each other, thereby letting you reuse only the one you need. But they *behave* as though they do. When the user changes the information in the spreadsheet, the bar chart reflects the changes immediately, and vice versa.

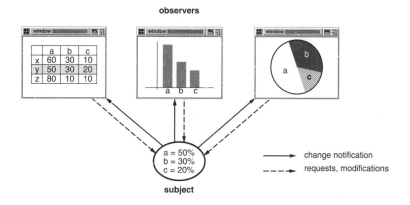

This behavior implies that the spreadsheet and bar chart are dependent on the data object and therefore should be notified of any change in its state. And there's no reason to limit the number of dependent objects to two; there may be any number of different user interfaces to the same data.

The Observer pattern describes how to establish these relationships. The key objects in this pattern are **subject** and **observer**. A subject may have any number of dependent observers. All observers are notified whenever the subject undergoes a change in state. In response, each observer will query the subject to synchronize its state with the subject's state.

This kind of interaction is also known as **publish-subscribe**. The subject is the publisher of notifications. It sends out these notifications without having to know who its observers are. Any number of observers can subscribe to receive notifications.

Applicability

Use the Observer pattern in any of the following situations:

- When an abstraction has two aspects, one dependent on the other. Encapsulating these aspects in separate objects lets you vary and reuse them independently.

- When a change to one object requires changing others, and you don't know how many objects need to be changed.

- When an object should be able to notify other objects without making assumptions about who these objects are. In other words, you don't want these objects tightly coupled.

Structure

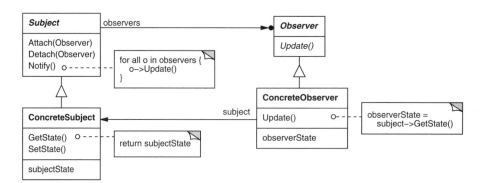

Participants

- **Subject**
  - knows its observers. Any number of Observer objects may observe a subject.
  - provides an interface for attaching and detaching Observer objects.

- **Observer**
  - defines an updating interface for objects that should be notified of changes ı subject.

    teSubject

    res state of interest to ConcreteObserver objects.

    ds a notification to its observers when its state changes.

    teObserver

    intains a reference to a ConcreteSubject object.

    res state that should stay consistent with the subject's.

    plements the Observer updating interface to keep its state consistent ɔh the subject's.

ions

teSubject notifies its observers whenever a change occurs that could s observers' state inconsistent with its own.

ɔeing informed of a change in the concrete subject, a ConcreteObserver nay query the subject for information. ConcreteObserver uses this in-on to reconcile its state with that of the subject.

lowing interaction diagram illustrates the collaborations between a and two observers:

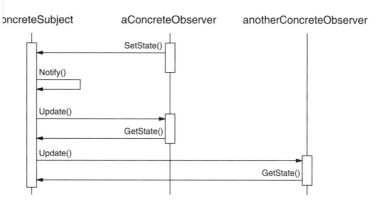

Note how the Observer object that initiates the change request postpones its update until it gets a notification from the subject. Notify is not always called by the subject. It can be called by an observer or by another kind of object entirely. The Implementation section discusses some common variations.

Consequences

The Observer pattern lets you vary subjects and observers independently. You can reuse subjects without reusing their observers, and vice versa. It lets you add observers without modifying the subject or other observers.

Further benefits and liabilities of the Observer pattern include the following:

1. *Abstract coupling between Subject and Observer.* All a subject knows is that it has a list of observers, each conforming to the simple interface of the abstract Observer class. The subject doesn't know the concrete class of any observer. Thus the coupling between subjects and observers is abstract and minimal.

   Because Subject and Observer aren't tightly coupled, they can belong to different layers of abstraction in a system. A lower-level subject can communicate and inform a higher-level observer, thereby keeping the system's layering intact. If Subject and Observer are lumped together, then the resulting object must either span two layers (and violate the layering), or it must be forced to live in one layer or the other (which might compromise the layering abstraction).

2. *Support for broadcast communication.* Unlike an ordinary request, the notification that a subject sends needn't specify its receiver. The notification is broadcast automatically to all interested objects that subscribed to it. The subject doesn't care how many interested objects exist; its only responsibility is to notify its observers. This gives you the freedom to add and remove observers at any time. It's up to the observer to handle or ignore a notification.

3. *Unexpected updates.* Because observers have no knowledge of each other's presence, they can be blind to the ultimate cost of changing the subject. A seemingly innocuous operation on the subject may cause a cascade of updates to observers and their dependent objects. Moreover, dependency criteria that aren't well-defined or maintained usually lead to spurious updates, which can be hard to track down.

   This problem is aggravated by the fact that the simple update protocol provides no details on *what* changed in the subject. Without additional protocol to help observers discover what changed, they may be forced to work hard to deduce the changes.

Implementation

Several issues related to the implementation of the dependency mechanism are discussed in this section.

where `interest` specifies the event of interest. At notification time, the subject supplies the changed aspect to its observers as a parameter to the Update operation. For example:

```
void Observer::Update(Subject*, Aspect& interest);
```

8. *Encapsulating complex update semantics.* When the dependency relationship between subjects and observers is particularly complex, an object that maintains these relationships might be required. We call such an object a **Change-Manager**. Its purpose is to minimize the work required to make observers reflect a change in their subject. For example, if an operation involves changes to several interdependent subjects, you might have to ensure that their observers are notified only after *all* the subjects have been modified to avoid notifying observers more than once.

ChangeManager has three responsibilities:

   (a) It maps a subject to its observers and provides an interface to maintain this mapping. This eliminates the need for subjects to maintain references to their observers and vice versa.

   (b) It defines a particular update strategy.

   (c) It updates all dependent observers at the request of a subject.

The following diagram depicts a simple ChangeManager-based implementation of the Observer pattern. There are two specialized ChangeManagers. SimpleChangeManager is naive in that it always updates all observers of each subject. In contrast, DAGChangeManager handles directed-acyclic graphs of dependencies between subjects and their observers. A DAGChangeManager is preferable to a SimpleChangeManager when an observer observes more than one subject. In that case, a change in two or more subjects might cause redundant updates. The DAGChangeManager ensures the observer receives just one update. SimpleChangeManager is fine when multiple updates aren't an issue.

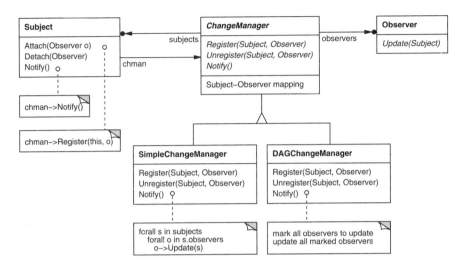

ChangeManager is an instance of the Mediator (273) pattern. In general there is only one ChangeManager, and it is known globally. The Singleton (127) pattern would be useful here.

9. *Combining the Subject and Observer classes.* Class libraries written in languages that lack multiple inheritance (like Smalltalk) generally don't define separate Subject and Observer classes but combine their interfaces in one class. That lets you define an object that acts as both a subject and an observer without multiple inheritance. In Smalltalk, for example, the Subject and Observer interfaces are defined in the root class Object, making them available to all classes.

Sample Code

An abstract class defines the Observer interface:

```
class Subject;

class Observer {
public:
    virtual ~Observer();
    virtual void Update(Subject* theChangedSubject) = 0;
protected:
    Observer();
};
```

This implementation supports multiple subjects for each observer. The subject passed to the Update operation lets the observer determine which subject changed when it observes more than one.

Similarly, an abstract class defines the Subject interface:

```
class Subject {
public:
    virtual ~Subject();

    virtual void Attach(Observer*);
    virtual void Detach(Observer*);
    virtual void Notify();
protected:
    Subject();
private:
    List<Observer*> *_observers;
};

void Subject::Attach (Observer* o) {
    _observers->Append(o);
}

void Subject::Detach (Observer* o) {
    _observers->Remove(o);
}

void Subject::Notify () {
    ListIterator<Observer*> i(_observers);

    for (i.First(); !i.IsDone(); i.Next()) {
        i.CurrentItem()->Update(this);
    }
}
```

`ClockTimer` is a concrete subject for storing and maintaining the time of day. It notifies its observers every second. `ClockTimer` provides the interface for retrieving individual time units such as the hour, minute, and second.

```
class ClockTimer : public Subject {
public:
    ClockTimer();

    virtual int GetHour();
    virtual int GetMinute();
    virtual int GetSecond();

    void Tick();
};
```

The `Tick` operation gets called by an internal timer at regular intervals to provide an accurate time base. `Tick` updates the `ClockTimer`'s internal state and calls `Notify` to inform observers of the change:

```
void ClockTimer::Tick () {
    // update internal time-keeping state
    // ...
    Notify();
}
```

Now we can define a class `DigitalClock` that displays the time. It inherits its graphical functionality from a `Widget` class provided by a user interface toolkit. The Observer interface is mixed into the `DigitalClock` interface by inheriting from `Observer`.

```
class DigitalClock: public Widget, public Observer {
public:
    DigitalClock(ClockTimer*);
    virtual ~DigitalClock();

    virtual void Update(Subject*);
        // overrides Observer operation

    virtual void Draw();
        // overrides Widget operation;
        // defines how to draw the digital clock
private:
    ClockTimer* _subject;
};

DigitalClock::DigitalClock (ClockTimer* s) {
    _subject = s;
    _subject->Attach(this);
}

DigitalClock::~DigitalClock () {
    _subject->Detach(this);
}
```

Before the `Update` operation draws the clock face, it checks to make sure the notifying subject is the clock's subject:

```
void DigitalClock::Update (Subject* theChangedSubject) {
    if (theChangedSubject == _subject) {
        Draw();
    }
}

void DigitalClock::Draw () {
    // get the new values from the subject

    int hour = _subject->GetHour();
    int minute = _subject->GetMinute();
    // etc.

    // draw the digital clock
}
```

An `AnalogClock` class can be defined in the same way.

```
class AnalogClock : public Widget, public Observer {
public:
    AnalogClock(ClockTimer*);
    virtual void Update(Subject*);
    virtual void Draw();
    // ...
};
```

The following code creates an `AnalogClock` and a `DigitalClock` that always show the same time:

```
ClockTimer* timer = new ClockTimer;
AnalogClock* analogClock = new AnalogClock(timer);
DigitalClock* digitalClock = new DigitalClock(timer);
```

Whenever the `timer` ticks, the two clocks will be updated and will redisplay themselves appropriately.

Known Uses

The first and perhaps best-known example of the Observer pattern appears in Smalltalk Model/View/Controller (MVC), the user interface framework in the Smalltalk environment [KP88]. MVC's Model class plays the role of Subject, while View is the base class for observers. Smalltalk, ET++ [WGM88], and the THINK class library [Sym93b] provide a general dependency mechanism by putting Subject and Observer interfaces in the parent class for all other classes in the system.

Other user interface toolkits that employ this pattern are InterViews [LVC89], the Andrew Toolkit [P+88], and Unidraw [VL90]. InterViews defines Observer and Observable (for subjects) classes explicitly. Andrew calls them "view" and "data object," respectively. Unidraw splits graphical editor objects into View (for observers) and Subject parts.

Related Patterns

Mediator (273): By encapsulating complex update semantics, the ChangeManager acts as mediator between subjects and observers.

Singleton (127): The ChangeManager may use the Singleton pattern to make it unique and globally accessible.

STATE   Object Behavioral

Intent

Allow an object to alter its behavior when its internal state changes. The object will appear to change its class.

Also Known As

Objects for States

Motivation

Consider a class TCPConnection that represents a network connection. A TCP-Connection object can be in one of several different states: Established, Listening, Closed. When a TCPConnection object receives requests from other objects, it responds differently depending on its current state. For example, the effect of an Open request depends on whether the connection is in its Closed state or its Established state. The State pattern describes how TCPConnection can exhibit different behavior in each state.

The key idea in this pattern is to introduce an abstract class called TCPState to represent the states of the network connection. The TCPState class declares an interface common to all classes that represent different operational states. Subclasses of TCPState implement state-specific behavior. For example, the classes TCPEstablished and TCPClosed implement behavior particular to the Established and Closed states of TCPConnection.

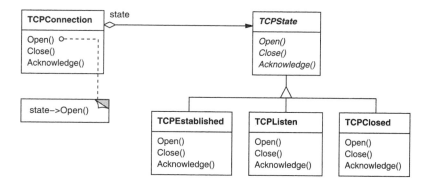

The class TCPConnection maintains a state object (an instance of a subclass of TCPState) that represents the current state of the TCP connection. The class TCP-

Connection delegates all state-specific requests to this state object. TCPConnection uses its TCPState subclass instance to perform operations particular to the state of the connection.

Whenever the connection changes state, the TCPConnection object changes the state object it uses. When the connection goes from established to closed, for example, TCPConnection will replace its TCPEstablished instance with a TCPClosed instance.

Applicability

Use the State pattern in either of the following cases:

- An object's behavior depends on its state, and it must change its behavior at run-time depending on that state.

- Operations have large, multipart conditional statements that depend on the object's state. This state is usually represented by one or more enumerated constants. Often, several operations will contain this same conditional structure. The State pattern puts each branch of the conditional in a separate class. This lets you treat the object's state as an object in its own right that can vary independently from other objects.

Structure

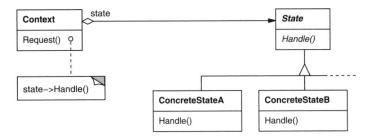

Participants

- **Context** (TCPConnection)
  - defines the interface of interest to clients.
  - maintains an instance of a ConcreteState subclass that defines the current state.
- **State** (TCPState)
  - defines an interface for encapsulating the behavior associated with a particular state of the Context.

- **ConcreteState subclasses** (TCPEstablished, TCPListen, TCPClosed)
  - each subclass implements a behavior associated with a state of the Context.

Collaborations

- Context delegates state-specific requests to the current ConcreteState object.
- A context may pass itself as an argument to the State object handling the request. This lets the State object access the context if necessary.
- Context is the primary interface for clients. Clients can configure a context with State objects. Once a context is configured, its clients don't have to deal with the State objects directly.
- Either Context or the ConcreteState subclasses can decide which state succeeds another and under what circumstances.

Consequences

The State pattern has the following consequences:

1. *It localizes state-specific behavior and partitions behavior for different states.* The State pattern puts all behavior associated with a particular state into one object. Because all state-specific code lives in a State subclass, new states and transitions can be added easily by defining new subclasses.

   An alternative is to use data values to define internal states and have Context operations check the data explicitly. But then we'd have look-alike conditional or case statements scattered throughout Context's implementation. Adding a new state could require changing several operations, which complicates maintenance.

   The State pattern avoids this problem but might introduce another, because the pattern distributes behavior for different states across several State subclasses. This increases the number of classes and is less compact than a single class. But such distribution is actually good if there are many states, which would otherwise necessitate large conditional statements.

   Like long procedures, large conditional statements are undesirable. They're monolithic and tend to make the code less explicit, which in turn makes them difficult to modify and extend. The State pattern offers a better way to structure state-specific code. The logic that determines the state transitions doesn't reside in monolithic `if` or `switch` statements but instead is partitioned between the State subclasses. Encapsulating each state transition and action in a class elevates the idea of an execution state to full object status. That imposes structure on the code and makes its intent clearer.

2. *It makes state transitions explicit.* When an object defines its current state solely in terms of internal data values, its state transitions have no explicit representation; they only show up as assignments to some variables. Introducing separate objects for different states makes the transitions more explicit.

Also, State objects can protect the Context from inconsistent internal states, because state transitions are atomic from the Context's perspective—they happen by rebinding *one* variable (the Context's State object variable), not several [dCLF93].

3. *State objects can be shared.* If State objects have no instance variables—that is, the state they represent is encoded entirely in their type—then contexts can share a State object. When states are shared in this way, they are essentially flyweights (see Flyweight (195)) with no intrinsic state, only behavior.

Implementation

The State pattern raises a variety of implementation issues:

1. *Who defines the state transitions?* The State pattern does not specify which participant defines the criteria for state transitions. If the criteria are fixed, then they can be implemented entirely in the Context. It is generally more flexible and appropriate, however, to let the State subclasses themselves specify their successor state and when to make the transition. This requires adding an interface to the Context that lets State objects set the Context's current state explicitly.

   Decentralizing the transition logic in this way makes it easy to modify or extend the logic by defining new State subclasses. A disadvantage of de-centralization is that one State subclass will have knowledge of at least one other, which introduces implementation dependencies between subclasses.

2. *A table-based alternative.* In *C++ Programming Style* [Car92], Cargill describes another way to impose structure on state-driven code: He uses tables to map inputs to state transitions. For each state, a table maps every possible input to a succeeding state. In effect, this approach converts conditional code (and virtual functions, in the case of the State pattern) into a table look-up.

   The main advantage of tables is their regularity: You can change the transition criteria by modifying data instead of changing program code. There are some disadvantages, however:

   • A table look-up is often less efficient than a (virtual) function call.

   • Putting transition logic into a uniform, tabular format makes the transition criteria less explicit and therefore harder to understand.

   • It's usually difficult to add actions to accompany the state transitions. The table-driven approach captures the states and their transitions, but it must be augmented to perform arbitrary computation on each transition.

   The key difference between table-driven state machines and the State pattern can be summed up like this: The State pattern models state-specific behavior, whereas the table-driven approach focuses on defining state transitions.

3. *Creating and destroying State objects.* A common implementation trade-off worth considering is whether (1) to create State objects only when they are needed and destroy them thereafter versus (2) creating them ahead of time and never destroying them.

   The first choice is preferable when the states that will be entered aren't known at run-time, *and* contexts change state infrequently. This approach avoids creating objects that won't be used, which is important if the State objects store a lot of information. The second approach is better when state changes occur rapidly, in which case you want to avoid destroying states, because they may be needed again shortly. Instantiation costs are paid once up-front, and there are no destruction costs at all. This approach might be inconvenient, though, because the Context must keep references to all states that might be entered.

4. *Using dynamic inheritance.* Changing the behavior for a particular request could be accomplished by changing the object's class at run-time, but this is not possible in most object-oriented programming languages. Exceptions include Self [US87] and other delegation-based languages that provide such a mechanism and hence support the State pattern directly. Objects in Self can delegate operations to other objects to achieve a form of dynamic inheritance. Changing the delegation target at run-time effectively changes the inheritance structure. This mechanism lets objects change their behavior and amounts to changing their class.

Sample Code

The following example gives the C++ code for the TCP connection example described in the Motivation section. This example is a simplified version of the TCP protocol; it doesn't describe the complete protocol or all the states of TCP connections.[8]

First, we define the class TCPConnection, which provides an interface for transmitting data and handles requests to change state.

```
class TCPOctetStream;
class TCPState;

class TCPConnection {
public:
    TCPConnection();

    void ActiveOpen();
    void PassiveOpen();
    void Close();
```

---

[8] This example is based on the TCP connection protocol described by Lynch and Rose [LR93].

```
        void Send();
        void Acknowledge();
        void Synchronize();

        void ProcessOctet(TCPOctetStream*);
    private:
        friend class TCPState;
        void ChangeState(TCPState*);
    private:
        TCPState* _state;
    };
```

TCPConnection keeps an instance of the TCPState class in the _state member variable. The class TCPState duplicates the state-changing interface of TCPConnection. Each TCPState operation takes a TCPConnection instance as a parameter, letting TCPState access data from TCPConnection and change the connection's state.

```
    class TCPState {
    public:
        virtual void Transmit(TCPConnection*, TCPOctetStream*);
        virtual void ActiveOpen(TCPConnection*);
        virtual void PassiveOpen(TCPConnection*);
        virtual void Close(TCPConnection*);
        virtual void Synchronize(TCPConnection*);
        virtual void Acknowledge(TCPConnection*);
        virtual void Send(TCPConnection*);
    protected:
        void ChangeState(TCPConnection*, TCPState*);
    };
```

TCPConnection delegates all state-specific requests to its TCPState instance _state. TCPConnection also provides an operation for changing this variable to a new TCPState. The constructor for TCPConnection initializes the object to the TCPClosed state (defined later).

```
        TCPConnection::TCPConnection () {
            _state = TCPClosed::Instance();
        }

        void TCPConnection::ChangeState (TCPState* s) {
            _state = s;
        }

        void TCPConnection::ActiveOpen () {
            _state->ActiveOpen(this);
        }

        void TCPConnection::PassiveOpen () {
            _state->PassiveOpen(this);
        }
```

```
void TCPConnection::Close () {
    _state->Close(this);
}


void TCPConnection::Acknowledge () {
    _state->Acknowledge(this);
}


void TCPConnection::Synchronize () {
    _state->Synchronize(this);
}
```

`TCPState` implements default behavior for all requests delegated to it. It can also change the state of a `TCPConnection` with the `ChangeState` operation. `TCPState` is declared a friend of `TCPConnection` to give it privileged access to this operation.

```
void TCPState::Transmit (TCPConnection*, TCPOctetStream*) { }
void TCPState::ActiveOpen (TCPConnection*) { }
void TCPState::PassiveOpen (TCPConnection*) { }
void TCPState::Close (TCPConnection*) { }
void TCPState::Synchronize (TCPConnection*) { }


void TCPState::ChangeState (TCPConnection* t, TCPState* s) {
    t->ChangeState(s);
}
```

Subclasses of `TCPState` implement state-specific behavior. A TCP connection can be in many states: Established, Listening, Closed, etc., and there's a subclass of `TCPState` for each state. We'll discuss three subclasses in detail: `TCPEstablished`, `TCPListen`, and `TCPClosed`.

```
class TCPEstablished : public TCPState {
public:
    static TCPState* Instance();

    virtual void Transmit(TCPConnection*, TCPOctetStream*);
    virtual void Close(TCPConnection*);
};


class TCPListen : public TCPState {
public:
    static TCPState* Instance();

    virtual void Send(TCPConnection*);
    // ...
};
```

```
class TCPClosed : public TCPState {
public:
    static TCPState* Instance();

    virtual void ActiveOpen(TCPConnection*);
    virtual void PassiveOpen(TCPConnection*);
    // ...
};
```

TCPState subclasses maintain no local state, so they can be shared, and only one instance of each is required. The unique instance of each TCPState subclass is obtained by the static Instance operation.[9]

Each TCPState subclass implements state-specific behavior for valid requests in the state:

```
void TCPClosed::ActiveOpen (TCPConnection* t) {
    // send SYN, receive SYN, ACK, etc.

    ChangeState(t, TCPEstablished::Instance());
}


void TCPClosed::PassiveOpen (TCPConnection* t) {
    ChangeState(t, TCPListen::Instance());
}


void TCPEstablished::Close (TCPConnection* t) {
    // send FIN, receive ACK of FIN

    ChangeState(t, TCPListen::Instance());
}


void TCPEstablished::Transmit (
    TCPConnection* t, TCPOctetStream* o
) {
    t->ProcessOctet(o);
}


void TCPListen::Send (TCPConnection* t) {
    // send SYN, receive SYN, ACK, etc.

    ChangeState(t, TCPEstablished::Instance());
}
```

After performing state-specific work, these operations call the ChangeState operation to change the state of the TCPConnection. TCPConnection itself doesn't know a thing about the TCP connection protocol; it's the TCPState subclasses that define each state transition and action in TCP.

---

[9] This makes each TCPState subclass a Singleton (see Singleton (127)).

Known Uses

Johnson and Zweig [JZ91] characterize the State pattern and its application to TCP connection protocols.

Most popular interactive drawing programs provide "tools" for performing operations by direct manipulation. For example, a line-drawing tool lets a user click and drag to create a new line. A selection tool lets the user select shapes. There's usually a palette of such tools to choose from. The user thinks of this activity as picking up a tool and wielding it, but in reality the editor's behavior changes with the current tool: When a drawing tool is active we create shapes; when the selection tool is active we select shapes; and so forth. We can use the State pattern to change the editor's behavior depending on the current tool.

We can define an abstract Tool class from which to define subclasses that implement tool-specific behavior. The drawing editor maintains a current Tool object and delegates requests to it. It replaces this object when the user chooses a new tool, causing the behavior of the drawing editor to change accordingly.

This technique is used in both the HotDraw [Joh92] and Unidraw [VL90] drawing editor frameworks. It allows clients to define new kinds of tools easily. In HotDraw, the DrawingController class forwards the requests to the current Tool object. In Unidraw, the corresponding classes are Viewer and Tool. The following class diagram sketches the Tool and DrawingController interfaces:

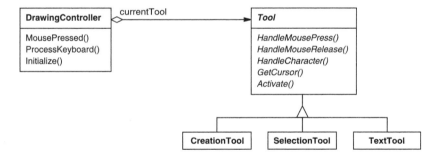

Coplien's Envelope-Letter idiom [Cop92] is related to State. Envelope-Letter is a technique for changing an object's class at run-time. The State pattern is more specific, focusing on how to deal with an object whose behavior depends on its state.

Related Patterns

The Flyweight (195) pattern explains when and how State objects can be shared.

State objects are often Singletons (127).

STRATEGY   Object Behavioral

Intent

Define a family of algorithms, encapsulate each one, and make them interchangeable. Strategy lets the algorithm vary independently from clients that use it.

Also Known As

Policy

Motivation

Many algorithms exist for breaking a stream of text into lines. Hard-wiring all such algorithms into the classes that require them isn't desirable for several reasons:

- Clients that need linebreaking get more complex if they include the linebreaking code. That makes clients bigger and harder to maintain, especially if they support multiple linebreaking algorithms.

- Different algorithms will be appropriate at different times. We don't want to support multiple linebreaking algorithms if we don't use them all.

- It's difficult to add new algorithms and vary existing ones when linebreaking is an integral part of a client.

We can avoid these problems by defining classes that encapsulate different linebreaking algorithms. An algorithm that's encapsulated in this way is called a **strategy**.

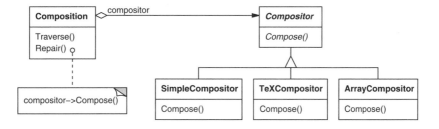

Suppose a Composition class is responsible for maintaining and updating the linebreaks of text displayed in a text viewer. Linebreaking strategies aren't implemented by the class Composition. Instead, they are implemented separately by subclasses of the abstract Compositor class. Compositor subclasses implement different strategies:

- **SimpleCompositor** implements a simple strategy that determines linebreaks one at a time.

- **TeXCompositor** implements the TEX algorithm for finding linebreaks. This strategy tries to optimize linebreaks globally, that is, one paragraph at a time.

- **ArrayCompositor** implements a strategy that selects breaks so that each row has a fixed number of items. It's useful for breaking a collection of icons into rows, for example.

A Composition maintains a reference to a Compositor object. Whenever a Composition reformats its text, it forwards this responsibility to its Compositor object. The client of Composition specifies which Compositor should be used by installing the Compositor it desires into the Composition.

Applicability

Use the Strategy pattern when

- many related classes differ only in their behavior. Strategies provide a way to configure a class with one of many behaviors.

- you need different variants of an algorithm. For example, you might define algorithms reflecting different space/time trade-offs. Strategies can be used when these variants are implemented as a class hierarchy of algorithms [HO87].

- an algorithm uses data that clients shouldn't know about. Use the Strategy pattern to avoid exposing complex, algorithm-specific data structures.

- a class defines many behaviors, and these appear as multiple conditional statements in its operations. Instead of many conditionals, move related conditional branches into their own Strategy class.

Structure

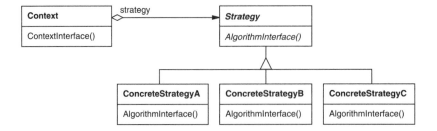

Participants

- **Strategy** (Compositor)
    - declares an interface common to all supported algorithms. Context uses this interface to call the algorithm defined by a ConcreteStrategy.
- **ConcreteStrategy** (SimpleCompositor, TeXCompositor, ArrayCompositor)
    - implements the algorithm using the Strategy interface.
- **Context** (Composition)
    - is configured with a ConcreteStrategy object.
    - maintains a reference to a Strategy object.
    - may define an interface that lets Strategy access its data.

Collaborations

- Strategy and Context interact to implement the chosen algorithm. A context may pass all data required by the algorithm to the strategy when the algorithm is called. Alternatively, the context can pass itself as an argument to Strategy operations. That lets the strategy call back on the context as required.
- A context forwards requests from its clients to its strategy. Clients usually create and pass a ConcreteStrategy object to the context; thereafter, clients interact with the context exclusively. There is often a family of ConcreteStrategy classes for a client to choose from.

Consequences

The Strategy pattern has the following benefits and drawbacks:

1. *Families of related algorithms.* Hierarchies of Strategy classes define a family of algorithms or behaviors for contexts to reuse. Inheritance can help factor out common functionality of the algorithms.

2. *An alternative to subclassing.* Inheritance offers another way to support a variety of algorithms or behaviors. You can subclass a Context class directly to give it different behaviors. But this hard-wires the behavior into Context. It mixes the algorithm implementation with Context's, making Context harder to understand, maintain, and extend. And you can't vary the algorithm dynamically. You wind up with many related classes whose only difference is the algorithm or behavior they employ. Encapsulating the algorithm in separate Strategy classes lets you vary the algorithm independently of its context, making it easier to switch, understand, and extend.

3. *Strategies eliminate conditional statements.* The Strategy pattern offers an alternative to conditional statements for selecting desired behavior. When different behaviors are lumped into one class, it's hard to avoid using conditional

statements to select the right behavior. Encapsulating the behavior in separate Strategy classes eliminates these conditional statements.

For example, without strategies, the code for breaking text into lines could look like

```
void Composition::Repair () {
    switch (_breakingStrategy) {
    case SimpleStrategy:
        ComposeWithSimpleCompositor();
        break;
    case TeXStrategy:
        ComposeWithTeXCompositor();
        break;
    // ...
    }
    // merge results with existing composition, if necessary
}
```

The Strategy pattern eliminates this case statement by delegating the line-breaking task to a Strategy object:

```
void Composition::Repair () {
    _compositor->Compose();
    // merge results with existing composition, if necessary
}
```

Code containing many conditional statements often indicates the need to apply the Strategy pattern.

4. *A choice of implementations.* Strategies can provide different implementations of the *same* behavior. The client can choose among strategies with different time and space trade-offs.

5. *Clients must be aware of different Strategies.* The pattern has a potential drawback in that a client must understand how Strategies differ before it can select the appropriate one. Clients might be exposed to implementation issues. Therefore you should use the Strategy pattern only when the variation in behavior is relevant to clients.

6. *Communication overhead between Strategy and Context.* The Strategy interface is shared by all ConcreteStrategy classes whether the algorithms they implement are trivial or complex. Hence it's likely that some ConcreteStrategies won't use all the information passed to them through this interface; simple ConcreteStrategies may use none of it! That means there will be times when the context creates and initializes parameters that never get used. If this is an issue, then you'll need tighter coupling between Strategy and Context.

7. *Increased number of objects.* Strategies increase the number of objects in an application. Sometimes you can reduce this overhead by implementing strategies as stateless objects that contexts can share. Any residual state is maintained by the context, which passes it in each request to the Strategy

object. Shared strategies should not maintain state across invocations. The Flyweight (195) pattern describes this approach in more detail.

Implementation

Consider the following implementation issues:

1. *Defining the Strategy and Context interfaces.* The Strategy and Context interfaces must give a ConcreteStrategy efficient access to any data it needs from a context, and vice versa.

   One approach is to have Context pass data in parameters to Strategy operations—in other words, take the data to the strategy. This keeps Strategy and Context decoupled. On the other hand, Context might pass data the Strategy doesn't need.

   Another technique has a context pass *itself* as an argument, and the strategy requests data from the context explicitly. Alternatively, the strategy can store a reference to its context, eliminating the need to pass anything at all. Either way, the strategy can request exactly what it needs. But now Context must define a more elaborate interface to its data, which couples Strategy and Context more closely.

   The needs of the particular algorithm and its data requirements will determine the best technique.

2. *Strategies as template parameters.* In C++ templates can be used to configure a class with a strategy. This technique is only applicable if (1) the Strategy can be selected at compile-time, and (2) it does not have to be changed at run-time. In this case, the class to be configured (e.g., `Context`) is defined as a template class that has a `Strategy` class as a parameter:

```
template <class AStrategy>
class Context {
    void Operation() { theStrategy.DoAlgorithm(); }
    // ...
private:
    AStrategy theStrategy;
};
```

   The class is then configured with a `Strategy` class when it's instantiated:

```
class MyStrategy {
public:
    void DoAlgorithm();
};

Context<MyStrategy> aContext;
```

   With templates, there's no need to define an abstract class that defines the interface to the `Strategy`. Using `Strategy` as a template parameter also lets you bind a `Strategy` to its `Context` statically, which can increase efficiency.

3. *Making Strategy objects optional.* The Context class may be simplified if it's meaningful *not* to have a Strategy object. Context checks to see if it has a Strategy object before accessing it. If there is one, then Context uses it normally. If there isn't a strategy, then Context carries out default behavior. The benefit of this approach is that clients don't have to deal with Strategy objects at all *unless* they don't like the default behavior.

Sample Code

We'll give the high-level code for the Motivation example, which is based on the implementation of Composition and Compositor classes in InterViews [LCI+92].

The `Composition` class maintains a collection of `Component` instances, which represent text and graphical elements in a document. A composition arranges component objects into lines using an instance of a `Compositor` subclass, which encapsulates a linebreaking strategy. Each component has an associated natural size, stretchability, and shrinkability. The stretchability defines how much the component can grow beyond its natural size; shrinkability is how much it can shrink. The composition passes these values to a compositor, which uses them to determine the best location for linebreaks.

```
class Composition {
public:
    Composition(Compositor*);
    void Repair();
private:
    Compositor* _compositor;
    Component* _components;     // the list of components
    int _componentCount;        // the number of components
    int _lineWidth;             // the Composition's line width
    int* _lineBreaks;           // the position of linebreaks
                                // in components
    int _lineCount;             // the number of lines
};
```

When a new layout is required, the composition asks its compositor to determine where to place linebreaks. The composition passes the compositor three arrays that define natural sizes, stretchabilities, and shrinkabilities of the components. It also passes the number of components, how wide the line is, and an array that the compositor fills with the position of each linebreak. The compositor returns the number of calculated breaks.

The `Compositor` interface lets the composition pass the compositor all the information it needs. This is an example of "taking the data to the strategy":

```
class Compositor {
public:
    virtual int Compose(
        Coord natural[], Coord stretch[], Coord shrink[],
        int componentCount, int lineWidth, int breaks[]
    ) = 0;
protected:
    Compositor();
};
```

Note that `Compositor` is an abstract class. Concrete subclasses define specific linebreaking strategies.

The composition calls its compositor in its `Repair` operation. `Repair` first initializes arrays with the natural size, stretchability, and shrinkability of each component (the details of which we omit for brevity). Then it calls on the compositor to obtain the linebreaks and finally lays out the components according to the breaks (also omitted):

```
void Composition::Repair () {
    Coord* natural;
    Coord* stretchability;
    Coord* shrinkability;
    int componentCount;
    int* breaks;

    // prepare the arrays with the desired component sizes
    // ...

    // determine where the breaks are:
    int breakCount;
    breakCount = _compositor->Compose(
        natural, stretchability, shrinkability,
        componentCount, _lineWidth, breaks
    );

    // lay out components according to breaks
    // ...
}
```

Now let's look at the `Compositor` subclasses. `SimpleCompositor` examines components a line at a time to determine where breaks should go:

```
class SimpleCompositor : public Compositor {
public:
    SimpleCompositor();

    virtual int Compose(
        Coord natural[], Coord stretch[], Coord shrink[],
        int componentCount, int lineWidth, int breaks[]
    );
    // ...
};
```

`TeXCompositor` uses a more global strategy. It examines a *paragraph* at a time, taking into account the components' size and stretchability. It also tries to give an even "color" to the paragraph by minimizing the whitespace between components.

```
class TeXCompositor : public Compositor {
public:
    TeXCompositor();

    virtual int Compose(
        Coord natural[], Coord stretch[], Coord shrink[],
        int componentCount, int lineWidth, int breaks[]
    );
    // ...
};
```

`ArrayCompositor` breaks the components into lines at regular intervals.

```
class ArrayCompositor : public Compositor {
public:
    ArrayCompositor(int interval);

    virtual int Compose(
        Coord natural[], Coord stretch[], Coord shrink[],
        int componentCount, int lineWidth, int breaks[]
    );
    // ...
};
```

These classes don't use all the information passed in `Compose`. `SimpleCompositor` ignores the stretchability of the components, taking only their natural widths into account. `TeXCompositor` uses all the information passed to it, whereas `ArrayCompositor` ignores everything.

To instantiate `Composition`, you pass it the compositor you want to use:

```
Composition* quick = new Composition(new SimpleCompositor);
Composition* slick = new Composition(new TeXCompositor);
Composition* iconic = new Composition(new ArrayCompositor(100));
```

`Compositor`'s interface is carefully designed to support all layout algorithms that subclasses might implement. You don't want to have to change this interface with every new subclass, because that will require changing existing subclasses. In general, the Strategy and Context interfaces determine how well the pattern achieves its intent.

Known Uses

Both ET++ [WGM88] and InterViews use strategies to encapsulate different line-breaking algorithms as we've described.

In the RTL System for compiler code optimization [JML92], strategies define different register allocation schemes (RegisterAllocator) and instruction set scheduling policies (RISCscheduler, CISCscheduler). This provides flexibility in targeting the optimizer for different machine architectures.

The ET++SwapsManager calculation engine framework computes prices for different financial instruments [EG92]. Its key abstractions are Instrument and Yield-Curve. Different instruments are implemented as subclasses of Instrument. Yield-Curve calculates discount factors, which determine the present value of future cash flows. Both of these classes delegate some behavior to Strategy objects. The framework provides a family of ConcreteStrategy classes for generating cash flows, valuing swaps, and calculating discount factors. You can create new calculation engines by configuring Instrument and YieldCurve with the different ConcreteStrategy objects. This approach supports mixing and matching existing Strategy implementations as well as defining new ones.

The Booch components [BV90] use strategies as template arguments. The Booch collection classes support three different kinds of memory allocation strategies: managed (allocation out of a pool), controlled (allocations/deallocations are protected by locks), and unmanaged (the normal memory allocator). These strategies are passed as template arguments to a collection class when it's instantiated. For example, an UnboundedCollection that uses the unmanaged strategy is instantiated as `UnboundedCollection<MyItemType*, Unmanaged>`.

RApp is a system for integrated circuit layout [GA89, AG90]. RApp must lay out and route wires that connect subsystems on the circuit. Routing algorithms in RApp are defined as subclasses of an abstract Router class. Router is a Strategy class.

Borland's ObjectWindows [Bor94] uses strategies in dialogs boxes to ensure that the user enters valid data. For example, numbers might have to be in a certain range, and a numeric entry field should accept only digits. Validating that a string is correct can require a table look-up.

ObjectWindows uses Validator objects to encapsulate validation strategies. Validators are examples of Strategy objects. Data entry fields delegate the validation strategy to an optional Validator object. The client attaches a validator to a field if validation is required (an example of an optional strategy). When the dialog is closed, the entry fields ask their validators to validate the data. The class library provides validators for common cases, such as a RangeValidator for numbers. New client-specific validation strategies can be defined easily by subclassing the Validator class.

Related Patterns

Flyweight (195): Strategy objects often make good flyweights.

TEMPLATE METHOD   Class Behavioral

Intent

Define the skeleton of an algorithm in an operation, deferring some steps to subclasses. Template Method lets subclasses redefine certain steps of an algorithm without changing the algorithm's structure.

Motivation

Consider an application framework that provides Application and Document classes. The Application class is responsible for opening existing documents stored in an external format, such as a file. A Document object represents the information in a document once it's read from the file.

Applications built with the framework can subclass Application and Document to suit specific needs. For example, a drawing application defines DrawApplication and DrawDocument subclasses; a spreadsheet application defines Spreadsheet-Application and SpreadsheetDocument subclasses.

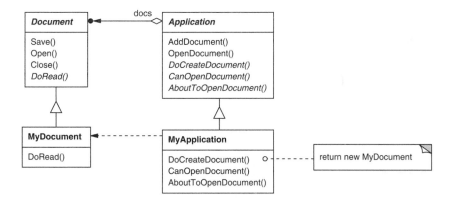

The abstract Application class defines the algorithm for opening and reading a document in its OpenDocument operation:

```
void Application::OpenDocument (const char* name) {
    if (!CanOpenDocument(name)) {
        // cannot handle this document
        return;
    }
```

```
        Document* doc = DoCreateDocument();

    if (doc) {
        _docs->AddDocument(doc);
        AboutToOpenDocument(doc);
        doc->Open();
        doc->DoRead();
    }
}
```

OpenDocument defines each step for opening a document. It checks if the document can be opened, creates the application-specific Document object, adds it to its set of documents, and reads the Document from a file.

We call OpenDocument a **template method**. A template method defines an algorithm in terms of abstract operations that subclasses override to provide concrete behavior. Application subclasses define the steps of the algorithm that check if the document can be opened (CanOpenDocument) and that create the Document (DoCreateDocument). Document classes define the step that reads the document (DoRead). The template method also defines an operation that lets Application subclasses know when the document is about to be opened (AboutToOpenDocument), in case they care.

By defining some of the steps of an algorithm using abstract operations, the template method fixes their ordering, but it lets Application and Document subclasses vary those steps to suit their needs.

Applicability

The Template Method pattern should be used

- to implement the invariant parts of an algorithm once and leave it up to subclasses to implement the behavior that can vary.

- when common behavior among subclasses should be factored and localized in a common class to avoid code duplication. This is a good example of "refactoring to generalize" as described by Opdyke and Johnson [OJ93]. You first identify the differences in the existing code and then separate the differences into new operations. Finally, you replace the differing code with a template method that calls one of these new operations.

- to control subclasses extensions. You can define a template method that calls "hook" operations (see Consequences) at specific points, thereby permitting extensions only at those points.

Structure

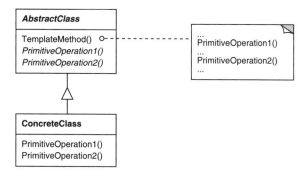

Participants

- **AbstractClass** (Application)
  - defines abstract **primitive operations** that concrete subclasses define to implement steps of an algorithm.
  - implements a template method defining the skeleton of an algorithm. The template method calls primitive operations as well as operations defined in AbstractClass or those of other objects.
- **ConcreteClass** (MyApplication)
  - implements the primitive operations to carry out subclass-specific steps of the algorithm.

Collaborations

- ConcreteClass relies on AbstractClass to implement the invariant steps of the algorithm.

Consequences

Template methods are a fundamental technique for code reuse. They are particularly important in class libraries, because they are the means for factoring out common behavior in library classes.

Template methods lead to an inverted control structure that's sometimes referred to as "the Hollywood principle," that is, "Don't call us, we'll call you" [Swe85]. This refers to how a parent class calls the operations of a subclass and not the other way around.

Template methods call the following kinds of operations:

- concrete operations (either on the ConcreteClass or on client classes);

- concrete AbstractClass operations (i.e., operations that are generally useful to subclasses);

- primitive operations (i.e., abstract operations);

- factory methods (see Factory Method (107)); and

- **hook operations**, which provide default behavior that subclasses can extend if necessary. A hook operation often does nothing by default.

It's important for template methods to specify which operations are hooks (*may* be overridden) and which are abstract operations (*must* be overridden). To reuse an abstract class effectively, subclass writers must understand which operations are designed for overriding.

A subclass can *extend* a parent class operation's behavior by overriding the operation and calling the parent operation explicitly:

```
void DerivedClass::Operation () {
    ParentClass::Operation();
    // DerivedClass extended behavior
}
```

Unfortunately, it's easy to forget to call the inherited operation. We can transform such an operation into a template method to give the parent control over how subclasses extend it. The idea is to call a hook operation from a template method in the parent class. Then subclasses can then override this hook operation:

```
void ParentClass::Operation () {
    // ParentClass behavior
    HookOperation();
}
```

`HookOperation` does nothing in `ParentClass`:

```
void ParentClass::HookOperation () { }
```

Subclasses override `HookOperation` to extend its behavior:

```
void DerivedClass::HookOperation () {
    // derived class extension
}
```

Implementation

Three implementation issues are worth noting:

1. *Using C++ access control.* In C++, the primitive operations that a template method calls can be declared protected members. This ensures that they are only called by the template method. Primitive operations that *must* be

overridden are declared pure virtual. The template method itself should not be overridden; therefore you can make the template method a nonvirtual member function.

2. *Minimizing primitive operations.* An important goal in designing template methods is to minimize the number of primitive operations that a subclass must override to flesh out the algorithm. The more operations that need overriding, the more tedious things get for clients.

3. *Naming conventions.* You can identify the operations that should be overridden by adding a prefix to their names. For example, the MacApp framework for Macintosh applications [App89] prefixes template method names with "Do-": "DoCreateDocument", "DoRead", and so forth.

Sample Code

The following C++ example shows how a parent class can enforce an invariant for its subclasses. The example comes from NeXT's AppKit [Add94]. Consider a class `View` that supports drawing on the screen. `View` enforces the invariant that its subclasses can draw into a view only after it becomes the "focus," which requires certain drawing state (for example, colors and fonts) to be set up properly.

We can use a `Display` template method to set up this state. `View` defines two concrete operations, `SetFocus` and `ResetFocus`, that set up and clean up the drawing state, respectively. `View`'s `DoDisplay` hook operation performs the actual drawing. `Display` calls `SetFocus` before `DoDisplay` to set up the drawing state; `Display` calls `ResetFocus` afterwards to release the drawing state.

```
void View::Display () {
    SetFocus();
    DoDisplay();
    ResetFocus();
}
```

To maintain the invariant, the `View`'s clients always call `Display`, and `View` subclasses always override `DoDisplay`.

`DoDisplay` does nothing in `View`:

```
void View::DoDisplay () { }
```

Subclasses override it to add their specific drawing behavior:

```
void MyView::DoDisplay () {
    // render the view's contents
}
```

Known Uses

Template methods are so fundamental that they can be found in almost every abstract class. Wirfs-Brock et al. [WBWW90, WBJ90] provide a good overview and discussion of template methods.

Related Patterns

Factory Methods (107) are often called by template methods. In the Motivation example, the factory method DoCreateDocument is called by the template method OpenDocument.

Strategy (315): Template methods use inheritance to vary part of an algorithm. Strategies use delegation to vary the entire algorithm.

VISITOR   Object Behavioral

Intent

Represent an operation to be performed on the elements of an object structure. Visitor lets you define a new operation without changing the classes of the elements on which it operates.

Motivation

Consider a compiler that represents programs as abstract syntax trees. It will need to perform operations on abstract syntax trees for "static semantic" analyses like checking that all variables are defined. It will also need to generate code. So it might define operations for type-checking, code optimization, flow analysis, checking for variables being assigned values before they're used, and so on. Moreover, we could use the abstract syntax trees for pretty-printing, program restructuring, code instrumentation, and computing various metrics of a program.

Most of these operations will need to treat nodes that represent assignment statements differently from nodes that represent variables or arithmetic expressions. Hence there will be one class for assignment statements, another for variable accesses, another for arithmetic expressions, and so on. The set of node classes depends on the language being compiled, of course, but it doesn't change much for a given language.

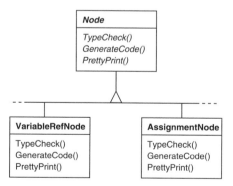

This diagram shows part of the Node class hierarchy. The problem here is that distributing all these operations across the various node classes leads to a system that's hard to understand, maintain, and change. It will be confusing to have type-checking code mixed with pretty-printing code or flow analysis code. Moreover, adding a new operation usually requires recompiling all of these classes. It would be better if each new operation could be added separately, and the node classes were independent of the operations that apply to them.

We can have both by packaging related operations from each class in a separate object, called a **visitor**, and passing it to elements of the abstract syntax tree as it's traversed. When an element "accepts" the visitor, it sends a request to the visitor that encodes the element's class. It also includes the element as an argument. The visitor will then execute the operation for that element—-the operation that used to be in the class of the element.

For example, a compiler that didn't use visitors might type-check a procedure by calling the TypeCheck operation on its abstract syntax tree. Each of the nodes would implement TypeCheck by calling TypeCheck on its components (see the preceding class diagram). If the compiler type-checked a procedure using visitors, then it would create a TypeCheckingVisitor object and call the Accept operation on the abstract syntax tree with that object as an argument. Each of the nodes would implement Accept by calling back on the visitor: an assignment node calls VisitAssignment operation on the visitor, while a variable reference calls VisitVariableReference. What used to be the TypeCheck operation in class AssignmentNode is now the VisitAssignment operation on TypeCheckingVisitor.

To make visitors work for more than just type-checking, we need an abstract parent class NodeVisitor for all visitors of an abstract syntax tree. NodeVisitor must declare an operation for each node class. An application that needs to compute program metrics will define new subclasses of NodeVisitor and will no longer need to add application-specific code to the node classes. The Visitor pattern encapsulates the operations for each compilation phase in a Visitor associated with that phase.

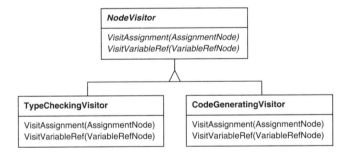

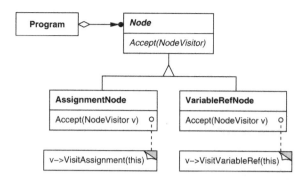

With the Visitor pattern, you define two class hierarchies: one for the elements being operated on (the Node hierarchy) and one for the visitors that define operations on the elements (the NodeVisitor hierarchy). You create a new operation by adding a new subclass to the visitor class hierarchy. As long as the grammar that the compiler accepts doesn't change (that is, we don't have to add new Node subclasses), we can add new functionality simply by defining new NodeVisitor subclasses.

Applicability

Use the Visitor pattern when

- an object structure contains many classes of objects with differing interfaces, and you want to perform operations on these objects that depend on their concrete classes.

- many distinct and unrelated operations need to be performed on objects in an object structure, and you want to avoid "polluting" their classes with these operations. Visitor lets you keep related operations together by defining them in one class. When the object structure is shared by many applications, use Visitor to put operations in just those applications that need them.

- the classes defining the object structure rarely change, but you often want to define new operations over the structure. Changing the object structure classes requires redefining the interface to all visitors, which is potentially costly. If the object structure classes change often, then it's probably better to define the operations in those classes.

Structure

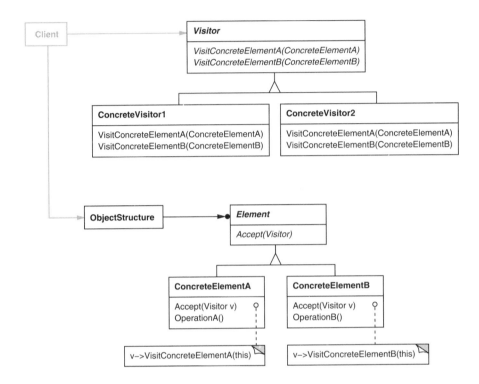

Participants

- **Visitor** (NodeVisitor)

  – declares a Visit operation for each class of ConcreteElement in the object structure. The operation's name and signature identifies the class that sends the Visit request to the visitor. That lets the visitor determine the concrete class of the element being visited. Then the visitor can access the element directly through its particular interface.

- **ConcreteVisitor** (TypeCheckingVisitor)

  – implements each operation declared by Visitor. Each operation implements a fragment of the algorithm defined for the corresponding class of object in the structure. ConcreteVisitor provides the context for the algorithm and stores its local state. This state often accumulates results during the traversal of the structure.

- **Element** (Node)

  – defines an Accept operation that takes a visitor as an argument.

- **ConcreteElement** (AssignmentNode,VariableRefNode)

  – implements an Accept operation that takes a visitor as an argument.

- **ObjectStructure** (Program)

  – can enumerate its elements.

  – may provide a high-level interface to allow the visitor to visit its elements.

  – may either be a composite (see Composite (163)) or a collection such as a list or a set.

Collaborations

- A client that uses the Visitor pattern must create a ConcreteVisitor object and then traverse the object structure, visiting each element with the visitor.

- When an element is visited, it calls the Visitor operation that corresponds to its class. The element supplies itself as an argument to this operation to let the visitor access its state, if necessary.

  The following interaction diagram illustrates the collaborations between an object structure, a visitor, and two elements:

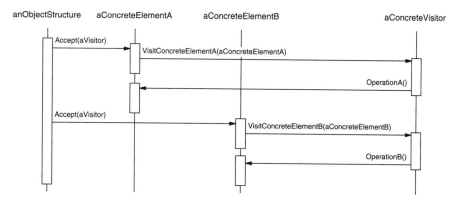

Consequences

Some of the benefits and liabilities of the Visitor pattern are as follows:

1. *Visitor makes adding new operations easy.* Visitors make it easy to add operations that depend on the components of complex objects. You can define a new operation over an object structure simply by adding a new visitor. In contrast, if you spread functionality over many classes, then you must change each class to define a new operation.

2. *A visitor gathers related operations and separates unrelated ones.* Related behavior isn't spread over the classes defining the object structure; it's localized in a visitor. Unrelated sets of behavior are partitioned in their own visitor

subclasses. That simplifies both the classes defining the elements and the algorithms defined in the visitors. Any algorithm-specific data structures can be hidden in the visitor.

3. *Adding new ConcreteElement classes is hard.* The Visitor pattern makes it hard to add new subclasses of Element. Each new ConcreteElement gives rise to a new abstract operation on Visitor and a corresponding implementation in every ConcreteVisitor class. Sometimes a default implementation can be provided in Visitor that can be inherited by most of the ConcreteVisitors, but this is the exception rather than the rule.

   So the key consideration in applying the Visitor pattern is whether you are mostly likely to change the algorithm applied over an object structure or the classes of objects that make up the structure. The Visitor class hierarchy can be difficult to maintain when new ConcreteElement classes are added frequently. In such cases, it's probably easier just to define operations on the classes that make up the structure. If the Element class hierarchy is stable, but you are continually adding operations or changing algorithms, then the Visitor pattern will help you manage the changes.

4. *Visiting across class hierarchies.* An iterator (see Iterator (257)) can visit the objects in a structure as it traverses them by calling their operations. But an iterator can't work across object structures with different types of elements. For example, the Iterator interface defined on page 263 can access only objects of type `Item`:

```
template <class Item>
class Iterator {
    // ...
    Item CurrentItem() const;
};
```

   This implies that all elements the iterator can visit have a common parent class `Item`.

   Visitor does not have this restriction. It can visit objects that don't have a common parent class. You can add any type of object to a Visitor interface. For example, in

```
class Visitor {
public:
    // ...
    void VisitMyType(MyType*);
    void VisitYourType(YourType*);
};
```

   `MyType` and `YourType` do not have to be related through inheritance at all.

5. *Accumulating state.* Visitors can accumulate state as they visit each element in the object structure. Without a visitor, this state would be passed as extra arguments to the operations that perform the traversal, or they might appear as global variables.

6. *Breaking encapsulation.* Visitor's approach assumes that the ConcreteElement interface is powerful enough to let visitors do their job. As a result, the pattern often forces you to provide public operations that access an element's internal state, which may compromise its encapsulation.

Implementation

Each object structure will have an associated Visitor class. This abstract visitor class declares a VisitConcreteElement operation for each class of ConcreteElement defining the object structure. Each Visit operation on the Visitor declares its argument to be a particular ConcreteElement, allowing the Visitor to access the interface of the ConcreteElement directly. ConcreteVisitor classes override each Visit operation to implement visitor-specific behavior for the corresponding ConcreteElement class.

The Visitor class would be declared like this in C++:

```
class Visitor {
public:
    virtual void VisitElementA(ElementA*);
    virtual void VisitElementB(ElementB*);

    // and so on for other concrete elements
protected:
    Visitor();
};
```

Each class of ConcreteElement implements an `Accept` operation that calls the matching `Visit...` operation on the visitor for that ConcreteElement. Thus the operation that ends up getting called depends on both the class of the element and the class of the visitor.[10]

The concrete elements are declared as

```
class Element {
public:
    virtual ~Element();
    virtual void Accept(Visitor&) = 0;
protected:
    Element();
};
```

---

[10] We could use function overloading to give these operations the same simple name, like `Visit`, since the operations are already differentiated by the parameter they're passed. There are pros and cons to such overloading. On the one hand, it reinforces the fact that each operation involves the same analysis, albeit on a different argument. On the other hand, that might make what's going on at the call site less obvious to someone reading the code. It really boils down to whether you believe function overloading is good or not.

```
class ElementA : public Element {
public:
    ElementA();
    virtual void Accept(Visitor& v) { v.VisitElementA(this); }
};

class ElementB : public Element {
public:
    ElementB();
    virtual void Accept(Visitor& v) { v.VisitElementB(this); }
};
```

A `CompositeElement` class might implement `Accept` like this:

```
class CompositeElement : public Element {
public:
    virtual void Accept(Visitor&);
private:
    List<Element*>* _children;
};

void CompositeElement::Accept (Visitor& v) {
    ListIterator<Element*> i(_children);

    for (i.First(); !i.IsDone(); i.Next()) {
        i.CurrentItem()->Accept(v);
    }
    v.VisitCompositeElement(this);
}
```

Here are two other implementation issues that arise when you apply the Visitor pattern:

1. *Double dispatch.* Effectively, the Visitor pattern lets you add operations to classes without changing them. Visitor achieves this by using a technique called **double-dispatch**. It's a well-known technique. In fact, some programming languages support it directly (CLOS, for example). Languages like C++ and Smalltalk support **single-dispatch**.

   In single-dispatch languages, two criteria determine which operation will fulfill a request: the name of the request and the type of receiver. For example, the operation that a GenerateCode request will call depends on the type of node object you ask. In C++, calling `GenerateCode` on an instance of `VariableRefNode` will call `VariableRefNode::GenerateCode` (which generates code for a variable reference). Calling `GenerateCode` on an `AssignmentNode` will call `AssignmentNode::GenerateCode` (which will generate code for an assignment). The operation that gets executed depends both on the kind of request and the type of the receiver.

   "Double-dispatch" simply means the operation that gets executed depends on the kind of request and the types of *two* receivers. `Accept` is a double-dispatch operation. Its meaning depends on two types: the Visitor's and the

Element's. Double-dispatching lets visitors request different operations on each class of element.[11]

This is the key to the Visitor pattern: The operation that gets executed depends on both the type of Visitor and the type of Element it visits. Instead of binding operations statically into the Element interface, you can consolidate the operations in a Visitor and use `Accept` to do the binding at run-time. Extending the Element interface amounts to defining one new Visitor subclass rather than many new Element subclasses.

2. *Who is responsible for traversing the object structure?* A visitor must visit each element of the object structure. The question is, how does it get there? We can put responsibility for traversal in any of three places: in the object structure, in the visitor, or in a separate iterator object (see Iterator (257)).

    Often the object structure is responsible for iteration. A collection will simply iterate over its elements, calling the Accept operation on each. A composite will commonly traverse itself by having each Accept operation traverse the element's children and call Accept on each of them recursively.

    Another solution is to use an iterator to visit the elements. In C++, you could use either an internal or external iterator, depending on what is available and what is most efficient. In Smalltalk, you usually use an internal iterator using `do:` and a block. Since internal iterators are implemented by the object structure, using an internal iterator is a lot like making the object structure responsible for iteration. The main difference is that an internal iterator will not cause double-dispatching—it will call an operation on the *visitor* with an *element* as an argument as opposed to calling an operation on the *element* with the *visitor* as an argument. But it's easy to use the Visitor pattern with an internal iterator if the operation on the visitor simply calls the operation on the element without recursing.

    You could even put the traversal algorithm in the visitor, although you'll end up duplicating the traversal code in each ConcreteVisitor for each aggregate ConcreteElement. The main reason to put the traversal strategy in the visitor is to implement a particularly complex traversal, one that depends on the results of the operations on the object structure. We'll give an example of such a case in the Sample Code.

Sample Code

Because visitors are usually associated with composites, we'll use the `Equipment` classes defined in the Sample Code of Composite (163) to illustrate the Visitor pattern. We will use Visitor to define operations for computing the inventory of materials and the total cost for a piece of equipment. The `Equipment` classes are

---

[11] If we can have *double*-dispatch, then why not *triple* or *quadruple*, or any other number? Actually, double-dispatch is just a special case of **multiple dispatch**, in which the operation is chosen based on any number of types. (CLOS actually supports multiple dispatch.) Languages that support double- or multiple dispatch lessen the need for the Visitor pattern.

so simple that using Visitor isn't really necessary, but they make it easy to see what's involved in implementing the pattern.

Here again is the `Equipment` class from Composite (163). We've augmented it with an `Accept` operation to let it work with a visitor.

```
class Equipment {
public:
    virtual ~Equipment();

    const char* Name() { return _name; }

    virtual Watt Power();
    virtual Currency NetPrice();
    virtual Currency DiscountPrice();

    virtual void Accept(EquipmentVisitor&);
protected:
    Equipment(const char*);
private:
    const char* _name;
};
```

The `Equipment` operations return the attributes of a piece of equipment, such as its power consumption and cost. Subclasses redefine these operations appropriately for specific types of equipment (e.g., a chassis, drives, and planar boards).

The abstract class for all visitors of equipment has a virtual function for each subclass of equipment, as shown next. All of the virtual functions do nothing by default.

```
class EquipmentVisitor {
public:
    virtual ~EquipmentVisitor();

    virtual void VisitFloppyDisk(FloppyDisk*);
    virtual void VisitCard(Card*);
    virtual void VisitChassis(Chassis*);
    virtual void VisitBus(Bus*);

    // and so on for other concrete subclasses of Equipment
protected:
    EquipmentVisitor();
};
```

`Equipment` subclasses define `Accept` in basically the same way: It calls the `EquipmentVisitor` operation that corresponds to the class that received the `Accept` request, like this:

```
void FloppyDisk::Accept (EquipmentVisitor& visitor) {
    visitor.VisitFloppyDisk(this);
}
```

Equipment that contains other equipment (in particular, subclasses of Com-positeEquipment in the Composite pattern) implements Accept by iterating over its children and calling Accept on each of them. Then it calls the Visit operation as usual. For example, Chassis::Accept could traverse all the parts in the chassis as follows:

```
void Chassis::Accept (EquipmentVisitor& visitor) {
    for (
        ListIterator<Equipment*> i(_parts);
        !i.IsDone();
        i.Next()
    ) {
        i.CurrentItem()->Accept(visitor);
    }
    visitor.VisitChassis(this);
}
```

Subclasses of EquipmentVisitor define particular algorithms over the equipment structure. The PricingVisitor computes the cost of the equipment structure. It computes the net price of all simple equipment (e.g., floppies) and the discount price of all composite equipment (e.g., chassis and buses).

```
class PricingVisitor : public EquipmentVisitor {
public:
    PricingVisitor();

    Currency& GetTotalPrice();

    virtual void VisitFloppyDisk(FloppyDisk*);
    virtual void VisitCard(Card*);
    virtual void VisitChassis(Chassis*);
    virtual void VisitBus(Bus*);
    // ...
private:
    Currency _total;
};

void PricingVisitor::VisitFloppyDisk (FloppyDisk* e) {
    _total += e->NetPrice();
}

void PricingVisitor::VisitChassis (Chassis* e) {
    _total += e->DiscountPrice();
}
```

PricingVisitor will compute the total cost of all nodes in the equipment structure. Note that PricingVisitor chooses the appropriate pricing policy for a class of equipment by dispatching to the corresponding member function. What's more, we can change the pricing policy of an equipment structure just by changing the PricingVisitor class.

We can define a visitor for computing inventory like this:

```
class InventoryVisitor : public EquipmentVisitor {
public:
    InventoryVisitor();

    Inventory& GetInventory();

    virtual void VisitFloppyDisk(FloppyDisk*);
    virtual void VisitCard(Card*);
    virtual void VisitChassis(Chassis*);
    virtual void VisitBus(Bus*);
    // ...

private:
    Inventory _inventory;
};
```

The `InventoryVisitor` accumulates the totals for each type of equipment in the object structure. `InventoryVisitor` uses an `Inventory` class that defines an interface for adding equipment (which we won't bother defining here).

```
void InventoryVisitor::VisitFloppyDisk (FloppyDisk* e) {
    _inventory.Accumulate(e);
}

void InventoryVisitor::VisitChassis (Chassis* e) {
    _inventory.Accumulate(e);
}
```

Here's how we can use an `InventoryVisitor` on an equipment structure:

```
Equipment* component;
InventoryVisitor visitor;

component->Accept(visitor);
cout << "Inventory "
    << component->Name()
    << visitor.GetInventory();
```

Now we'll show how to implement the Smalltalk example from the Interpreter pattern (see page 248) with the Visitor pattern. Like the previous example, this one is so small that Visitor probably won't buy us much, but it provides a good illustration of how to use the pattern. Further, it illustrates a situation in which iteration is the visitor's responsibility.

The object structure (regular expressions) is made of four classes, and all of them have an `accept:` method that takes the visitor as an argument. In class `SequenceExpression`, the `accept:` method is

```
accept: aVisitor
    ^ aVisitor visitSequence: self
```

In class RepeatExpression, the accept: method sends the visitRepeat: message. In class AlternationExpression, it sends the visitAlternation: message. In class LiteralExpression, it sends the visitLiteral: message.

The four classes also must have accessing functions that the visitor can use. For SequenceExpression these are expression1 and expression2; for AlternationExpression these are alternative1 and alternative2; for RepeatExpression it is repetition; and for LiteralExpression these are components.

The ConcreteVisitor class is REMatchingVisitor. It is responsible for the traversal because its traversal algorithm is irregular. The biggest irregularity is that a RepeatExpression will repeatedly traverse its component. The class REMatchingVisitor has an instance variable inputState. Its methods are essentially the same as the match: methods of the expression classes in the Interpreter pattern except they replace the argument named inputState with the expression node being matched. However, they still return the set of streams that the expression would match to identify the current state.

```
visitSequence: sequenceExp
    inputState := sequenceExp expression1 accept: self.
    ^ sequenceExp expression2 accept: self.


visitRepeat: repeatExp
    | finalState |
    finalState := inputState copy.
    [inputState isEmpty]
        whileFalse:
            [inputState := repeatExp repetition accept: self.
            finalState addAll: inputState].
    ^ finalState


visitAlternation: alternateExp
    | finalState originalState |
    originalState := inputState.
    finalState := alternateExp alternative1 accept: self.
    inputState := originalState.
    finalState addAll: (alternateExp alternative2 accept: self).
    ^ finalState
```

```
visitLiteral: literalExp
    | finalState tStream |
    finalState := Set new.
    inputState
        do:
            [:stream | tStream := stream copy.
                (tStream nextAvailable:
                    literalExp components size
                ) = literalExp components
                    ifTrue: [finalState add: tStream]
            ].
    ^ finalState
```

Known Uses

The Smalltalk-80 compiler has a Visitor class called ProgramNodeEnumerator. It's used primarily for algorithms that analyze source code. It isn't used for code generation or pretty-printing, although it could be.

IRIS Inventor [Str93] is a toolkit for developing 3-D graphics applications. Inventor represents a three-dimensional scene as a hierarchy of nodes, each representing either a geometric object or an attribute of one. Operations like rendering a scene or mapping an input event require traversing this hierarchy in different ways. Inventor does this using visitors called "actions." There are different visitors for rendering, event handling, searching, filing, and determining bounding boxes.

To make adding new nodes easier, Inventor implements a double-dispatch scheme for C++. The scheme relies on run-time type information and a two-dimensional table in which rows represent visitors and columns represent node classes. The cells store a pointer to the function bound to the visitor and node class.

Mark Linton coined the term "Visitor" in the X Consortium's Fresco Application Toolkit specification [LP93].

Related Patterns

Composite (163): Visitors can be used to apply an operation over an object structure defined by the Composite pattern.

Interpreter (243): Visitor may be applied to do the interpretation.

Discussion of Behavioral Patterns

Encapsulating Variation

Encapsulating variation is a theme of many behavioral patterns. When an aspect of a program changes frequently, these patterns define an object that encapsulates that aspect. Then other parts of the program can collaborate with the object whenever they depend on that aspect. The patterns usually define an abstract class that describes the encapsulating object, and the pattern derives its name from that object.[12] For example,

- a Strategy object encapsulates an algorithm (Strategy (315)),

- a State object encapsulates a state-dependent behavior (State (305)),

- a Mediator object encapsulates the protocol between objects (Mediator (273)), and

- an Iterator object encapsulates the way you access and traverse the components of an aggregate object (Iterator (257)).

These patterns describe aspects of a program that are likely to change. Most patterns have two kinds of objects: the new object(s) that encapsulate the aspect, and the existing object(s) that use the new ones. Usually the functionality of new objects would be an integral part of the existing objects were it not for the pattern. For example, code for a Strategy would probably be wired into the strategy's Context, and code for a State would be implemented directly in the state's Context.

But not all object behavioral patterns partition functionality like this. For example, Chain of Responsibility (223) deals with an arbitrary number of objects (i.e., a chain), all of which may already exist in the system.

Chain of Responsibility illustrates another difference in behavioral patterns: Not all define static communication relationships between classes. Chain of Responsibility prescribes communication between an open-ended number of objects. Other patterns involve objects that are passed around as arguments.

Objects as Arguments

Several patterns introduce an object that's *always* used as an argument. One of these is Visitor (331). A Visitor object is the argument to a polymorphic Accept operation on the objects it visits. The visitor is never considered a part of those objects, even though the conventional alternative to the pattern is to distribute Visitor code across the object structure classes.

---

[12] This theme runs through other kinds of patterns, too. AbstractFactory (87), Builder (97), and Prototype (117) all encapsulate knowledge about how objects are created. Decorator (175) encapsulates responsibility that can be added to an object. Bridge (151) separates an abstraction from its implementation, letting them vary independently.

Other patterns define objects that act as magic tokens to be passed around and invoked at a later time. Both Command (233) and Memento (283) fall into this category. In Command, the token represents a request; in Memento, it represents the internal state of an object at a particular time. In both cases, the token can have a complex internal representation, but the client is never aware of it. But even here there are differences. Polymorphism is important in the Command pattern, because executing the Command object is a polymorphic operation. In contrast, the Memento interface is so narrow that a memento can only be passed as a value. So it's likely to present no polymorphic operations at all to its clients.

Should Communication be Encapsulated or Distributed?

Mediator (273) and Observer (293) are competing patterns. The difference between them is that Observer distributes communication by introducing Observer and Subject objects, whereas a Mediator object encapsulates the communication between other objects.

In the Observer pattern, there is no single object that encapsulates a constraint. Instead, the Observer and the Subject must cooperate to maintain the constraint. Communication patterns are determined by the way observers and subjects are interconnected: a single subject usually has many observers, and sometimes the observer of one subject is a subject of another observer. The Mediator pattern centralizes rather than distributes. It places the responsibility for maintaining a constraint squarely in the mediator.

We've found it easier to make reusable Observers and Subjects than to make reusable Mediators. The Observer pattern promotes partitioning and loose coupling between Observer and Subject, and that leads to finer-grained classes that are more apt to be reused.

On the other hand, it's easier to understand the flow of communication in Mediator than in Observer. Observers and subjects are usually connected shortly after they're created, and it's hard to see how they are connected later in the program. If you know the Observer pattern, then you understand that the way observers and subjects are connected is important, and you also know what connections to look for. However, the indirection that Observer introduces will still make a system harder to understand.

Observers in Smalltalk can be parameterized with messages to access the Subject state, and so they are even more reusable than they are in C++. This makes Observer more attractive than Mediator in Smalltalk. Thus a Smalltalk programmer will often use Observer where a C++ programmer would use Mediator.

Decoupling Senders and Receivers

When collaborating objects refer to each other directly, they become dependent on each other, and that can have an adverse impact on the layering and reusability of a system. Command, Observer, Mediator, and Chain of Responsibility address how you can decouple senders and receivers, but with different trade-offs.

The Command pattern supports decoupling by using a Command object to define the binding between a sender and receiver:

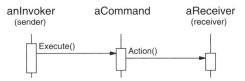

The Command object provides a simple interface for issuing the request (that is, the Execute operation). Defining the sender-receiver connection in a separate object lets the sender work with different receivers. It keeps the sender decoupled from the receivers, making senders easy to reuse. Moreover, you can reuse the Command object to parameterize a receiver with different senders. The Command pattern nominally requires a subclass for each sender-receiver connection, although the pattern describes implementation techniques that avoid subclassing.

The Observer pattern decouples senders (subjects) from receivers (observers) by defining an interface for signaling changes in subjects. Observer defines a looser sender-receiver binding than Command, since a subject may have multiple observers, and their number can vary at run-time.

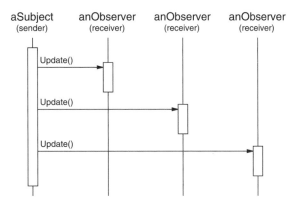

The Subject and Observer interfaces in the Observer pattern are designed for communicating changes. Therefore the Observer pattern is best for decoupling objects when there are data dependencies between them.

The Mediator pattern decouples objects by having them refer to each other indirectly through a Mediator object.

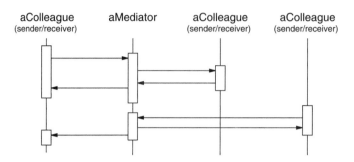

A Mediator object routes requests between Colleague objects and centralizes their communication. Consequently, colleagues can only talk to each other through the Mediator interface. Because this interface is fixed, the Mediator might have to implement its own dispatching scheme for added flexibility. Requests can be encoded and arguments packed in such a way that colleagues can request an open-ended set of operations.

The Mediator pattern can reduce subclassing in a system, because it centralizes communication behavior in one class instead of distributing it among subclasses. However, *ad hoc* dispatching schemes often decrease type safety.

Finally, the Chain of Responsibility pattern decouples the sender from the receiver by passing the request along a chain of potential receivers:

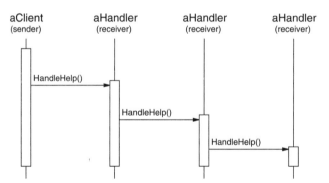

Since the interface between senders and receivers is fixed, Chain of Responsibility may also require a custom dispatching scheme. Hence it has the same type-safety drawbacks as Mediator. Chain of Responsibility is a good way to decouple the sender and the receiver if the chain is already part of the system's structure, and one of several objects may be in a position to handle the request. Moreover, the pattern offers added flexibility in that the chain can be changed or extended easily.

Summary

With few exceptions, behavioral design patterns complement and reinforce each other. A class in a chain of responsibility, for example, will probably include at least one application of Template Method (325). The template method can use primitive operations to determine whether the object should handle the request and to choose the object to forward to. The chain can use the Command pattern to represent requests as objects. Interpreter (243) can use the State pattern to define parsing contexts. An iterator can traverse an aggregate, and a visitor can apply an operation to each element in the aggregate.

Behavioral patterns work well with other patterns, too. For example, a system that uses the Composite (163) pattern might use a visitor to perform operations on components of the composition. It could use Chain of Responsibility to let components access global properties through their parent. It could also use Decorator (175) to override these properties on parts of the composition. It could use the Observer pattern to tie one object structure to another and the State pattern to let a component change its behavior as its state changes. The composition itself might be created using the approach in Builder (97), and it might be treated as a Prototype (117) by some other part of the system.

Well-designed object-oriented systems are just like this—they have multiple patterns embedded in them—but not because their designers necessarily thought in these terms. Composition at the *pattern* level rather than the class or object levels lets us achieve the same synergy with greater ease.

Chapter 6

Conclusion

It's possible to argue that this book hasn't accomplished much. After all, it doesn't present any algorithms or programming techniques that haven't been used before. It doesn't give a rigorous method for designing systems, nor does it develop a new theory of design—it just documents existing designs. You could conclude that it makes a reasonable tutorial, perhaps, but it certainly can't offer much to an experienced object-oriented designer.

We hope you think differently. Cataloging design patterns is important. It gives us standard names and definitions for the techniques we use. If we don't study design patterns in software, we won't be able to improve them, and it'll be harder to come up with new ones.

This book is only a start. It contains some of the most common design patterns that expert object-oriented designers use, and yet people hear and learn about them solely by word of mouth or by studying existing systems. Early drafts of the book prompted other people to write down the design patterns they use, and it should prompt even more in its current form. We hope this will mark the start of a movement to document the expertise of software practitioners.

This chapter discusses the impact we think design patterns will have, how they are related to other work in design, and how you can get involved in finding and cataloging patterns.

6.1 What to Expect from Design Patterns

Here are several ways in which the design patterns in this book can affect the way you design object-oriented software, based on our day-to-day experience with them.

A Common Design Vocabulary

Studies of expert programmers for conventional languages have shown that knowledge and experience isn't organized simply around syntax but in larger conceptual structures such as algorithms, data structures and idioms [AS85, Cop92, Cur89, SS86], and plans for fulfilling a particular goal [SE84]. Designers probably don't think about the notation they're using for recording the design as much as they try to match the current design situation against plans, algorithms, data structures, and idioms they have learned in the past.

Computer scientists name and catalog algorithms and data structures, but we don't often name other kinds of patterns. Design patterns provide a common vocabulary for designers to use to communicate, document, and explore design alternatives. Design patterns make a system seem less complex by letting you talk about it at a higher level of abstraction than that of a design notation or programming language. Design patterns raise the level at which you design and discuss design with your colleagues.

Once you've absorbed the design patterns in this book, your design vocabulary will almost certainly change. You will speak directly in terms of the names of the design patterns. You'll find yourself saying things like, "Let's use an Observer here," or, "Let's make a Strategy out of these classes."

A Documentation and Learning Aid

Knowing the design patterns in this book makes it easier to understand existing systems. Most large object-oriented systems use these design patterns. People learning object-oriented programming often complain that the systems they're working with use inheritance in convoluted ways and that it's difficult to follow the flow of control. In large part this is because they do not understand the design patterns in the system. Learning these design patterns will help you understand existing object-oriented systems.

These design patterns can also make you a better designer. They provide solutions to common problems. If you work with object-oriented systems long enough, you'll probably learn these design patterns on your own. But reading the book will help you learn them much faster. Learning these patterns will help a novice act more like an expert.

Moreover, describing a system in terms of the design patterns that it uses will make it a lot easier to understand. Otherwise, people will have to reverse-engineer the design to unearth the patterns it uses. Having a common vocabulary means you don't have to describe the whole design pattern; you can just name it and expect your reader to know it. A reader who doesn't know the patterns will have to look them up at first, but that's still easier than reverse-engineering.

We use these patterns in our own designs, and we've found them invaluable. Yet we use the patterns in arguably naive ways. We use them to pick names for classes, to think about and teach good design, and to describe designs in terms of the sequence of design patterns we applied [BJ94]. It's easy to imagine more sophisticated ways of using patterns, such as pattern-based CASE tools or hypertext documents. But patterns are a big help even without sophisticated tools.

An Adjunct to Existing Methods

Object-oriented design methods are supposed to promote good design, to teach new designers how to design well, and to standardize the way designs are developed. A design method typically defines a set of notations (usually graphical) for modeling various aspects of a design, along with a set of rules that govern how and when to use each notation. Design methods usually describe problems that occur in a design, how to resolve them, and how to evaluate design. But they haven't been able to capture the experience of expert designers.

We believe our design patterns are an important piece that's been missing from object-oriented design methods. The design patterns show how to use primitive techniques such as objects, inheritance, and polymorphism. They show how to parameterize a system with an algorithm, a behavior, a state, or the kind of objects it's supposed to create. Design patterns provide a way to describe more of the "why" of a design and not just record the results of your decisions. The Applicability, Consequences, and Implementation sections of the design patterns help guide you in the decisions you have to make.

Design patterns are especially useful in turning an analysis model into an implementation model. Despite many claims that promise a smooth transition from object-oriented analysis to design, in practice the transition is anything but smooth. A flexible and reusable design will contain objects that aren't in the analysis model. The programming language and class libraries you use affect the design. Analysis models often must be redesigned to make them reusable. Many of the design patterns in the catalog address these issues, which is why we call them *design* patterns.

A full-fledged design method requires more kinds of patterns than just design patterns. There can also be analysis patterns, user interface design patterns, or performance-tuning patterns. But the design patterns are an essential part, one that's been missing until now.

A Target for Refactoring

One of the problems in developing reusable software is that it often has to be reorganized or **refactored** [OJ90]. Design patterns help you determine how to reorganize a design, and they can reduce the amount of refactoring you need to do later.

The lifecycle of object-oriented software has several phases. Brian Foote identifies these phases as the **prototyping**, **expansionary**, and **consolidating** phases [Foo92].

The prototyping phase is a flurry of activity as the software is brought to life through rapid prototyping and incremental changes, until it meets an initial set of requirements and reaches adolescence. At this point, the software usually consists of class hierarchies that closely reflect entities in the initial problem domain. The main kind of reuse is white-box reuse by inheritance.

Once the software has reached adolescence and is put into service, its evolution is governed by two conflicting needs: (1) the software must satisfy more requirements, and (2) the software must be more reusable. New requirements usually add new classes and operations and perhaps whole class hierarchies. The software goes through an expansionary phase to meet new requirements. This can't continue for long, however. Eventually the software will become too inflexible and arthritic for further change. The class hierarchies will no longer match any problem domain. Instead they'll reflect many problem domains, and classes will define many unrelated operations and instance variables.

To continue to evolve, the software must be reorganized in a process known as *refactoring*. This is the phase in which frameworks often emerge. Refactoring involves tearing apart classes into special- and general-purpose components, moving operations up or down the class hierarchy, and rationalizing the interfaces of classes. This consolidation phase produces many new kinds of objects, often by decomposing existing objects and using object composition instead of inheritance. Hence black-box reuse replaces white-box reuse. The continual need to satisfy more requirements along with the need for more reuse propels object-oriented software through repeated phases of expansion and consolidation—expansion as new requirements are satisfied, and consolidation as the software becomes more general.

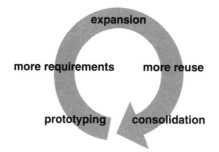

This cycle is unavoidable. But good designers are aware of the changes that can prompt refactorings. Good designers also know class and object structures that can help avoid refactorings—their designs are robust in the face of requirement changes. A thorough requirements analysis will highlight those requirements that are likely to change during the life of the software, and a good design will be robust to them.

Our design patterns capture many of the structures that result from refactoring. Using these patterns early in the life of a design prevents later refactorings. But even if you don't see how to apply a pattern until after you've built your system, the pattern can still show you how to change it. Design patterns thus provide targets for your refactorings.

6.2   A Brief History

The catalog began as a part of Erich's Ph.D. thesis [Gam91, Gam92]. Roughly half of the current patterns were in his thesis. By OOPSLA '91 it was officially an independent catalog, and Richard had joined Erich to work on it. John started working on it soon thereafter. By OOPSLA '92, Ralph had joined the group. We worked hard to make the catalog fit for publication at ECOOP '93, but soon we realized that a 90-page paper was not going to be accepted. So we summarized the catalog and submitted the summary, which was accepted. We decided to turn the catalog into a book shortly thereafter.

Our names for the patterns have changed a little along the way. "Wrapper" became "Decorator," "Glue" became "Facade," "Solitaire" became "Singleton," and "Walker" became "Visitor." A couple of patterns got dropped because they didn't seem important enough. But otherwise the set of patterns in the catalog has changed little since the end of 1992. The patterns themselves, however, have evolved tremendously.

In fact, noticing that something is a pattern is the easy part. All four of us are actively working on building object-oriented systems, and we've found that it's easy to spot patterns when you look at enough systems. But *finding* patterns is much easier than *describing* them.

If you build systems and then reflect on what you build, you will see patterns in what you do. But it's hard to describe patterns so that people who don't know them will understand them and realize why they are important. Experts immediately recognized the value of the catalog in its early stages. But the only ones who could understand the patterns were those who had already used them.

Since one of the main purposes of the book was to teach object-oriented design to new designers, we knew we had to improve the catalog. We expanded the average size of a pattern from less than 2 to more than 10 pages by including a detailed motivating example and sample code. We also started examining the trade-offs and the various ways of implementing the pattern. This made the patterns easier to learn.

Another important change over the past year has been a greater emphasis on the problem that a pattern solves. It's easiest to see a pattern as a solution, as a technique that can be adapted and reused. It's harder to see when it is *appropriate*—to characterize the problems it solves and the context in which it's the best solution. In general, it's easier to see *what* someone is doing than to know *why*, and the "why" for a pattern is the problem it solves. Knowing the purpose of a pattern is important too, because it helps us choose patterns to apply. It also helps us understand the design of existing systems. A pattern author must determine and characterize the problem that the pattern solves, even if you have to do it after you've discovered its solution.

6.3   The Pattern Community

We aren't the only ones interested in writing books that catalog the patterns experts use. We are a part of a larger community interested in patterns in general and software-related patterns in particular. Christopher Alexander is the architect who first studied patterns in buildings and communities and developed a "pattern language" for generating them. His work has inspired us time and again. So it's fitting and worthwhile to compare our work to his. Then we'll look at others' work in software-related patterns.

Alexander's Pattern Languages

There are many ways in which our work is like Alexander's. Both are based on observing existing systems and looking for patterns in them. Both have templates for describing patterns (although our templates are quite different). Both rely on natural language and lots of examples to describe patterns rather than formal languages, and both give rationales for each pattern.

But there are just as many ways in which our works are different:

1. People have been making buildings for thousands of years, and there are many classic examples to draw upon. We have been making software systems for a relatively short time, and few are considered classics.

2. Alexander gives an order in which his patterns should be used; we have not.

3. Alexander's patterns emphasize the problems they address, whereas design patterns describe the solutions in more detail.

4. Alexander claims his patterns will generate complete buildings. We do not claim that our patterns will generate complete programs.

When Alexander claims you can design a house simply by applying his patterns one after another, he has goals similar to those of object-oriented design methodologists who give step-by-step rules for design. Alexander doesn't deny the need for creativity; some of his patterns require understanding the living habits of the people who will use the building, and his belief in the "poetry" of design implies a level of expertise beyond the pattern language itself.[1] But his description of how patterns generate designs implies that a pattern language can make the design process deterministic and repeatable.

The Alexandrian point of view has helped us focus on design trade-offs—the different "forces" that help shape a design. His influence made us work harder to understand the applicability and consequences of our patterns. It also kept us from worrying about defining a formal representation of patterns. Although such a representation might make automating patterns possible, at this stage it's more important to explore the space of design patterns than to formalize it.

---

[1] See "The poetry of the language" [AIS+77].

From Alexander's point of view, the patterns in this book do not form a pattern language. Given the variety of software systems that people build, it's hard to see how we could provide a "complete" set of patterns, one that offers step-by-step instructions for designing an application. We can do that for certain classes of applications, such as report-writing or making a forms-entry system. But our catalog is just a collection of related patterns; we can't pretend it's a pattern language.

In fact, we think it's unlikely that there will *ever* be a complete pattern language for software. But it's certainly possible to make one that is *more* complete. Additions would have to include frameworks and how to use them [Joh92], patterns for user interface design [BJ94], analysis patterns [Coa92], and all the other aspects of developing software. Design patterns are just a part of a larger pattern language for software.

Patterns in Software

Our first collective experience in the study of software architecture was at an OOPSLA '91 workshop led by Bruce Anderson. The workshop was dedicated to developing a handbook for software architects. (Judging from this book, we suspect "architecture encyclopedia" will be a more appropriate name than "architecture handbook.") That first workshop has led to a series of meetings, the most recent of which being the first conference on Pattern Languages of Programs held in August 1994. This has created a community of people interested in documenting software expertise.

Of course, others have had this goal as well. Donald Knuth's *The Art of Computer Programming* [Knu73] was one of the first attempts to catalog software knowledge, though he focused on describing algorithms. Even so, the task proved too great to finish. The *Graphics Gems* series [Gla90, Arv91, Kir92] is another catalog of design knowledge, though it too tends to focus on algorithms. The Domain Specific Software Architecture program sponsored by the U.S. Department of Defense [GM92] concentrates on gathering architectural information. The knowledge-based software engineering community tries to represent software-related knowledge in general. There are many other groups with goals at least a little like ours.

James Coplien's *Advanced C++: Programming Styles and Idioms* [Cop92] has influenced us, too. The patterns in his book tend to be more C++-specific than our design patterns, and his book contains lots of lower-level patterns as well. But there is some overlap, as we point out in our patterns. Jim has been active in the pattern community. He's currently working on patterns that describe people's roles in software development organizations.

There are a lot of other places in which to find descriptions of patterns. Kent Beck was one of the first people in the software community to advocate Christopher Alexander's work. In 1993 he started writing a column in *The Smalltalk Report* on Smalltalk patterns. Peter Coad has also been collecting patterns for some time. His paper on patterns seems to us to contain mostly analysis patterns [Coa92]; we haven't seen his latest patterns, though we know he is still working on them. We've heard of several books on patterns that are in the works, but we haven't seen any of them, either. All we can do is let you know they're coming. One of these books will be from the Pattern Languages of Programs conference.

6.4   An Invitation

What can you do if you are interested in patterns? First, use them and look for other patterns that fit the way you design. A lot of books and articles about patterns will be coming out in the next few years, so there will be plenty of sources for new patterns. Develop your vocabulary of patterns, and use it. Use it when you talk with other people about your designs. Use it when you think and write about them.

Second, be a critical consumer. The design pattern catalog is the result of hard work, not just ours but that of dozens of reviewers who gave us feedback. If you spot a problem or believe more explanation is needed, contact us. The same goes for any other catalog of patterns: Give the authors feedback! One of the great things about patterns is that they move design decisions out of the realm of vague intuition. They let authors be explicit about the trade-offs they make. This makes it easier to see what is wrong with their patterns and to argue with them. Take advantage of that.

Third, look for patterns you use, and write them down. Make them a part of your documentation. Show them to other people. You don't have to be in a research lab to find patterns. In fact, finding relevant patterns is nearly impossible if you don't have practical experience. Feel free to write your own catalog of patterns...but make sure someone else helps you beat them into shape!

6.5   A Parting Thought

The best designs will use many design patterns that dovetail and intertwine to produce a greater whole. As Christopher Alexander says:

> It is possible to make buildings by stringing together patterns, in a rather loose way. A building made like this, is an assembly of patterns. It is not dense. It is not profound. But it is also possible to put patterns together in such a way that many patterns overlap in the same physical space: the building is very dense; it has many meanings captured in a small space; and through this density, it becomes profound.
>
> *A Pattern Language* [AIS+77, page *xli*]

Appendix A

Glossary

abstract class A class whose primary purpose is to define an interface. An abstract class defers some or all of its implementation to subclasses. An abstract class cannot be instantiated.

abstract coupling Given a class A that maintains a reference to an abstract class B, class A is said to be *abstractly coupled* to B. We call this abstract coupling because A refers to a *type* of object, not a concrete object.

abstract operation An operation that declares a signature but doesn't implement it. In C++, an abstract operation corresponds to a **pure virtual member function**.

acquaintance relationship A class that refers to another class has an *acquaintance* with that class.

aggregate object An object that's composed of subobjects. The subobjects are called the aggregate's **parts**, and the aggregate is responsible for them.

aggregation relationship The relationship of an aggregate object to its parts. A class defines this relationship for its instances (e.g., aggregate objects).

black-box reuse A style of reuse based on object composition. Composed objects reveal no internal details to each other and are thus analogous to "black boxes."

class A class defines an object's interface and implementation. It specifies the object's internal representation and defines the operations the object can perform.

class diagram A diagram that depicts classes, their internal structure and operations, and the static relationships between them.

class operation An operation targeted to a class and not to an individual object. In C++, class operations are are called **static member functions**.

concrete class A class having no abstract operations. It can be instantiated.

constructor In C++, an operation that is automatically invoked to initialize new instances.

coupling The degree to which software components depend on each other.

delegation An implementation mechanism in which an object forwards or *delegates* a request to another object. The delegate carries out the request on behalf of the original object.

design pattern A design pattern systematically names, motivates, and explains a general design that addresses a recurring design problem in object-oriented systems. It describes the problem, the solution, when to apply the solution, and its consequences. It also gives implementation hints and examples. The solution is a general arrangement of objects and classes that solve the problem. The solution is customized and implemented to solve the problem in a particular context.

destructor In C++, an operation that is automatically invoked to finalize an object that is about to be deleted.

dynamic binding The run-time association of a request to an object and one of its operations. In C++, only virtual functions are dynamically bound.

encapsulation The result of hiding a representation and implementation in an object. The representation is not visible and cannot be accessed directly from outside the object. Operations are the only way to access and modify an object's representation.

framework A set of cooperating classes that makes up a reusable design for a specific class of software. A framework provides architectural guidance by partitioning the design into abstract classes and defining their responsibilities and collaborations. A developer customizes the framework to a particular application by subclassing and composing instances of framework classes.

friend class In C++, a class that has the same access rights to the operations and data of a class as that class itself.

inheritance A relationship that defines one entity in terms of another. **Class inheritance** defines a new class in terms of one or more parent classes. The new class inherits its interface and implementation from its parents. The new class is called a **subclass** or (in C++) a **derived class**. Class inheritance combines **interface inheritance** and **implementation inheritance**. Interface inheritance defines a new interface in terms of one or more existing interfaces. Implementation inheritance defines a new implementation in terms of one or more existing implementations.

instance variable A piece of data that defines part of an object's representation. C++ uses the term **data member**.

interaction diagram A diagram that shows the flow of requests between objects.

interface The set of all signatures defined by an object's operations. The interface describes the set of requests to which an object can respond.

metaclass Classes are objects in Smalltalk. A metaclass is the class of a class object.

mixin class A class designed to be combined with other classes through inheritance. Mixin classes are usually abstract.

object A run-time entity that packages both data and the procedures that operate on that data.

object composition Assembling or *composing* objects to get more complex behavior.

object diagram A diagram that depicts a particular object structure at run-time.

object reference A value that identifies another object.

operation An object's data can be manipulated only by its operations. An object performs an operation when it receives a request. In C++, operations are called **member functions**. Smalltalk uses the term **method**.

overriding Redefining an operation (inherited from a parent class) in a subclass.

parameterized type A type that leaves some constituent types unspecified. The unspecified types are supplied as parameters at the point of use. In C++, parameterized types are called **templates**.

parent class The class from which another class inherits. Synonyms are **superclass** (Smalltalk), **base class** (C++), and **ancestor class**.

polymorphism The ability to substitute objects of matching interface for one another at run-time.

private inheritance In C++, a class inherited solely for its implementation.

protocol Extends the concept of an interface to include the allowable sequences of requests.

receiver The target object of a request.

request An object performs an operation when it receives a corresponding request from another object. A common synonym for request is **message**.

signature An operation's signature defines its name, parameters, and return value.

subclass A class that inherits from another class. In C++, a subclass is called a **derived class**.

subsystem An independent group of classes that collaborate to fulfill a set of responsibilities.

subtype A type is a subtype of another if its interface contains the interface of the other type.

supertype The parent type from which a type inherits.

toolkit A collection of classes that provides useful functionality but does not define the design of an application.

type The name of a particular interface.

white-box reuse A style of reuse based on class inheritance. A subclass reuses the interface and implementation of its parent class, but it may have access to otherwise private aspects of its parent.

Appendix B

Guide to Notation

We use diagrams throughout the book to illustrate important ideas. Some diagrams are informal, like a screen shot of a dialog box or a schematic showing a tree of objects. But the design patterns in particular use more formal notations to denote relationships and interactions between classes and objects. This appendix describes these notations in detail.

We use three different diagrammatic notations:

1. A **class diagram** depicts classes, their structure, and the static relationships between them.

2. An **object diagram** depicts a particular object structure at run-time.

3. An **interaction diagram** shows the flow of requests between objects.

Each design pattern includes at least one class diagram. The other notations are used as needed to supplement the discussion. The class and object diagrams are based on OMT (Object Modeling Technique) [RBP+91, Rum94].[1] The interaction diagrams are taken from Objectory [JCJO92] and the Booch method [Boo94]. These notations are summarized on the inside back cover of the book.

B.1 Class Diagram

Figure B.1a shows the OMT notation for abstract and concrete classes. A class is denoted by a box with the class name in bold type at the top. The key operations of the class appear below the class name. Any instance variables appear below the operations.

---

[1] OMT uses the term "object diagram" to refer to class diagrams. We use "object diagram" exclusively to refer to diagrams of object structures.

Type information is optional; we use the C++ convention, which puts the type name before the name of the operation (to signify the return type), instance variable, or actual parameter. Slanted type indicates that the class or operation is abstract.

In some design patterns it's helpful to see where client classes reference Participant classes. When a pattern includes a Client class as one of its participants (meaning the client has a responsibility in the pattern), the Client appears as an ordinary class. This is true in Flyweight (195), for example. When the pattern does not include a Client participant (i.e., clients have no responsibilities in the pattern), but including it nevertheless clarifies which pattern participants interact with clients, then the Client class is shown in gray, as shown in Figure B.1b. An example is Proxy (207). A gray Client also makes it clear that we haven't accidentally omitted the Client from the Participants discussion.

Figure B.1c shows various relationships between classes. The OMT notation for class inheritance is a triangle connecting a subclass (LineShape in the figure) to its parent class (Shape). An object reference representing a part-of or aggregation relationship is indicated by an arrowheaded line with a diamond at the base. The arrow points to the class that is aggregated (e.g., Shape). An arrowheaded line without the diamond denotes acquaintance (e.g., a LineShape keeps a reference to a Color object, which other shapes may share). A name for the reference may appear near the base to distinguish it from other references.[2]

Another useful thing to show is which classes instantiate which others. We use a dashed arrowheaded line to indicate this, since OMT doesn't support it. We call this the "creates" relationship. The arrow points to the class that's instantiated. In Figure B.1c, CreationTool creates LineShape objects.

OMT also defines a filled circle to mean "more than one." When the circle appears at the head of a reference, it means multiple objects are being referenced or aggregated. Figure B.1c shows that Drawing aggregates multiple objects of type Shape.

Finally, we've augmented OMT with pseudocode annotations to let us sketch the implementations of operations. Figure B.1d shows the pseudocode annotation for the Draw operation on the Drawing class.

B.2   Object Diagram

An object diagram shows instances exclusively. It provides a snapshot of the objects in a design pattern. The objects are named "a*Something*", where *Something* is the class of the object. Our symbol for an object (modified slightly from standard OMT) is a rounded

---

[2] OMT also defines **associations** between classes, which appear as plain lines between class boxes. Associations are bidirectional. Although associations are appropriate during analysis, we feel they're too high-level for expressing the relationships in design patterns, simply because associations must be mapped down to object references or pointers during design. Object references are intrinsically directed and are therefore better suited to the relationships that concern us. For example, Drawing knows about Shapes, but the Shapes don't know about the Drawing they're in. You can't express this relationship with associations alone.

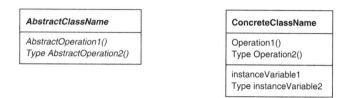

(a) Abstract and concrete classes

(b) Participant Client class (left) and implicit Client class (right)

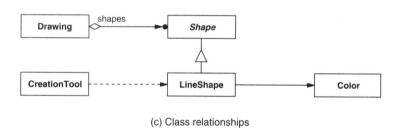

(c) Class relationships

(d) Pseudocode annotation

Figure B.1: Class diagram notation

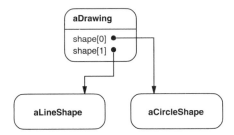

Figure B.2: Object diagram notation

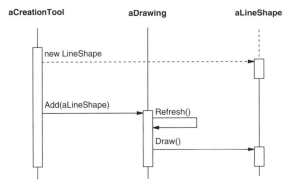

Figure B.3: Interaction diagram notation

box with a line separating the object name from any object references. Arrows indicate the object referenced. Figure B.2 shows an example.

B.3   Interaction Diagram

An interaction diagram shows the order in which requests between objects get executed. Figure B.3 is an interaction diagram that shows how a shape gets added to a drawing.

Time flows from top to bottom in an interaction diagram. A solid vertical line indicates the lifetime of a particular object. The naming convention for objects is the same as for object diagrams—the class name prefixed by the letter "a" (e.g., aShape). If the object doesn't get instantiated until after the beginning of time as recorded in the diagram, then its vertical line appears dashed until the point of creation.

A vertical rectangle shows that an object is active; that is, it is handling a request. The operation can send requests to other objects; these are indicated with a horizontal arrow pointing to the receiving object. The name of the request is shown above the arrow. A request to create an object is shown with a dashed arrowheaded line. A request to the sending object itself points back to the sender.

Figure B.3 shows that the first request is from aCreationTool to create aLineShape. Later, aLineShape is Added to aDrawing, which prompts aDrawing to send a Refresh request to itself. Note that aDrawing sends a Draw request to aLineShape as part of the Refresh operation.

Appendix C

Foundation Classes

This appendix documents the foundation classes we use in the C++ sample code of several design patterns. We've intentionally kept the classes simple and minimal. We describe the following classes:

- `List`, an ordered list of objects.

- `Iterator`, the interface for accessing an aggregate's objects in a sequence.

- `ListIterator`, an iterator for traversing a `List`.

- `Point`, a two-dimensional point.

- `Rect`, an axis-aligned rectangle.

Some newer C++ standard types may not be available on all compilers. In particular, if your compiler doesn't define `bool`, then define it manually as

```
typedef int bool;
const int true = 1;
const int false = 0;
```

C.1 List

The `List` class template provides a basic container for storing an ordered list of objects. `List` stores elements by value, which means it works for built-in types as well as class instances. For example, `List<int>` declares a list of `int`s. But most of the patterns use `List` to store pointers to objects, as in `List<Glyph*>`. That way `List` can be used for heterogeneous lists.

For convenience, `List` also provides synonyms for stack operations, which make code that uses `List` for stacks more explicit without defining another class.

```
template <class Item>
class List {
public:
    List(long size = DEFAULT_LIST_CAPACITY);
    List(List&);
    ~List();
    List& operator=(const List&);

    long Count() const;
    Item& Get(long index) const;
    Item& First() const;
    Item& Last() const;
    bool Includes(const Item&) const;

    void Append(const Item&);
    void Prepend(const Item&);

    void Remove(const Item&);
    void RemoveLast();
    void RemoveFirst();
    void RemoveAll();

    Item& Top() const;
    void Push(const Item&);
    Item& Pop();
};
```

The following sections describe these operations in greater detail.

Construction, Destruction, Initialization, and Assignment

`List(long size)`

> initializes the list. The `size` parameter is a hint for the initial number of elements.

`List(List&)`

> overrides the default copy constructor so that member data are initialized properly.

`~List()`

> frees the list's internal data structures but *not* the elements in the list. The class is not designed for subclassing; therefore the destructor isn't virtual.

`List& operator=(const List&)`

> implements the assignment operation to assign member data properly.

Accessing

These operations provide basic access to the list's elements.

`long Count() const`

 returns the number of objects in the list.

`Item& Get(long index) const`

 returns the object at the given index.

`Item& First() const`

 returns the first object in the list.

`Item& Last() const`

 returns the last object in the list.

Adding

`void Append(const Item&)`

 adds the argument to the list, making it the last element.

`void Prepend(const Item&)`

 adds the argument to the list, making it the first element.

Removing

`void Remove(const Item&)`

 removes the given element from the list. This operation requires that the type of elements in the list supports the `==` operator for comparison.

`void RemoveFirst()`

 removes the first element from the list.

`void RemoveLast()`

 removes the last element from the list.

`void RemoveAll()`

 removes all elements from the list.

Stack Interface

```
Item& Top() const
```
    returns the top element (when the List is viewed as a stack).

```
void Push(const Item&)
```
    pushes the element onto the stack.

```
Item& Pop()
```
    pops the top element from the stack.

C.2   Iterator

`Iterator` is an abstract class that defines a traversal interface for aggregates.

```
template <class Item>
class Iterator {
public:
    virtual void First() = 0;
    virtual void Next() = 0;
    virtual bool IsDone() const = 0;
    virtual Item CurrentItem() const = 0;
protected:
    Iterator();
};
```

The operations do the following:

```
virtual void First()
```
    positions the iterator to the first object in the aggregate.

```
virtual void Next()
```
    positions the iterator to the next object in the sequence.

```
virtual bool IsDone() const
```
    returns `true` when there are no more objects in the sequence.

```
virtual Item CurrentItem() const
```
    returns the object at the current position in the sequence.

C.3   ListIterator

`ListIterator` implements the `Iterator` interface to traverse List objects. Its constructor takes a list to traverse as an argument.

```
template <class Item>
class ListIterator : public Iterator<Item> {
public:
    ListIterator(const List<Item>* aList);

    virtual void First();
    virtual void Next();
    virtual bool IsDone() const;
    virtual Item CurrentItem() const;
};
```

C.4   Point

Point represents a point in a two-dimensional Cartesian coordinate space. Point supports some minimal vector arithmetic. The coordinates of a Point are defined as

```
typedef float Coord;
```

Point's operations are self-explanatory.

```
class Point {
public:
    static const Point Zero;

    Point(Coord x = 0.0, Coord y = 0.0);

    Coord X() const;   void X(Coord x);
    Coord Y() const;   void Y(Coord y);

    friend Point operator+(const Point&, const Point&);
    friend Point operator-(const Point&, const Point&);
    friend Point operator*(const Point&, const Point&);
    friend Point operator/(const Point&, const Point&);

    Point& operator+=(const Point&);
    Point& operator-=(const Point&);
    Point& operator*=(const Point&);
    Point& operator/=(const Point&);

    Point operator-();

    friend bool operator==(const Point&, const Point&);
    friend bool operator!=(const Point&, const Point&);

    friend ostream& operator<<(ostream&, const Point&);
    friend istream& operator>>(istream&, Point&);
};
```

The static member Zero represents Point(0, 0).

C.5   Rect

Rect represents an axis-aligned rectangle. A Rect is defined by an origin point and an extent (that is, width and height). The Rect operations are self-explanatory.

```
class Rect {
public:
    static const Rect Zero;

    Rect(Coord x, Coord y, Coord w, Coord h);
    Rect(const Point& origin, const Point& extent);

    Coord Width() const;    void Width(Coord);
    Coord Height() const;   void Height(Coord);
    Coord Left() const;     void Left(Coord);
    Coord Bottom() const;   void Bottom(Coord);

    Point& Origin() const; void Origin(const Point&);
    Point& Extent() const; void Extent(const Point&);

    void MoveTo(const Point&);
    void MoveBy(const Point&);

    bool IsEmpty() const;
    bool Contains(const Point&) const;
};
```

The static member Zero is equivalent to the rectangle

```
Rect(Point(0, 0), Point(0, 0));
```

Bibliography

[Add94]   Addison-Wesley, Reading, MA. *NEXTSTEP General Reference: Release 3, Volumes 1 and 2*, 1994.

[AG90]   D.B. Anderson and S. Gossain. Hierarchy evolution and the software lifecycle. In *TOOLS '90 Conference Proceedings*, pages 41–50, Paris, June 1990. Prentice Hall.

[AIS+77] Christopher Alexander, Sara Ishikawa, Murray Silverstein, Max Jacobson, Ingrid Fiksdahl-King, and Shlomo Angel. *A Pattern Language*. Oxford University Press, New York, 1977.

[App89]   Apple Computer, Inc., Cupertino, CA. *Macintosh Programmers Workshop Pascal 3.0 Reference*, 1989.

[App92]   Apple Computer, Inc., Cupertino, CA. *Dylan. An object-oriented dynamic language*, 1992.

[Arv91]   James Arvo. *Graphics Gems II*. Academic Press, Boston, MA, 1991.

[AS85]   B. Adelson and E. Soloway. The role of domain experience in software design. *IEEE Transactions on Software Engineering*, 11(11):1351–1360, 1985.

[BE93]   Andreas Birrer and Thomas Eggenschwiler. Frameworks in the financial engineering domain: An experience report. In *European Conference on Object-Oriented Programming*, pages 21–35, Kaiserslautern, Germany, July 1993. Springer-Verlag.

[BJ94]   Kent Beck and Ralph Johnson. Patterns generate architectures. In *European Conference on Object-Oriented Programming*, pages 139–149, Bologna, Italy, July 1994. Springer-Verlag.

[Boo94]   Grady Booch. *Object-Oriented Analysis and Design with Applications*. Benjamin/Cummings, Redwood City, CA, 1994. Second Edition.

[Bor81]   A. Borning. The programming language aspects of ThingLab—a constraint-oriented simulation laboratory. *ACM Transactions on Programming Languages and Systems*, 3(4):343–387, October 1981.

[Bor94]   Borland International, Inc., Scotts Valley, CA. *A Technical Comparison of Borland ObjectWindows 2.0 and Microsoft MFC 2.5*, 1994.

[BV90]   Grady Booch and Michael Vilot. The design of the C++ Booch components. In *Object-Oriented Programming Systems, Languages, and Applications Conference Proceedings*, pages 1–11, Ottawa, Canada, October 1990. ACM Press.

[Cal93]   Paul R. Calder. *Building User Interfaces with Lightweight Objects*. PhD thesis, Stanford University, 1993.

[Car89]   J. Carolan. Constructing bullet-proof classes. In *Proceedings C++ at Work '89*. SIGS Publications, 1989.

[Car92]   Tom Cargill. *C++ Programming Style*. Addison-Wesley, Reading, MA, 1992.

[CIRM93]   Roy H. Campbell, Nayeem Islam, David Raila, and Peter Madeany. Designing and implementing Choices: An object-oriented system in C++. *Communications of the ACM*, 36(9):117–126, September 1993.

[CL90]   Paul R. Calder and Mark A. Linton. Glyphs: Flyweight objects for user interfaces. In *ACM User Interface Software Technologies Conference*, pages 92–101, Snowbird, UT, October 1990.

[CL92]   Paul R. Calder and Mark A. Linton. The object-oriented implementation of a document editor. In *Object-Oriented Programming Systems, Languages, and Applications Conference Proceedings*, pages 154–165, Vancouver, British Columbia, Canada, October 1992. ACM Press.

[Coa92]   Peter Coad. Object-oriented patterns. *Communications of the ACM*, 35(9):152–159, September 1992.

[Coo92]   William R. Cook. Interfaces and specifications for the Smalltalk-80 collection classes. In *Object-Oriented Programming Systems, Languages, and Applications Conference Proceedings*, pages 1–15, Vancouver, British Columbia, Canada, October 1992. ACM Press.

[Cop92]   James O. Coplien. *Advanced C++ Programming Styles and Idioms*. Addison-Wesley, Reading, MA, 1992.

[Cur89]   Bill Curtis. Cognitive issues in reusing software artifacts. In Ted J. Biggerstaff and Alan J. Perlis, editors, *Software Reusability, Volume II: Applications and Experience*, pages 269–287. Addison-Wesley, Reading, MA, 1989.

[dCLF93]   Dennis de Champeaux, Doug Lea, and Penelope Faure. *Object-Oriented System Development*. Addison-Wesley, Reading, MA, 1993.

[Deu89]   L. Peter Deutsch. Design reuse and frameworks in the Smalltalk-80 system. In Ted J. Biggerstaff and Alan J. Perlis, editors, *Software Reusability, Volume II: Applications and Experience*, pages 57–71. Addison-Wesley, Reading, MA, 1989.

[Ede92] D. R. Edelson. Smart pointers: They're smart, but they're not pointers. In *Proceedings of the 1992 USENIX C++ Conference*, pages 1–19, Portland, OR, August 1992. USENIX Association.

[EG92] Thomas Eggenschwiler and Erich Gamma. The ET++SwapsManager: Using object technology in the financial engineering domain. In *Object-Oriented Programming Systems, Languages, and Applications Conference Proceedings*, pages 166–178, Vancouver, British Columbia, Canada, October 1992. ACM Press.

[ES90] Margaret A. Ellis and Bjarne Stroustrup. *The Annotated C++ Reference Manual*. Addison-Wesley, Reading, MA, 1990.

[Foo92] Brian Foote. A fractal model of the lifecycles of reusable objects. *OOPSLA '92 Workshop on Reuse*, October 1992. Vancouver, British Columbia, Canada.

[GA89] S. Gossain and D.B. Anderson. Designing a class hierarchy for domain representation and reusability. In *TOOLS '89 Conference Proceedings*, pages 201–210, CNIT Paris—La Defense, France, November 1989. Prentice Hall.

[Gam91] Erich Gamma. *Object-Oriented Software Development based on ET++: Design Patterns, Class Library, Tools* (in German). PhD thesis, University of Zurich *Institut für Informatik*, 1991.

[Gam92] Erich Gamma. *Object-Oriented Software Development based on ET++: Design Patterns, Class Library, Tools* (in German). Springer-Verlag, Berlin, 1992.

[Gla90] Andrew Glassner. *Graphics Gems*. Academic Press, Boston, MA, 1990.

[GM92] M. Graham and E. Mettala. The Domain-Specific Software Architecture Program. In *Proceedings of DARPA Software Technology Conference, 1992*, pages 204–210, April 1992. Also published in *CrossTalk, The Journal of Defense Software Engineering*, pages 19–21, 32, October 1992.

[GR83] Adele J. Goldberg and David Robson. *Smalltalk-80: The Language and Its Implementation*. Addison-Wesley, Reading, MA, 1983.

[HHMV92] Richard Helm, Tien Huynh, Kim Marriott, and John Vlissides. An object-oriented architecture for constraint-based graphical editing. In *Proceedings of the Third Eurographics Workshop on Object-Oriented Graphics*, pages 1–22, Champéry, Switzerland, October 1992. Also available as IBM Research Division Technical Report RC 18524 (79392).

[HO87] Daniel C. Halbert and Patrick D. O'Brien. Object-oriented development. *IEEE Software*, 4(5):71–79, September 1987.

[ION94] IONA Technologies, Ltd., Dublin, Ireland. *Programmer's Guide for Orbix, Version 1.2*, 1994.

[JCJO92] Ivar Jacobson, Magnus Christerson, Patrik Jonsson, and Gunnar Over-gaard. *Object-Oriented Software Engineering—A Use Case Driven Approach.* Addison-Wesley, Wokingham, England, 1992.

[JF88] Ralph E. Johnson and Brian Foote. Designing reusable classes. *Journal of Object-Oriented Programming*, 1(2):22–35, June/July 1988.

[JML92] Ralph E. Johnson, Carl McConnell, and J. Michael Lake. The RTL system: A framework for code optimization. In Robert Giegerich and Susan L. Graham, editors, *Code Generation—Concepts, Tools, Techniques. Proceedings of the International Workshop on Code Generation*, pages 255–274, Dagstuhl, Germany, 1992. Springer-Verlag.

[Joh92] Ralph Johnson. Documenting frameworks using patterns. In *Object-Oriented Programming Systems, Languages, and Applications Conference Proceedings*, pages 63–76, Vancouver, British Columbia, Canada, October 1992. ACM Press.

[JZ91] Ralph E. Johnson and Jonathan Zweig. Delegation in C++. *Journal of Object-Oriented Programming*, 4(11):22–35, November 1991.

[Kir92] David Kirk. *Graphics Gems III.* Harcourt, Brace, Jovanovich, Boston, MA, 1992.

[Knu73] Donald E. Knuth. *The Art of Computer Programming, Volumes 1, 2, and 3.* Addison-Wesley, Reading, MA, 1973.

[Knu84] Donald E. Knuth. *The TEXbook.* Addison-Wesley, Reading, MA, 1984.

[Kof93] Thomas Kofler. Robust iterators in ET++. *Structured Programming*, 14:62–85, March 1993.

[KP88] Glenn E. Krasner and Stephen T. Pope. A cookbook for using the model-view controller user interface paradigm in Smalltalk-80. *Journal of Object-Oriented Programming*, 1(3):26–49, August/September 1988.

[LaL94] Wilf LaLonde. *Discovering Smalltalk.* Benjamin/Cummings, Redwood City, CA, 1994.

[LCI+92] Mark Linton, Paul Calder, John Interrante, Steven Tang, and John Vlissides. *InterViews Reference Manual.* CSL, Stanford University, 3.1 edition, 1992.

[Lea88] Doug Lea. libg++, the GNU C++ library. In *Proceedings of the 1988 USENIX C++ Conference*, pages 243–256, Denver, CO, October 1988. USENIX Association.

[LG86] Barbara Liskov and John Guttag. *Abstraction and Specification in Program Development.* McGraw-Hill, New York, 1986.

[Lie85] Henry Lieberman. There's more to menu systems than meets the screen. In *SIGGRAPH Computer Graphics*, pages 181–189, San Francisco, CA, July 1985.

[Lie86] Henry Lieberman. Using prototypical objects to implement shared behavior in object-oriented systems. In *Object-Oriented Programming Systems, Languages, and Applications Conference Proceedings*, pages 214–223, Portland, OR, November 1986.

[Lin92] Mark A. Linton. Encapsulating a C++ library. In *Proceedings of the 1992 USENIX C++ Conference*, pages 57–66, Portland, OR, August 1992. ACM Press.

[LP93] Mark Linton and Chuck Price. Building distributed user interfaces with Fresco. In *Proceedings of the 7th X Technical Conference*, pages 77–87, Boston, MA, January 1993.

[LR93] Daniel C. Lynch and Marshall T. Rose. *Internet System Handbook*. Addison-Wesley, Reading, MA, 1993.

[LVC89] Mark A. Linton, John M. Vlissides, and Paul R. Calder. Composing user interfaces with InterViews. *Computer*, 22(2):8–22, February 1989.

[Mar91] Bruce Martin. The separation of interface and implementation in C++. In *Proceedings of the 1991 USENIX C++ Conference*, pages 51–63, Washington, D.C., April 1991. USENIX Association.

[McC87] Paul McCullough. Transparent forwarding: First steps. In *Object-Oriented Programming Systems, Languages, and Applications Conference Proceedings*, pages 331–341, Orlando, FL, October 1987. ACM Press.

[Mey88] Bertrand Meyer. *Object-Oriented Software Construction*. Series in Computer Science. Prentice Hall, Englewood Cliffs, NJ, 1988.

[Mur93] Robert B. Murray. *C++ Strategies and Tactics*. Addison-Wesley, Reading, MA, 1993.

[OJ90] William F. Opdyke and Ralph E. Johnson. Refactoring: An aid in designing application frameworks and evolving object-oriented systems. In *SOOPPA Conference Proceedings*, pages 145–161, Marist College, Poughkeepsie, NY, September 1990. ACM Press.

[OJ93] William F. Opdyke and Ralph E. Johnson. Creating abstract superclasses by refactoring. In *Proceedings of the 21st Annual Computer Science Conference (ACM CSC '93)*, pages 66–73, Indianapolis, IN, February 1993.

[P+88] Andrew J. Palay et al. The Andrew Toolkit: An overview. In *Proceedings of the 1988 Winter USENIX Technical Conference*, pages 9–21, Dallas, TX, February 1988. USENIX Association.

[Par90] ParcPlace Systems, Mountain View, CA. *ObjectWorks\Smalltalk Release 4 Users Guide*, 1990.

[Pas86] Geoffrey A. Pascoe.   Encapsulators: A new software paradigm in Smalltalk-80. In *Object-Oriented Programming Systems, Languages, and Applications Conference Proceedings*, pages 341–346, Portland, OR, October 1986. ACM Press.

[Pug90] William Pugh. Skiplists: A probabilistic alternative to balanced trees. *Communications of the ACM*, 33(6):668–676, June 1990.

[RBP+91] James Rumbaugh, Michael Blaha, William Premerlani, Frederick Eddy, and William Lorenson.   *Object-Oriented Modeling and Design*.   Prentice Hall, Englewood Cliffs, NJ, 1991.

[Rum94] James Rumbaugh. The life of an object model: How the object model changes during development.   *Journal of Object-Oriented Programming*, 7(1):24–32, March/April 1994.

[SE84] Elliot Soloway and Kate Ehrlich.   Empirical studies of programming knowledge. *IEEE Transactions on Software Engineering*, 10(5):595–609, September 1984.

[Sha90] Yen-Ping Shan. MoDE: A UIMS for Smalltalk. In *ACM OOPSLA/ECOOP '90 Conference Proceedings*, pages 258–268, Ottawa, Ontario, Canada, October 1990. ACM Press.

[Sny86] Alan Snyder. Encapsulation and inheritance in object-oriented languages. In *Object-Oriented Programming Systems, Languages, and Applications Conference Proceedings*, pages 38–45, Portland, OR, November 1986. ACM Press.

[SS86] James C. Spohrer and Elliot Soloway. Novice mistakes: Are the folk wisdoms correct? *Communications of the ACM*, 29(7):624–632, July 1986.

[SS94] Douglas C. Schmidt and Tatsuya Suda. The Service Configurator Framework: An extensible architecture for dynamically configuring concurrent, multi-service network daemons. In *Proceeding of the Second International Workshop on Configurable Distributed Systems*, pages 190–201, Pittsburgh, PA, March 1994. IEEE Computer Society.

[Str91] Bjarne Stroustrup.   *The C++ Programming Language*.   Addison-Wesley, Reading, MA, 1991. Second Edition.

[Str93] Paul S. Strauss. IRIS Inventor, a 3D graphics toolkit. In *Object-Oriented Programming Systems, Languages, and Applications Conference Proceedings*, pages 192–200, Washington, D.C., September 1993. ACM Press.

[Str94] Bjarne Stroustrup.   *The Design and Evolution of C++*.   Addison-Wesley, Reading, MA, 1994.

[Sut63] I.E. Sutherland. *Sketchpad: A Man-Machine Graphical Communication System*. PhD thesis, MIT, 1963.

[Swe85] Richard E. Sweet. The Mesa programming environment. *SIGPLAN Notices*, 20(7):216–229, July 1985.

[Sym93a] Symantec Corporation, Cupertino, CA. *Bedrock Developer's Architecture Kit*, 1993.

[Sym93b] Symantec Corporation, Cupertino, CA. *THINK Class Library Guide*, 1993.

[Sza92] Duane Szafron. SPECTalk: An object-oriented data specification language. In *Technology of Object-Oriented Languages and Systems (TOOLS 8)*, pages 123–138, Santa Barbara, CA, August 1992. Prentice Hall.

[US87] David Ungar and Randall B. Smith. Self: The power of simplicity. In *Object-Oriented Programming Systems, Languages, and Applications Conference Proceedings*, pages 227–242, Orlando, FL, October 1987. ACM Press.

[VL88] John M. Vlissides and Mark A. Linton. Applying object-oriented design to structured graphics. In *Proceedings of the 1988 USENIX C++ Conference*, pages 81–94, Denver, CO, October 1988. USENIX Association.

[VL90] John M. Vlissides and Mark A. Linton. Unidraw: A framework for building domain-specific graphical editors. *ACM Transactions on Information Systems*, 8(3):237–268, July 1990.

[WBJ90] Rebecca Wirfs-Brock and Ralph E. Johnson. A survey of current research in object-oriented design. *Communications of the ACM*, 33(9):104–124, 1990.

[WBWW90] Rebecca Wirfs-Brock, Brian Wilkerson, and Lauren Wiener. *Designing Object-Oriented Software*. Prentice Hall, Englewood Cliffs, NJ, 1990.

[WGM88] André Weinand, Erich Gamma, and Rudolf Marty. ET++—An object-oriented application framework in C++. In *Object-Oriented Programming Systems, Languages, and Applications Conference Proceedings*, pages 46–57, San Diego, CA, September 1988. ACM Press.

Index

Names of design patterns appear in small capitals: e.g., ADAPTER. Page numbers in **bold** indicate the definition of a term. Numbers in *italics* indicate a diagram for the term. Letters after a diagram's page number indicate the kind of diagram: a *"c"* denotes a class diagram, an *"i"* denotes an interaction diagram, and an *"o"* denotes an object diagram. For example, *88co* means that a class and object diagram appears on page 88.

A

abstract class **15**, *16c*, **359**, 364, *365c*
abstract coupling, *see* coupling, abstract
    in OBSERVER 296
ABSTRACT FACTORY **87**
    extensibility of 91
    in catalog summary 8
    Lexi's use of 51
    used to configure a subsystem 193
Abstract Factory
    participant of ABSTRACT FACTORY *88c*, 89
abstract operation, *see* operation, abstract
    use to implement ADAPTER 144
abstract syntax tree 244, 251, 331
    class structure for *244c, 331c*
    constructing in Smalltalk 250
    object structure for *244o*
AbstractExpression
    participant of INTERPRETER *245c*, 245
Abstraction
    participant of BRIDGE *153c*, 154
AbstractProduct
    participant of ABSTRACT FACTORY *88c*, 89
accumulating state 336
acquaintance **22**, **359**
    C++, defined in 23
    compared with aggregation 23
    Smalltalk, defined in 23
Action, *see* COMMAND

active iterator, *see* iterator, active
Ada 4, 21
Adaptee
    participant of ADAPTER 141, *141c*
ADAPTER **139**
    compared with BRIDGE 161, 219
    compared with DECORATOR 184
    compared with PROXY 216
    in catalog summary 8
Adapter
    participant of ADAPTER 141, *141c*
adapter **140**
    class adapter 141, *141c*
    object adapter 141, *141c*
    parameterized 145
    pluggable, *see* pluggable adapter
    two-way **143**, *143c*
adorner 179
Aggregate
    participant of ITERATOR 259, *259c*
aggregate object 257
aggregation **22**, **359**
    C++, defined in 23
    compared with acquaintance 23
    notation for 23
    Smalltalk, defined in 23
Alexander, Christopher *xiii*, 2, 356, 358

transaction 236
transparent enclosure 43, *see also* DECORATOR
traversal of aggregate objects, *see also* ITERATOR
 across class hierarchies 336
 assigning responsibility for in VISITOR 339
 inorder, preorder, postorder 262
TreeAccessorDelegate 145, *145c*
TreeDisplay 142, 144, *144c, 145c*
two-way adapter, *see* adapter, two-way
type **13**
 compared with class 16
 C++, definition in 17
 Eiffel, definition in 17
 Smalltalk, definition in 17
 subtype **13**
 supertype **13**
type-checking 332
 to identify requests at run-time 228
 see also dynamic_cast
TypeCheckingVisitor *332c*

U

undo/redo 59–60, 62–64, 235, 238, 283, 287
 avoiding error accumulation during 239
Unidraw
 use of ADAPTER 143
 use of CHAIN OF RESPONSIBILITY 232
 use of COMMAND 232, 242
 use of FACTORY METHOD 111
 use of ITERATOR 270
 use of MEDIATOR 282
 use of MEMENTO 289
 use of OBSERVER 303
 use of PROTOTYPE 126
 use of STATE 313
UnsharedConcreteFlyweight
 participant of FLYWEIGHT 199
updates
 encapsulating complex 299
 limiting unexpected 296
 protocol for in OBSERVER 296
 triggering 297

V

Validator 323
VariableExp 252
VariableRefNode *333c*
ViewManager 281, *281o*

Virtual Constructor, *see* FACTORY METHOD
virtual memory framework 192
virtual proxy, *see* proxy, virtual
VISITOR **331**
 combined with INTERPRETER 247, 255
 in catalog summary 9
 interaction diagram for Lexi 74
 use in Lexi 76
 use in compiler example 190, 331
 use of delegation in 21
Visitor 75, 337
 participant of VISITOR 334, *334c*
visitor 74, **332**
VisualComponent 176, *176c*, 180
vocabulary, defining common 352

W

Wall *82c*, 83
white-box reuse, *see* reuse, white-box
Widget *224c*, 230, *275c*, 278
widget 48, 87
 Glyph hierarchy 50
WidgetFactory 87
Window *20c*, 39, *54c, 55c*, 152, 156
 configuring with WindowImp 57–58
 interface 53
window systems 35
 support in Lexi 51
WindowImp 55, *55c*, 152, *152c*, 157
 subclasses 55
Windows, *see* Microsoft Windows
WindowSystemFactory 57
Wrapper, *see* ADAPTER, DECORATOR
WYSIWYG 33

X

X Window System 52, 56, 57, 151, 158
XIconWindow 151, *151c*
XWindow 151, *151c*
XWindowImp 152, *152c*, 158

Related Patterns Resources

0-201-63498-8

Use the contents of the *Design Patterns* book to create your own design documents and reusable components. The CD contains:

- 23 patterns to cut and paste into your design documents
- Sample code demonstrating pattern implementation
- Complete *Design Patterns* content in standard HTML format, with numerous hyper-linked cross references
- Access through a standard web browser
- Java-based dynamic search engine

0-201-18462-1

The classic work has been tailored and enhanced to address the specific needs of the Smalltalk programmer. The original catalog of simple and succinct solutions has been written in Smalltalk code, and the material is discussed from the perspective of the Smalltalk programmer. This book provides efficient solutions to your Smalltalk design problems, ultimately helping you become a better software designer.

0-201-43293-5

This succinct, example-driven book demystifies the fine points of patterns, placing them in the broader context of basic object-oriented design principles. It dispels many of the misconceptions about patterns that have spread in the software development community—clearly articulating what patterns are and how they ease the development process. The book also presents themes and variations on several established patterns, yielding many new insights.

Also available from Addison-Wesley:

0-201-89542-0	Analysis Patterns: Reusable Object Models
0-201-60734-4	Pattern Languages of Program Design
0-201-89527-7	Pattern Languages of Program Design 2
0-201-31011-2	Pattern Languages of Program Design 3

For more information on Addison-Wesley's **Software Patterns Series**, please see:
http://www.awl.com/cseng/sps/

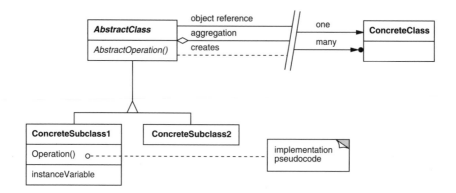

Class Diagram Notation

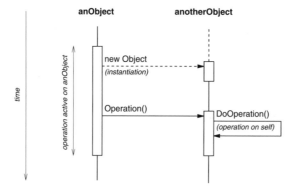

Object Diagram Notation

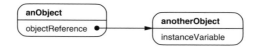

Interaction Diagram Notation